Historic Alabama Hotels and Resorts

Historic

Alabama Hotels and Resorts

JAMES F. SULZBY, Jr.

UNIVERSITY OF ALABAMA PRESS
TUSCALOOSA AND LONDON

To Dr. Guy E. Snavely

Tuscaloosa, Alabama 35487-0380

Library of Congress Catalog Card Number 60-11419
ISBN 0-8173-5309-7

Manufactured in the United States of America

First Paperback edition 1989

Second printing 1994

Foreword

I commend to the reader these stories of the old watering places, taverns, country hotels and camp meeting places of the Alabama of earlier days.

Mr. Sulzby tells in an inimitable way many of the handed-down traditions of those who gathered at these resorts with the foremost intention of a pleasant stay. The visitors sometimes chose to say that they gathered to benefit their health, but the story of these old localities when it is analyzed through the reminiscences of those who went, through the advertisements that sought patronage for these hotels, proves that the social life made the drawing cards which pulled people there.

The author has clearly demonstrated that he has done considerable research, not only in published sources but through interviews with the descendants of those who owned these places and the descendants of those who visited them, and has attempted to relive through his descriptions a life which was glamorous and romantic in the day when business was not so much a part of living as it is today.

The author uses quotations liberally in the presenting of his story, but otherwise he paraphrases the descriptions and recollections of those days in a way which makes this volume entertaining.

PETER A. BRANNON

Department of Archives and History,
Montgomery, Alabama

Contents

CONTENTS

CONTENTS

CONTENTS

1

The Alabama House STEVENSON

Railroads established Stevenson, a town in the northeastern corner of the state, in Jackson County. Vernon K. Stevenson, one of the surveyors of the route for the Nashville and Chattanooga Railroad, together with John F. Anderson, founded the town in 1853, although there were settlers who had lived there for twenty-five years or more.

The Nashville and Chattanooga Railroad (now Nashville, Chattanooga and St. Louis Railroad) was the first built through Jackson County. It was incorporated under the laws of Tennessee in 1845, and was authorized by an act of the legislature of Alabama in 1850 to construct its line through the northern part of Jackson County and to build a bridge across the Tennessee River. The part of the railroad in Jackson County, built in 1852-53, was completed to Chattanooga in 1854.

The Memphis and Charleston Railroad (now part of the Southern Railway System) was chartered in Tennessee in 1846 and in Alabama in 1850. An act of the Alabama legislature in 1856 granted a right-of-way through state lands for an extension of the road from Stevenson to form a through line to Chattanooga. The road was opened for service in 1857, after an agreement with the Nashville and Chattanooga for use of that road's tracks between Stevenson and Chattanooga.

Where the two railroads connected, the new town of Stevenson was established and lots laid off for building sites. Soon stores and houses were constructed. With people buying lots and new construction underway, Stevenson enjoyed a prosperous beginning.

One of the earliest buildings in Stevenson was the Alabama House, the town's first hotel. It was a three-story frame building with a porch at the front of each of the floors, and there were over fifty rooms. It was located on the site of the present Stevenson Drug Company. J. D. Boren was the hotel-keeper at the time of the War Between the States. Living in the hotel at that time were W. Bopes from England, a farmer; J. M. Russell, a tanner; S. H. Pankey, a grocer; Andnid Heinson, born in Denmark, a carpenter; S. Heijmon, born in Russia, a merchant; N. A. Johnson, a retail grocer; B. F. Dunlap, a physician; Edward Rosewater and James M. Lancaster, telegraph operators; and J. M. McDonald, born in Scotland, a laborer.

During the War Between the States, Stevenson was a busy place. The Alabama House, during the Union advance that ended in Chickamauga, was headquarters for the Union forces. General Alexander McDowell McCook, commanding the old Twentieth Army Corps, took possession of the hotel as temporary headquarters on the movement of the Army of the Cumberland from Tullahoma. On August 29, 1863, between Stevenson and Caperton's Ferry on the Tennessee River, McCook gathered his boats and pontoons, hidden under the dense foliage of overhanging trees, and launched them into and across the river. The troops marched over Sand Mountain and at length into Lookout Valley, where the scattered corps were concentrated along Chickamauga Creek, and the bloody struggle of September 19 and 20 was fought.

A regiment under the command of Colonel Kryzyanowski of Michigan was stationed at Stevenson during the winter of 1863-64, and once again the Alabama House was used as headquarters. The army left Alabama in early May, 1864, to join Sherman's main army in Georgia.

Early in the winter of 1864, Stevenson hummed with the movement of men, horses and supplies. Schofield's division of Thomas' army was concentrated at Stevenson for the campaign which culminated at the Battle of Nashville in the middle of December.

The Alabama House withstood the effects of the skirmishes which took place in and around Stevenson. The hotel served the Union forces to more advantage perhaps than it did the Confederates. When the town recovered from the effects of the war, many new buildings were constructed. Among these was a modern two-story brick building to be used as the Stevenson Hotel. The new hotel was built adjacent to the railroad tracks and connected to the depot by a wooden walkway. It was built in 1872 by John F. Anderson, the town's co-founder.

Throughout the life of the Alabama House, it was the largest building in Stevenson. For years, before and after the war, trains stopped in Stevenson for the passengers to take their meals at the town's only hotel. However, the Alabama House failed to keep pace with the growth of the town, and by 1875 it had been removed.

4

Alabama White Sulphur Springs

Like most states, Alabama can boast of its White Sulphur Springs, named for the sulphur water which made these resorts famous. The Alabama White Sulphur Springs resort is located in DeKalb County, barely within the state, adjacent to Georgia and within thirty-six miles of Chattanooga. These mineral springs were formerly known as Hanna Springs. The Alabama Great Southern Railroad (now part of the Southern Railway System) had a stop approximately two miles from the resort, at a station called Sulphur Springs.

This watering place in Wills Valley is located on an elevated site at the foot of Fox Ridge. Wills Valley is bordered on the east by Lookout Mountain and on the west by Sand Mountain. The resort is reached by a winding country road which has no nearby bridge for crossing the spring branch.

Alabama White Sulphur Springs has a picturesque history. Its ancient trees were known to the Cherokee Indians. Long before the War Between the States, an academy for "white settlers" was established there by Washington Bowling, a pioneer in the community. The springs, consisting of white sulphur, black sulphur, limestone, freestone, epsom and catarrh waters, were considered very healthful and the academy boys and girls were instructed in the virtues of the waters as well as in the Blueback Speller, Smith's Grammar and McGuffey Reader. The location was in the path of Union and Confederate troop movements during the war, and a few unimportant skirmishes took place there. The school was closed during Reconstruction days.

The Alabama White Sulphur Springs Hotel, consisting of eighty rooms, along with six cottages, was built in 1871 by Colonel A. B. Hanna of Rising Fawn, Georgia. Pine and poplar trees were cut and finished at a nearby sawmill owned by Colonel Hanna. The three-story hotel building was constructed on the traditional summer resort pattern with double verandas on three sides at each floor level, like decks on a river steamer. The kitchen annex was located at one end of the hotel. A large dining room accommodated over one hundred guests, for either dining or dancing.

The importance of the resort merited its listing in 1878 in the *Hand Book of Alabama* by Saffold Berney, under the classification of mineral springs and waters of Alabama. Only nine such listings are included in this publication.

Perhaps the 1880 season rings out as the most pretentious of all for the resort because of the splendid management by Major W. R. Davol, who came directly there from the Stanton House in Chattanooga. To begin the season, Major Davol extended invitations to prominent people throughout Alabama and Tennessee to attend the opening ball on Tuesday evening, June 15. Included in the entertainment for the evening was the Grand Balcony Promenade, which extended one-fifth of a mile in length. For the season, first-class accommodations at reasonable terms were advertised. Amusements included music, bowling, croquet, and archery.

Major Davol, in giving his personal attention to the desires of his guests, established the cuisine as the dominant feature of the resort. In addition, he advertised the resort as having "the finest waters in the world." During the season, the dinner menu each evening included a soup, three kinds of roast, three boiled meats, four cuts of cold meat, five entrees, seven relishes, seven vegetables, five pastries, six desserts, coffee, tea, buttermilk, and sweet milk. From the menu, guests were permitted to order to their tastes and capacities. Meals sent to rooms and children occupying seats at the first table were charged extra.

As to the hotel's wine list, Major Davol provided the finest champagnes, clarets, sherries and ports, both domestic and imported. The best grades of California aged wines were offered. The Carte Blanche brand of champagne was $4.00 a quart, while the American Dry was $1.00 a quart. Bass Pale ale, Younger's ale, London Porter, and Guiness XX Brown Stout all sold for thirty-five cents a bottle.

In 1901 Dabney H. Scoville purchased the resort and changed the name of the hotel to Lamine, his wife's name. The Lamine Hotel was advertised extensively. Trains, carriages and spring wagons brought summer guests from all over the South, a substantial part of the patronage coming from Chattanooga and Birmingham.

The children who accompanied their parents to the resort always looked forward to the double team, ten-passenger hack which met all trains at Sulphur Springs station. The hack, a traditional feature of the resort, is shown in the accompanying picture. The frame of the hack is preserved in a barn on the grounds.

Alabama White Sulphur Springs resort had several owners following its development by Colonel Hanna. These owners included George W. Davenport, Dabney H. Scoville and his wife, Lamine, R. F. Hadgins, W. M. Ratchford, Robert L. Blainist, and John Thomas Lupton and his wife, Elizabeth. Soon after Mr. and Mrs. Lupton purchased the resort property in 1929, it was donated to the Y.W.C.A. of Chattanooga for use as a summer camp.

The resort became known as Camp Elizabeth Lupton. The hotel building was used as living quarters for the campers, who came to enjoy the mountain air and summer activities. Mrs. Lupton provided equipment for sports, crafts and dramatics. The entire camp program taught that "living together in harmony and friendship was true democracy," and was aimed at strengthening character as well as bodies. For many years Mrs. M. L. Argo of Chattanooga was camp director. Over 10,000 Y.W.C.A. girls have enjoyed Camp Elizabeth Lupton.

It was the campers' fancy that the creaking hotel building be affectionately called "the old lady." It was "the old lady" who had loved and mothered so many children, but unfortunately it was found she was getting tired and aching in her joints. In fact, the building was in such poor repair that it was decided the 1953 season should be the last for the Y.W.C.A. campers there.

In 1954 the property was purchased by Raymond Hendrix, who has since died. He planned to donate the property to the Church of Christ to be used as a summer vacation Bible school. The property consisted of sixty-four acres of land, the hotel building, nine smaller buildings, a swimming pool, and the mineral springs. Plans called for the rehabilitation of the buildings. It is hoped that soon again squeals caused by plunges into the spring-fed pool will echo up the glen; gatherings around the campfires for worship will be seen; "Honor the Flag" ceremonies will be witnessed and vesper hymns sung.

Perhaps no resort in Alabama has seen more activity than the Alabama White Sulphur Springs. There is much to interest the visitors there now. It is the last remaining old resort hotel building of noteworthiness still standing in Alabama. It stands as a reminder, even in its present state of repair, of the old days when people frequented the watering places.

8

Albert Hotel SELMA

The history of the Hotel Albert in Selma dates back to February 15, 1854, when the legislature chartered the Broad Street Hotel Company. John M. Strong, Nathaniel Waller, James M. Huggins, James D. Monk, Samuel M. Chapman and Thomas W. Street were appointed commissioners to "open books on subscription to the capital stock of a company to be called The Broad Street Hotel of Selma," with the building to be located on Broad Street and Dallas Avenue. However, the commissioners failed in their efforts to dispose of $100,000 in capital stock necessary to construct the hotel.

On February 2, 1860, the legislature passed an act "to revise and amend the act incorporating the Broad Street Hotel Company of Selma." The first amendment added the names of C. E. Thomas, M. J. A. Keith, William S. Knox and James Lapsley to the original list of commissioners. The authorization for the issuance of capital stock was increased from $100,000 to $200,000, and the company was given the authority to sell bonds.

Construction of the Broad Street Hotel finally got under way in the latter part of 1860. James E. Sweet of Albany, New York, was the architect. In addition to drawing the plans for the building, he superintended its construction until he was called home in April, 1861, at the outbreak of the War Between the States. Major T. M. Wiley then supervised the construction from April until December, 1861, when work was suspended because of the war.

At this time the brick and frame work had been completed to the fourth floor, but the building was without a roof. Hall and Granger of Selma handled the brick work up to this point. The stone, quarried in Shelby County, was furnished and laid by Charles Neilson. The hotel is of Venetian architecture, following the design of the Palace of the Doges in Venice.

The Broad Street Hotel building played a minor role in the War Between the States when the Confederate and Union cavalrymen, at various times, stabled their horses in the hotel's ground floor area.

Selma enjoyed unusual prosperity in 1866. The city council paid $15,000 for the Central Masonic Institute building and presented it to Dallas County for use as the courthouse, following the removal of the county seat that year from Cahawba to Selma. The city also organized a paid fire department, purchased a steam fire engine, built and furnished a hospital, established a public school on the plan of Mobile and New Orleans, built a market house, permitted the construction of a street railroad, and extended the limits of the city under the provisions of the newly adopted city charter. The old fortification on the Summerfield and Range Line roads was leveled so as not to obstruct the public highway. During the year many new homes were built and businesses established in an effort to "rebuild the city" which had been left in ruins during occupation by federal forces under General Wilson.

But still the city, with all its speedy return to prosperity, was without an up-to-date hotel. Attention was called to the problem in the February 9, 1866, issue of the Selma *Daily Messenger:*

10 ALBERT HOTEL

> There is not a first class hotel in Selma — A first class hotel here is a necessity. We cannot do without one. Forty-five thousand dollars in cash has already been expended on the Broad Street Hotel; but the company by whom it was undertaken, crippled hopelessly by the war, is unable to finish it, and it stands there a reproach to the enterprise of our people. The company owns the lot, 220 x 240, on the principal street and in the very heart of the city; the walls of the building, 220 x 210, are up to the third story —here the work stopped. One Hundred thousand dollars will complete the building and furnish it in good style.

On June 15, 1866, the Broad Street Hotel Company sold the partially built hotel to Charles M. Shelly. On December 7 a new company, known as The National Hotel Company of Selma, was formed. The incorporators were Charles M. Shelly, Joseph Hardie, John White, Porter King, Boliver Eason, Thomas W. Shae, and William N. Boynton. These men were appointed commissioners to open books on subscription to capital stock in the company, with the understanding that $50,000 had to be subscribed before the company could become a corporate body.

In May, 1867, Mr. Shelly sold the property to The National Hotel Company of Selma. Work was resumed on the building, a roof was constructed, and with the completion of the first and second floors accommodations were available for guests. Facilities included eleven bedrooms, a bridal apartment, two parlors, and a skating rink. The skating rink was on the second floor, occupying the space originally designed for the spacious dining room. Besides the main office, commercial stores occupied the principal portion of the ground floor.

One of the outstanding features of the first floor lobby is the broad oaken stairway which curves gracefully to the right and left in leading to the second floor. The stairway is fronted with large, beautiful stained glass windows, lending additional elegance to the interior style and finish. A large rotunda surrounded by an oaken balustrade looks down on the lobby below to dominate the appearance of the main hallway.

Though the exterior walls of the third and fourth floors were finished, years elapsed before the interior work on these floors was completed. An impressive Venetian arcade on the second floor, facing Broad Street from above the arcade leading into the hotel entrance, is graced with fourteen columns. Directly above the second floor arcade, balconies on the third and fourth floor levels extended outward from the building. Above the roof line, directly over the two balconies, an octangular-shaped observation tower was erected.

By order of the city council, the hotel company was "allowed to pay half taxes" in 1868. This was intended to assist it financially because of the difficulties experienced in selling stock and bonds. Interest rates during this period were from twenty to twenty-five per cent.

In 1891 the hotel was purchased by a group of stockholders organized as the Hotel Albert Company, a name chosen to honor Albert G. Parrish, who was active in procuring the money to purchase the property. The company engaged J. G. Barnwell, an architect from Rome, Georgia, to furnish plans and direct the work of completing the hotel. Work was begun by John Z. Norris on December 14, 1891, including completion of all the ground floor stores on Broad Street. Mr. Parrish was able to get the city council to exempt city taxes on bonds issued to complete and furnish the Hotel Albert.

George O. Baker of Selma, a mining engineer who came there from Philadelphia before the War Between the States, invested heavily in the Hotel Albert enterprise. Mr. Baker and Albert G. Parrish both served on the Selma Public School Board, and schools have since been named for each of them.

With the completion of the building the ground floor consisted of the main office of the hotel, eight stores, a barber shop, billiard room, bar, and laundry, and the elevator entrance. On the second floor the skating rink was converted into a dining room, measuring forty-one by seventy-one feet, with bronze ceiling, oak wainscoting, and handsomely designed stained glass windows. Also located on the second floor were a large pantry, a children's dining room, the kitchen, public and private parlors, and a bridal apartment, in addition to the eleven bedrooms already in use. On the third floor there were thirty-eight bedrooms, and on the fourth floor, forty-three more.

From time to time improvements have been made to the building. The balconies on the third and fourth floors have been removed, as has the observation tower. A small arcade on the third floor, with six columns, is directly over the Broad Street entrance. This arcade adds greatly to the original design of the building and conforms to the Palace of the Doges architecture.

Among the interesting parts of the hotel, the reception parlors on the second floor are most noteworthy, and the antique furniture in them is worth a special trip to see.

Since 1930 the hotel has had but three managers. F. A. Cater served from 1930 to 1950, Cook Hearn from 1950 to 1952, and G. H. Mosher, the present manager, since 1952.

On Sunday, January 3, 1954, the public was invited by the manager, Mr. Mosher, to inspect the reconditioned hotel building, which had been completely modernized. The dining room area on the second floor had been converted into eleven bedrooms, each with bath; the kitchen had been made into two apartments; and the billiard room, bar and store rooms had been converted into a beauty shop. Many other improvements were made throughout the building, including the redecoration of all rooms. Automatic fire sprinkler protection is maintained throughout the hotel. Current officers of the Hotel Albert Company are H. W. Gamble, president; B. F. Wilson, secretary; and A. P. Elebash, treasurer.

Selma is so steeped in colorful history that its atmosphere remains distinctly Old South, despite all its progressive modernity. The Hotel Albert is rightly among the showplaces of that city, although its architecture is not in the southern tradition. Its distinctiveness as the only building of its sort in Alabama makes it interesting to visitors, and is a source of pride to residents of the town.

13

American Hotel GAINESVILLE

The land where Gainesville, in Sumter County, is now located was once owned by John Coleman, a white man who settled there the year before the Dancing Rabbit Treaty in 1832 and who became entitled to three hundred to four hundred acres of land by the treaty because he had a Choctaw wife. He at once offered to sell the land to George S. Gaines for $1,000 and the latter accepted, paying the first installment. Mr. Coleman told Mr. Gaines a few days later that Colonel Moses Lewis had since offered him $2,000 in cash, and remarked that the difference would have saved him from toil in his old age. Mr. Gaines had known him well since he came into the country as the government factor, and he suggested that Coleman go to Colonel Lewis, sell the property to him, and refund the advance he had received from Gaines. Colonel

Lewis bought the property, laid out the town and named it Gainesville because of his high regard for Mr. Gaines.

Before the construction of railroads in that section of the state, Gainesville was the most important cotton shipping point on the Tombigbee River. Flatboats and poleboats conveyed about 6,000 bales of cotton annually to the Mobile market. Between 1832 and 1838 the population of the town grew to nearly 4,000. It was during this period that the famous shower of meteors or "falling stars" occurred on November 13, 1833; and "Dark Sunday"—a solar eclipse—occurred on December 21, 1834. The meteor display furnished the title for Carl Carmer's book, *Stars Fell on Alabama.*

The Tombigbee River was a thoroughfare for river boats. Boats docking regularly at the Gainesville landing included the *Vincennes, Planter, Lamplighter, Lewis Case, Ophelia,* and *Gen. Sumter;* and later, the *Jas. L. Hewitt, Frances Lyon, Montgomery,* and *Gainesville.* Plantation owners for miles around came to Gainesville to ship their cotton or to board the packet for Mobile, 315 miles down the river, to stock up on items not obtainable in Gainesville. In addition to steamboat transportation, Gainesville was situated on the stage route from Columbus, Mississippi, to Selma and Montgomery. This important west Alabama line was operated by Jemison, Ficklin, Powell and Company, which used four-horse stages.

One of the largest buildings in Gainesville was the American Hotel, located on Yankee Street near the bluff, overlooking the river. It was built in 1836 by Martin Griswold, who kept it open for six years through the encouragement of Colonel W. W. Russell, a local merchant. In its next ten years of operation, the hotel had six proprietors, none of whom remained more than two years. On September 21, 1852, Robert Grattan McMahon, a local storekeeper, became the proprietor with the idea of remaining there for only three years. He stayed for more than twenty-five.

The American Hotel was a two-storied frame building with twenty rooms. A long hall extended the length of the building on the first floor with rooms on each side. The hotel had a dance hall on the second floor which was built on springs to assist the dancers with the "steps of the day." This dance floor was known throughout the state. A veranda at the front on both floors was a delightful place for the guests to look down upon the town. At one end of the veranda an enclosed stairway led to the second floor.

The hotel was the most pretentious building in Gainesville. Eight dormer windows extended from the front roof, and a bell tower above the roof line housed the bell which rang three time a day to announce the meals. The building was known for its white dressing and green-trimmed window blinds.

The bill-of-fare at the American Hotel made it famous. Because it had an underground storage area built of brick under the bluff near the hotel, fresh produce was always available, even out of season. Ice was usually kept during all seasons in this underground storage.

Mr. McMahon's genial manner and hearty welcome to his guests made them feel at home at the American. He dispersed a generous and liberal hospitality, taxing himself to the utmost and even beyond ordinary efforts to confer kindness, often upon the undeserving and those who proved unworthy. This was his nature. No personal friend ever paid for his hospitality. Mr. McMahon often said, "An up-country hotel won't pay." Often he was questioned as to continuous annual losses from his hotel, but with pride he would point to his slaves and state, "They are eating out of the hotel also and they look fine." It was not until the War Between the States that he made money.

During the war the hotel gave shelter to wounded soldiers. Mr. McMahon in a letter to his sister-in-law, Mrs. John McMahon, in Courtland, Alabama, dated April 20, 1861, wrote, "We have fifty-three of the poor wounded soldiers from Corinth—they are doing well and I have written Nate [her son who was a doctor] we could take fifty to one hundred more."

The Academy at Gainesville and the American Hotel were known jointly as the Buckner Hospital, and Dr. Francis Thornton of Kentucky was post surgeon. In the late spring of 1862, following the Battle of Shiloh, a large number of the soldiers wounded in that battle were cared for there. By the fall of 1862 Dr. W. T. McAllister was sent to Gainesville as surgeon in charge of the hospital. His assistants were Dr. S. W. Lee, then of Florida, Dr. R. D. Jackson of Selma, a Dr. Reese of Alabama, a Dr. Yates of Texas, and Mrs. Fannie A. Beers of New Orleans, a nurse. Mrs. Beers organized the nursing staff at the hospital and was in charge of the mess room, diets for the soldiers, laundry, linen room, renovation of garments, and nursing the wounded.

Mrs. Beers praised highly the co-operation of the fine women of Gainesville who came to the rescue of the hospital in supplying the needed linens. Before the hospital was completely organized, orders were received to transfer the facilities and staff to Ringgold, Georgia, because of the lack of hospital stores at Gainesville.

Later, in another letter to his sister-in-law in Courtland on December 5, 1864, Mr. McMahon stated, "We are having four large hospitals established here and among the surgeons will be Dr. Cress, the former surgeon with the 16th Alabama. . . ."

During the latter days of the war General Nathan Bedford Forrest and his cavalrymen, while being pursued by General Wilson, established headquarters at Gainesville on April 15, 1865. It was here that he learned of the surrender of General Lee's army at Appomattox Courthouse and of the fall of Mobile, followed soon by the negotiations of General Johnston with General Sherman. General Forrest knew that the end of the toilsome marches was at hand. On May 9, Brigadier General E. S. Dennis arrived at Gainesville as the federal commissioner to execute the proper paroles. General W. H. Jackson was appointed a commissioner to authenticate Confederate muster rolls and other necessary papers at Gainesville. Negotiations were handled at Citronelle by Confederate General Dick Taylor, but the soldiers were paroled at Gainesville. By May 16, approximately 8,000 officers and men had been paroled and permitted to return to their homes. The American Hotel was used by the officers who paroled the soldiers. A historical marker erected in Gainesville by the Alabama Historical Association commemorates the paroling of Forrest's men.

Mr. McMahon operated the American Hotel until March 1, 1875. In the Gainesville *Dispatch* of that date he advertised: "The subscriber having been in 'hotel harness' for twenty years, last September, and finding that it does not swell his purse, but rather collapses it, for this and other cogent reasons, has pulled down his 'hotel' sign and keeps only a private Boarding House. He will, though, entertain such friends as may call—if convenient."

In a letter written by Mr. McMahon to his nephew, Dr. Nate McMahon, in Courtland, one week after he announced the closing of his hotel, he said, "We have had an influx of shows and theatres for weeks past which kept me up until 12 and 1 O C and entirely consumed all my writing time. . . . You will see that I have taken down my Hotel sign, on account of the 'Civil Rights Bill'."

An editorial in the Gainesville *Dispatch* stated, "Robert Grattan McMahon, proprietor, a kind hearted gentleman, has discontinued his hotel after running it 20 years and retired from public business, but not to put people to inconvenience, will still entertain persons, who may insist on calling in a private way."

Mr. McMahon operated the boarding house until he died on May 8, 1880. At the time of his death he held the office of mayor of Gainesville. Following Mr. McMahon's death, his wife and his daughter, Mollie, and her husband, John Gilbert, made the hotel building their private home. Following the death of Mrs. McMahon, Mr. and Mrs. Gilbert continued to live there.

The American Hotel building was torn down in 1915. Before the building was removed, it became so dilapidated that it was dangerous.

18

Anniston Inn

In 1872 the Woodstock Iron Company was formed by General Daniel Tyler, Alfred L. Tyler, James Noble, Sr., and John W. Samuel, and William Noble. The first furnace of the company was completed and started in April, 1873, at Anniston, and the second was completed in August, 1879. By 1881, a cotton factory, the largest and finest in the state, was completed. In 1882 the car-wheel works of Noble Brothers were moved from Rome, Georgia, to Anniston.

Meanwhile, a model city had been laid out by the Woodstock Iron Company for Anniston. This included streets, drainage, water works, schools and an electric light plant. The company advertised, "the situation of Anniston is such that it cannot but be a healthy place." Perhaps the next most outstanding project of the company was the building of the Anniston Inn, a fine hostelry that cost the company $260,000. The dining room alone cost $27,000.

Plans for the inn were drawn by Stanford White and work on the building began in the fall of 1884. When it was completed and opened to the public under the proprietorship of Milo Butler & Son in April, 1885, the inn was advertised as "the completest hotel in the South, and no man who has not seen it has a right to dispute that claim. It is a graceful specimen of Queen Anne architecture. Its very appearance is an invitation to rest and ease." It was located between Fourteenth and Fifteenth Streets and between Moore and Gurnee Avenues.

The wide verandas extended entirely around the first three floors. Easy chairs were provided on each of the verandas for the guests to enjoy the breezes. The grounds consisted of twenty acres of beautifully landscaped lawn, in the center of which was a lake. Winding drives led to the entrance of the inn.

The interior finish was of solid wood polished like satin, relieved by unique tiles and rich tapestry. The square windows with their stained glass and artistic draperies softened the scene with a peculiarly fine effect. The parlors were magnificently furnished, and offered many tempting devices for the comfort of their occupants. The bedrooms were large and well ventilated, and from the second to the fifth floor were furnished in equal style and taste. The most beautiful room in this elegant establishment was the dining room. Its walls were of oak, with exquisitely carved ornaments. The glowing arches which spanned it in three places and the inlaid work which shone about the windows in various designs were among the many things the guests admired in this royal room. The tables were furnished with the clearest crystal, the brightest silver and the most beautiful china. The menu was in keeping with the elegance of the table settings.

The entire inn was lighted with both incandescent electric lights and gas. It was said to have been "the first hotel in the United States to be lighted throughout with incandescent lights."

Upon the opening of the inn, the Atlanta *Constitution* reported:

> The Anniston Inn has to-day been thrown open to the public, complete in every detail—nothing wanting, nothing lacking, nothing left undone—a perfect marvel of finish, painstaking work, of convenience, of comfort, luxury and taste; furnished as has not been surpassed in this or any other country.

The situation itself is everything that could be desired, commanding the most beautiful views in every direction, of the finest valley and mountain scenery in the South. The grounds have been laid off on every side and graded and sodded, shrubbery planted, walks graveled and rolled, drives paved, and the whole work made permanent and secure by the most thorough system of paving and draining. The architecture of the inn is Queen Anne. The first story is cut stone, the second of pressed brick, and the third and fourth and fifth of heavy framed work, covered with California redwood shingles and Georgia slate. The wide windows, heavy window frames, gables and large bay windows give a grand and picturesque effect.

The interior, from the first floor to the top, is one beautiful piece of cabinet work of oak, selected Southern pine, California redwood and walnut. The ceiling, floors, beams, wainscoting and windows, door casings, halls, offices, ladies and gentlemen's parlor, the sitting and dining room, have been finished and highly polished, bringing out the natural grain of the wood as perfectly as the finest finished furniture. The heavy girders supporting the ceiling of the dining room, ladies' parlor and rotunda have been encased in oak beautifully paneled and polished. The grand staircase is a masterpiece of workmanship and art; built of massive polished oak and flanked on every floor with beautiful stained-glass windows. The ladies' chambers are large, with wide windows, all opening so each window gives a view of the grand scenery beyond.

Every room from basement to the top floor, as well as the broad porch that extends for nearly a quarter of a mile around the building, is lighted by the Brush incandescent light, the whole arranged either for gas or electricity. The building is heated throughout by hot water conveyed through pipes and register in the rooms and halls, while the baths and water closets are supplied on every floor with abundance of clean water from the mountain water-works, and the entire building protected in case of fire by hose on each floor; water always on at a high pressure from the mountain reservoir. The elevators are run by hydraulic pressure from the same source.

The ladies' parlor is carpeted with heavy Wilton carpet; the windows draped with heavy Turcoman old gold and velvet curtains suspended by brass poles and brackets. The furniture is upholstered with blue and crimson silk plush; the tables are ebony beautifully inlaid; the chandeliers are yellow brass, with center-piece of beaten copper ornamented with silver. The fireplaces in parlor, gentlemen's sitting room and dining room are built of terra cotta; are very wide and old-fashioned, extending from floor to ceiling, and are ornamented with heavy brass andirons and fenders. The upper sash of the windows of first floor, as well as the doors to ladies' parlor and main hall, are stained glass; the windows and archways all draped with rich Turcoman curtains. The furniture of office and gentlemen's parlor is cherry, beautifully carved—the large arm and smokers' chairs, cherry, cushioned with olive green leather; the writing table, a desk of cherry, elegantly finished.

The dining room is a gem—a thing of beauty—well lighted with broad square and bay windows on every side—the upper sash, with small stained glass, being stationary; the lower being doors of large glass swinging on hinges, opening outward—all the windows being hung with heavy rich Turcoman curtains, the floor carpeted with heavy Hartford body Brussels carpets, as are the halls, office, gentlemen's parlor and smoking room, stairway, and every chamber in the inn.

The chambers are large and splendidly ventilated—windows of double width, protected by linen window shades on spring rollers; next with folding inside blinds. The windows of every chamber are draped with costly Madras curtains. Many of the suites of rooms have bay windows and broad tile fireplaces, with massive paneled mantels of polished yellow pine and beveled plate-glass mirrors. The furniture of chambers of highly polished cherry and ash, each bed furnished with a spring and hair mattress; the pillows and bolsters of feathers of best quality. The blankets, quilts and linens are of the finest quality, and in keeping with the surroundings.

The table linen is of the choicest quality; the silver plain, but massive; the china and glass are in keeping with the whole. Two hundred guests can be comfortably seated. The children's and servants' dining rooms are fitted up in the same manner as the main dining room. The inn has two large refrigerators on the ground floor capable of holding a car load of meat and fruit, and one large refrigerator for general storage, and a smaller one on kitchen floor for daily use.

On the first floor of the building known as the annex are the steam laundry, ironing room, bakery and boiler room, with two 40-horse-power locomotive boilers to heat the building and run the electric engines. On the second floor is the kitchen, serving room, china and silver room and pantry, all fitted in the most thorough manner. The two floors above are the servants' quarters, being a small inn of itself, the rooms being nicely furnished and carpeted, with bath rooms and closets on each floor.

The inn was managed by Harry Hardell, a well-known hotel operator from Philadelphia. Manager Hardell was ever mindful of making the Anniston Inn a most entrancing place for a short stay, especially for the people who were passing through on their way to Florida in the fall and returning northward in the spring. Since Anniston was also a halfway point between New York and New Orleans, it was advertised: "A stop here will break the fatigue of a long ride. The railroads will give travelers every facility for stopping over as long as they may desire, and will protect them in their through-rate tickets."

During the first two years of the hotel's operation, an orchestra from Macon, Georgia, was employed. Dances which were held twice a week featured the German and the Lancers, the favorite dances at that time. During the summer seasons in 1885 and 1886, a large number of young ladies from New Orleans and Mobile were present to enjoy the gay entertainment offered at the inn.

On August 13, 1888, Samuel Noble, vice president and general manager of the Woodstock Iron Company, died, and soon thereafter all the various companies which composed the parent company separated and independent companies were formed. The Anniston Inn was taken over by the Anniston City Land Company, and M. A. Butler was made manager.

A very outstanding social affair was held at the Anniston Inn when Adlai Stevenson, soon after his election as Vice President of the United States in 1893, came to Anniston and was entertained by Dr. T. W. Ayers. A dinner was given at the hotel in celebration of the national party's successful campaign, and also the triumph in the Fourth Congressional District of Alabama over the Populists and Republicans for the first time in thirty years.

The Southern Female University, which occupied the Lakeview Hotel building in Birmingham until 1894, closed as a result of the fire which destroyed that structure in that year. Through the efforts of the school's former president, Henry G. Lamar, the Anniston Inn was obtained and the school reopened, although its name was changed to the Anniston College for Young Ladies. Dr. A. J. Battle became president of the new college and served in this capacity until 1906, when he was succeeded by Dr. Clarence J. Owens, who served until 1909.

When the college was disbanded in 1909 and gave up its lease on the inn, the building was closed and it remained unused for the next eight years. The inn was reopened during World War I. O. N. Todd was the manager in 1917 and 1918, and was followed by A. Lamar Poindexter, who served as manager until 1922. With the establishment of Camp McClellan in Anniston, the inn became the assembly place for many social entertainments for the soldiers and their families. Dances were given regularly, and accommodations were also provided for guests who were there to visit the soldiers in camp.

When General John J. Pershing made his first trip to Camp McClellan in December, 1919, the local post of the American Legion entertained him at the Anniston Inn with a 'possum dinner. Colonel Harry N. Ayers, then the commander of the local post, luckily planned other entrees for the general, for it developed that he barely tasted the 'possum. Most of the grandees of Anniston and their ladies were invited to this dinner at $10.00 per place.

The inn continued to be "the wonder and admiration of visitors." Dancing in the dining room attracted the local people of Anniston, as did the script dance for the younger set on various occasions. Several local residents occupied rooms permanently at the inn. It was unfortunate the inn could not depend upon the patronage for which it was built, resort trade. The luxurious appointments and external attractions won for it the title, "the famous Anniston Inn." Because of its nearness to the old Union Station, it did enjoy some commercial patronage.

On January 2, 1923, the inn burned and only a portion of the building was saved. After the fire the City of Anniston acquired the property, and the remaining part of the building later became the property of the Axis Club, being deeded to the club for a small sum.

Had the fire not destroyed the hotel register, such names as Abraham Hewitt, Peter Cooper Hewitt, W. S. Gurnee, William Nelson Cromwell, and P. J. Goodhart, all northern capitalists, could be found repeatedly. Governor Herbert Lehman of New York was a frequent visitor to the inn.

Though it was considered the finest hotel in the South, it was an over-improvement. The land company struggled with it for nearly forty years, at a loss on the investment during most of them. Only ten years during this time was it operated for the purpose for which it was constructed. Its memory remains a tradition of the early days of Anniston, of which the early residents still rightly boast.

24

Aus-Kel Springs

Could I but paint descriptive scenes
Of Land-scape views on lawns of green,
Of ball grounds, parks and swimming pools,
With bathrooms tempered warm and cool,
I would sculpture high, write underneath
The "Aus-Kel" Springs, My masterpiece.

If you are in search of a summer home,
Where native birds sing sweet their song,
Come out and see the "Aus-Kel" Springs,
And join with nature there to sing,
The joy and peace that reigns above,
And as thyself, thy neighbor love.

—*Slocomb School Bulletin,* 1907-1908

The Aus-Kel Springs Hotel, located two miles southeast of Slocomb in Geneva County, was constructed in 1908 by J. C. Ausley and A. C. Kelly, partners in the Morris Lumber Company of Slocomb. The name of the hotel bore the first three letters of each owner's last name.

The springs, of blue colored lime water, boiling up through white sand, were located beneath a beautiful bluff, surrounded by a large grove of trees. It was found that the water from at least two of the springs contained minerals. This immediately gave inspiration to the enterprising gentlemen who owned the land to build a hotel, located a half-mile from the springs.

The hotel, containing a dozen rooms, was a two-story structure built of lumber taken from the surrounding forests. In connection with the hotel there were bath houses and two swimming pools, one for the men and one for the women, a quarter of a mile apart. A dance hall, skating rink, bowling alley and baseball diamond were added attractions for entertainment at Aus-Kel Springs.

Since Aus-Kel Springs was not on a main line railroad, the owners provided a private narrow-gauge dummy railroad to transport visitors to and from the springs. An open-air coach drawn by a steam locomotive made trips to Slocomb hourly during the day to pick up guests, as well as to meet the trains of the Central of Georgia Railroad. Transportation on the dummy line was for the convenience of hotel guests and visitors. Visitors were required to pay fifteen cents for a round trip.

The hotel operated on the American plan. However, guests who rented cottages had the privilege of taking their meals at the hotel.

Unfortunately, due to the inaccessibility of the resort, the hotel was short-lived. It was in the southern part of the state and generally the people of south Alabama were more interested in resorts with higher altitude.

The hotel closed its doors after the 1911 season, but thereafter the owners made the recreational facilities available to the people in and around Slocomb. It became well known as a popular picnic grounds. After the two-story hotel building remained idle for a few years, it burned to the ground.

Today the property is owned by Mr. and Mrs. Charles C. Smith. They have constructed a guest house which they are occupying as their home. An electric organ has been installed in their newly designed recreation room. They have built a modern bath house, constructed a new swimming pool which is supplied by water from the springs, built stables for their horses and improved the grounds, in preparation for a beautiful home to be built there in the near future.

Aus-Kel Springs Hotel and resort was built with the objective of attracting visitors from distant places as well as local people. The hope of attracting guests from out of the state for vacations was never realized; however, the hotel became a mecca for drummers. The place was beautiful, quiet and restful, and afforded much pleasure to those who visited there.

Aus-Kel Springs Hotel was perhaps the only hotel in Alabama which necessarily had to be reached by transportation made possible by its owners. The dummy line was a novelty for the children, who often made round trips for amusement. With the lumber company moving away in 1912, the hotel closed and the dummy line was removed. This meant the end of Aus-Kel Springs as a summer resort.

For years the residents of several towns nearby used the grounds for picnics and ball games.

Bailey Springs

In 1831 and 1832 Jonathan Bailey acquired 200 acres of land in Lauderdale County from the government. In 1843 he became interested in another forty-acre tract of land nearby, on which was located a small stream of water which emerged from the side of a precipitous hill and gradually accumulated in a flint basin below. This spring was fourteen miles from Tuscumbia, nine miles from Florence, and two-and-a-half miles from the stage road leading to Nashville. Mr. Bailey finally obtained this land from the government three years later, in 1846.

Dr. A. C. Farrar, a Jackson, Mississippi, physician, reported in 1854 that the spring, at the time of its discovery, had the following appearance: "On the surface of this small spring, could be seen, from time to time, a thick scum or pellicule of a dark brown color, which imparted to the touch unctious properties."

Several neighbors of Mr. Bailey were afflicted with sore eyes and they used the water from this spring as an external application. Their eyes were helped and finally cured. About this time Mr. Bailey's health, which had previously been good, for some reason became impaired. He was severely afflicted with dyspepsia of a most aggravated and intractable character. In vain he sought relief through the skill of the most eminent, approved and popular physicians of his neighborhood.

Mr. Bailey grew worse daily, and at length one of the medical gentlemen in attendance advised him to visit a mineral spring some fifty miles distant. So depressed were his spirits and so shattered his constitution, however, that he balked at the idea of leaving his home. He casually adverted to his own little spring, informing his physician of the cures it had effected for his neighbors, and suggested that perhaps it might benefit him as well. The doctor examined the water and gave him permission to use it, probably more as an experiment to amuse his patient and to give him mental quietude than as a serious attempt to cure him.

For some time Mr. Bailey suffered with a severe spinal pain, which made him restless by day and sleepless by night, but finally his pain was abated and then it ceased entirely. His appetite improved, his good health returned, and he was pronounced cured.

The next case was that of a gentleman from Tennessee who had scrofula, and the water was no less beneficial in his case. The fame of this spring had begun, and news of the wonderful effects of its water induced twenty patients to visit there in 1844, even before Mr. Bailey had rightful ownership of the property. Most of those who visited there were gratified with the effects, and the spring soon attracted the attention of the most eminent physicians of Lauderdale County. They became convinced that the water possessed valuable medicinal properties, and advised their scrofulous, dyspeptic and dropsical patients to use the water.

Each successive year added to the reputation of the water, and this once-neglected little fountain became the resort of rich and poor, young and old, sick and well. Its visitors hailed from such distant places as St. Louis, Louisville, Cincinnati, and Columbus, Mississippi, with no effort on the part of the proprietor to advertise the resort. By 1853 the number of visitors had multiplied beyond the ability of the proprietor to accommodate them.

Mr. Bailey continued to conduct the springs as the only proprietor until October, 1857, when he died of apoplexy. In 1858 the springs, houses and acreage were purchased by A. G. Ellis, under the name of Ellis & Company, for the sum of $35,000. Within three years, more than $40,000 was spent for a hotel and improvements to make Bailey Springs comfortable for the sick and delightful to the pleasure seeker. An advertisement said: "It is now what nature evidently intended it should be, one of the most beautiful, lovely and attractive watering places in the United States."

The springs were enclosed with a neat plank fence, which embraced about ten acres of ground, all of which was beautifully adorned with shade trees and shrubbery. The three springs were sheltered under one roof by a shed which measured 150 by 60 feet, giving sufficient room for 200 guests, under which invalids could exercise and be protected from "falling weather." The three springs, aside from the larger freestone spring, all differed from each other and contained separate and distinct medicinal qualities, but all were equally efficacious in the cure of disease. One spring frequently checked diarrhea while the other acted as a purgative.

For the 1858 season, which opened March 19 and extended to December 19, there were 1,550 registered guests at the hotel. Because of the famous cuisine, many guests when traveling in the extreme northern parts of Alabama went out of their way to eat meals at Bailey Springs.

It was a general custom in the registration of a family for the gentleman to register for himself and the lady, and to list the number of children and servants. Many of the guests brought along their servants when visiting the resort, while in other instances plantation owners often sent their slaves there to be cured of disease. A rather unusual entry appeared in the hotel register on May 12, 1859 — "The Holding Juvenile Continentals of Brooklyn, New York, Mr. W. L. Holding, Wife & Four Sons to stay all summer." Eight days later a man destined to make history signed his name in the register — "N. B. Forrest, Memphis." The next time he visited the hotel was on July 20, 1867, when he signed "Gen." as a prefix to his name. In the Florence *Gazette* of August 3, 1859, it was reported: "One hundred and fifty arrivals, not counting servants, were reported for the week of July 17, 1859 at Bailey Springs. They amused themselves with music, bowling, whist and cricket."

Ladies appeared at Bailey's elegantly appareled. For instance, there was the "Darro," created of white taffeta elaborately adorned with needlework. Its double tabs, beautifully proportioned, elicited admiration, and the scroll reverse with effective drop trimming was a beautiful novelty. The "Marion," the "Nightingale," and innumerable other diverting fashions were also often seen at the resort.

In 1860 it was advertised:

> The beautiful shades, walks, bowling saloons, both for ladies and gentlemen, billiard tables, bath houses, and shower baths, long needed, are now ready for visitors (the shower bath at the fall of the branch); together with a large number of well furnished and finished rooms, to say nothing of the accommodations, which will be the very best the country can afford; all under the superintendence of the best managers and stewards, who have been employed on account of their great experience and determination to see that none shall go away dissatisfied. A very superior band of musicians have been employed to amuse and delight the visitors, and give animation and soul to the lovers of music, who may wish to touch the fantastic toe and grace the large and spacious ball room.

Ellis & Company called attention to other amusements at Bailey Springs as follows:

> But, we are asked, "How can the well amuse themselves and spend their time at Bailey Springs?" We answer, by reading entertaining and useful books. They may also take pleasure trips to Florence, nine miles distant, at which place, during commencement exercises, no one could be better entertained. The Wesleyan University is located there, with over two hundred young men in attendance, and one of the most flourishing institutions in the South or West. The Female Synodical College, with nearly as many students, is also located in Florence—They may visit, one and a half miles from Florence the three large cotton factories—Or they may visit Wright & Rice's large casting and machine works about four miles from the Springs, where steam engines, gins, wagons, sugar mills, and all manner of castings are manufactured, from the steam engine to the claw hammer. . . . And last, they may visit the extensive woolen factory of Milner & Co., about six miles from the Springs. . . . These factories deserve the notice and patronage of the Southern people.

Ellis & Company also suggested other pastimes for the well to amuse themselves:

> If they have a taste of Geology, they may range the hills and valleys in search of specimens, many of which abound in this region; they may cross Shoal Creek and ascend a lofty limestone cliff, and view in it an excavation where, many years ago, the rites of sepulture were rendered to one of the red men of the forest. From Shoal Creek beautiful shells may be obtained; but if the reader has not taste for, or knowledge of Geology, he may turn his attention occasionally to the piscatory tribe; but he will sometimes meet with the fate of Dr. Franklin's friend, who got glorious nibbles and no fish. At others, he will be amply rewarded by an abundant supply of large white delicious trout.

But actually it was unnecessary for the guests to leave the resort for their entertainment, for on the grounds there was a large and well-constructed ten-pin alley, with double tables and expert attendants. There were secluded forest drives, romantic rambles and hunting grounds. Each evening the large ballroom was enlivened by the stirring music of a fine brass or string band.

The proprietors thought it best to offer to the public the certificates of persons actually cured or benefited by Bailey Springs waters, as well as opinions entertained by distinguished men; believing that such a course would be more convincing to the invalid, and perhaps would induce those who were afflicted to visit the springs. Here are a few certificates:

> I have been conversant with the history of Bailey Springs from their first discovery . . . in the extraordinary curative effect of the water on Mr. Bailey himself, and am prepared to say most unequivocally, I do believe in the curative qualities of the water. I have seen with my own eyes, specimens of humanity raised from depths of affliction and disease, that seemed to be almost miraculous. And to the afflicted, it is not a matter of small moment, that these Springs have as their attendant physician, Dr. B. F. Crittenden, whose long and well tried skill gives an additional confidence, and affords an immediate hand of relief to such as require his attention. I know the man.
>
> Felix Johnson, former President,
> LaGrange College, Alabama.

Bailey Springs, Ala., Sept. 5, 1859

Messrs. Ellis & Co.:

Gentlemen: I cheerfully comply with your request, to give you a statement of my case. I arrived at your springs on the tenth of July last, severely afflicted with the dropsy, having had it from the first of February. I was swollen to about twice my natural size, and had very little or no hopes of recovery from it, but after using the water of your rock spring, without the use of any medicine, I shall leave in the morning, feeling and believing that I am entirely cured.

With my best wishes, gentlemen, for your health and success.

I am yours, very respectfully,

Ephraim Tuttle, of Louisiana.

Case of Joshua Stamps, of Rogersville, Alabama. "He came to the springs about 1845, afflicted with dyspepsia. His condition was very low, and life despaired of. He had tried seven physicians, but all to no effect. In four weeks he was restored to health, and it continued good till the last sickness. These facts are known by Drs. Kyle and Crittenden, Major Sturdevant, and many of the citizens of Rogersville, to whom reference is made."

An extract from a letter written by Col. Sam Tate, President of the Memphis and Charleston Railroad Co., he says: "You are at liberty to refer to me in your pamphlet. For many diseases, I think, your springs exceed any in the world."

An extract from a letter written by Col. F. M. White, President of the Mississippi and Tennessee Railroad, he says: "You are at liberty to refer to me in regard to the virtues of the Bailey Springs waters. I am assured of their great medicinal qualities."

Col. Miles H. McGehee, of Victoria, Mississippi, who kept his negro servants there almost all the time for scrofula and dropsy, says: "I have never sent one in time and let him stay long enough, but that he got well at Bailey Springs."

The proprietors of Bailey Springs ascertained that "two-thirds of all the visitors to Bailey Springs are invalids. In the last two years [1859 and 1860], thirty-six hundred persons have visited them, which would show the large number of twenty-four hundred invalids—a large majority of whom were either cured or benefitted by the use of the water—and, astounding to relate, there has not been an average of ten deaths a year."

The War Between the States had its effect on Bailey Springs. For the season in 1861, there were 841 guests registered at the hotel; in 1862 there were 106; in 1863, only 65; and during 1864 the resort was closed. In 1865, at the close of the war, the hotel reopened and, during the remainder of the year, there were 65 guests there. Bailey Springs suffered another loss in 1864 in the death of A. G. Ellis. The property descended to his widow, three daughters and a son, who continued the operation of the health resort under the name of Ellis & Company.

Perhaps one of the most noted figures ever to live at Bailey Springs was Dr. Henry A. Moody, who received his degree at the University Medical School of Louisville, Kentucky, in 1866, and soon thereafter began the practice of medicine at the resort. Dr. Moody was married to Miss Virginia Ellis, the daughter of Mrs. A. G. Ellis. Dr. Moody lived approximately a mile from the resort but he maintained his office in the Ball Room Row, which was one of the busiest "rows" at Bailey Springs. Here he prescribed the water that most benefited each patient. His report on the medicinal values of Bailey Springs waters is summarized as follows: "From extensive experiences, I am convinced of the great medicinal value by the use of Bailey Springs water, and the healthful atmosphere, climatic conditions, shady walks, and hygienic environments add greatly to the value and usefulness of same." Dr. Moody practiced his profession at Bailey Springs until 1888, when he moved to Panola, Mississippi, for six years. He then returned to Alabama to occupy the chair of Materia Medica and Therapeutics in the School of Medicine, in the Medical College of Alabama (technically then a part of the University of Alabama), in Mobile. Dr. Moody was at one time the managing editor and a writer for the *Southern Medical Journal.*

During the 1866 season, there were 429 registered guests at Bailey Springs, and by the end of the season in 1870, patronage had increased to 759. The crowds grew larger from year to year, but the number never exceeded those of the ante-bellum era.

John B. Bachelder, in his publication *Popular Resorts and How to Reach Them,* listed Bailey Springs as "one of high reputation for many years and are annually patronized by large numbers. At Tuscumbia, the passenger wishing to reach Bailey Springs takes a branch road to Florence, and stage thence." Saffold Berney, in his *Hand Book of Alabama,* published in 1878, states: "Bailey Springs—Lauderdale county, 9 miles northeast of Florence; connected with Memphis and Charleston Railroad, at Florence, by daily stages; location high and healthful; water excellent for dyspepsia, dropsy, gravel, scrofula, and all kindred diseases."

The following is a characteristic advertisement among many found in the Florence *Gazette*:

> Bailey Springs, North Alabama . . . These celebrated springs are now open to the public . . . their wonderful power in curing dropsy, scrofula, dyspepsia, female diseases and all derangements of the skin and kidneys is too well known throughout the South to be here reiterated. . . . A magnificent ball room served by a first class band, will afford amusement and gratification to the votaries of Terpsichore. A well stocked Livery Stable will insure satisfactory teams to the lovers of the drive, Billiards and Tenpins and bath house, etc., lend their artificial attractions to a place preëminent in Natural scenery, fine hunting and fishing, and the most effective mineral and chalybeate waters in America. Rush Patton's Daily Omnibus Line connects with the Memphis and Charleston R. R. at South Florence.
>
> Ellis and Company, Bailey Springs.

Rates at the resort were never too expensive. The summer rates were higher than those in the spring, fall and winter. The off-season rates for board were as low as $1.20 per day. Many thought that from September until the time of the winter rains was the very best time to receive all the benefits possible from the waters; therefore, the hotel was open practically the entire year. The hotel and the "rows" were able to accommodate five hundred visitors. The several "rows" were known as the Memphis Row, Florence Row, Mississippi Row, the Ball Room Row, the Dining Row and the Office Row. The Dining and Office Rows were one-story buildings and all others were two-story. The hotel building was a two-story structure. One private cottage on the grounds was known as Senator Morgan's cottage. The senator and his daughter spent many summers there.

Upon the death of Mrs. A. G. Ellis in 1887, the resort descended to Captain William P. Ellis and Mrs. Virginia Ellis Moody, son and daughter, respectively, of Mrs. Ellis; and W. A. Ellis, a grandson. Mrs. William P. Ellis operated the resort personally following the death of her mother-in-law.

In 1893 the Bailey Springs University, for higher education of women, was established at the resort. William P. Ellis, Dr. Henry A. Moody, Charles H. Tatum and Ella B. Ellis organized the school. Dr. Henry A. Moody was made president. The board of six trustees was to be appointed by the governor. Free tuition in all departments, including vocal and instrumental music, drawing, painting, elocution, physical culture, stenography and typewriting, was offered to thirty-six white females of the state between the ages of fourteen and twenty-four. With respect to free scholarships, the charter stated that "no charges except for board, heat, lights, washing and servants' attendance were made; and the aggregate amount for these items could not exceed $13.00 for four weeks for each student."

The university was incorporated with the approval of the state legislature on December 13, 1894. The effects of the Panic of 1893-94 evidently caused the school to struggle, for the student body consisted of only eight preparatory students and twenty-eight collegiate students. One student graduated in 1894. The faculty consisted of nine professors and instructors. The library contained three hundred volumes.

On February 23, 1899, the state legislature exempted the Bailey Springs buildings and improvements from taxation, both state and county, upon the agreement that the university would offer sixty free scholarships, one from nearly every county in the state. Mainly because of the distance of the university from railroad facilities, it was never a commercial success, and by 1900 it was closed. The university, during its existence, never interfered with the activities of the resort during the summer months.

In 1901 the Bailey Springs properties were sold to Bayles B. Shane, who in 1903 sold his holdings to Mrs. J. W. Bedingfield. In the same year, Mrs. Bedingfield sold the resort to Mrs. Tommie W. Kilburn. The following year Mrs. Kilburn sold the resort to H. C. Williamson. The several owners before Mr. Williamson continued to lease the facilities to Mr. William P. Ellis.

Under the ownership of Mr. Williamson, his brother-in-law, Frederick H. Hatch, managed the hotel until 1910, the final season of operation. The next successor in title was Fred W. Beyer who, in 1914, purchased the springs and the abandoned buildings. In 1916 Mr. Beyer sold his holdings to W. M. Richardson, J. W. Young and F. A. Nolen for $18,000. In 1918 C. W. Ashcraft purchased Mr. Nolen's one-third interest. In 1919, the government acquired an easement to permanently flood part of the land which became a part of the Wilson Lake. In 1920 the hotel and other buildings at Bailey Springs burned.

In 1924, J. E. F. Westmoreland purchased the Bailey Springs property. The following year he sold it to Sam K. Kendall for $41,000. A mortgage for $36,000 was given as part of the consideration. In 1926, Mr. Kendall had a contract to sell the property to Dr. Courtney W. Shropshire of Birmingham, who attempted to organize Bailey Springs, Inc., a stock company to exploit Bailey Springs. The Bailey Springs Finance Corporation, with headquarters in the First National Bank building in Birmingham, acting as the fiscal agents for Bailey Springs, Inc., issued a brochure which presented pictures and descriptions of the proposed casino hotel, sanatorium, clubhouse, eighteen-hole golf course, swimming pool and bathing beach, riding academy, bridle paths, and residential park, and a plan for beautification of the grounds.

Bailey Springs, Inc., published the following statement:

> For several generations Bailey Springs was a favored resort for the aristocracy of the South, but it has never been developed in a way even remotely commensurate with its potentialities. In ante-bellum days the resort was exceedingly popular, but with the unfortunate Civil War and its consequent

impoverishment of the Confederate States, like so many other Southern enterprises, it became almost decadent, although in the years that have intervened, people from all over the South have sought renewed health and vigor from its potent springs.

Though well promoted, Bailey Springs, Inc., failed to attract the co-operation of the medical profession in the United States and Canada in subscription to its stock.

With Dr. Shropshire's failure to exercise the option with Sam Kendall to purchase the properties, Mr. Westmoreland foreclosed his mortgage in 1928, and regained title to the property at the sale. He then improved the springs and grounds and sold a large number of lots on the backwaters of Shoal Creek. Mr. and Mrs. Westmoreland are now deceased, and H. L. Reeder of Florence is the administrator of the Westmoreland estate. Under Mr. Reeder's supervision, practically all of the Bailey Springs properties have been sold, with the exception of a few scattered lots.

Perhaps the statement issued by Bailey Springs, Inc., regarding the popularity of the resort before and after the War Between the States, is true. During the 1890's, Bailey Springs served as a popular recreational place, frequented by the people of Florence and Sheffield especially. Week-end parties and dances attracted the local young people. In the latter years of the resort, guests continued to fill the hotel and "rows" during the summer months; however, the larger percentage came for the recreation rather than the mineral waters. But regardless of the reasons why the patrons came, they eventually visited the spring yard. Even with the facilities of the resort in a rather worn-out condition, guests came and came again. The favorable reputation of Bailey Springs, which was established in the ante-bellum era, remained until it closed a half-century later.

38

Battery Heights Hotel BRIDGEPORT

Bridgeport is situated in the extreme northeastern corner of Alabama, in Jackson County, less than four miles from the intersection of the Tennessee-Georgia-Alabama state lines, amid the beautiful hills on the west bank of the Tennessee River. It acquired its name from the Nashville, Chattanooga & St. Louis Railroad bridges across the river and the establishment of a river port for the exchange of shipments by rail and steamboats. The post office was established October 1, 1854, as Jonesville, but the name was changed to Bridgeport on December 15, 1854.

Occupying a commanding position, it became the center of important military movements in 1863. The convergence of the natural routes of travel at this point made it the place for concentrating and distributing supplies. The federal army in Chattanooga was fed and supplied with ammunition from Bridgeport.

When the federal forces had been driven back into Chattanooga from the bloody field of Chickamauga and were being vigorously besieged, their commanders began to appreciate the importance of the river as a possible avenue of relief. Captain Arthur Edwards, the assistant quartermaster, was sent to Bridgeport with a corps of mechanics and builders and ordered to construct floating vessels to meet the emergency. He built a small steamer, the *Chattanooga,* which was of great service in carrying supplies to Kelly's Ford (Ferry), and which probably saved Grant's army in Chattanooga from the necessity of evacuating the city. Eight other boats were constructed by the federal government at Bridgeport and at Chattanooga during the winter of 1863-64, including the *Chickamauga,* the *Wauhatchie,* the *Resaca,* the *Lookout,* the *Stone River,* the *Kingston,* the *Bridgeport,* and the *Missionary.*

In 1887 a boom struck Bridgeport and the growth of the town was swift and phenomenal. The town was incorporated on February 18, 1891, and Frank J. Kilpatrick, formerly of New York, was elected the first mayor. Mr. Kilpatrick influenced other eastern capitalists to come to Bridgeport and make investments in homes, business houses, and manufacturing establishments. The land sales were advertised in many parts of the United States, especially in San Francisco and Seattle, with the use of the slogan "Keep Your Eyes on Bridgeport."

In 1888, at the Point on Battery Hill, overlooking the Tennessee River from the heights which were fortified during the War Between the States, Mayor Kilpatrick built the beautiful Battery Heights Hotel. The view of the river and valley at this point is spectacular, with the river bending in a southerly direction. A scenic road was constructed to Battery Hill and the Point.

The three-story hotel was erected to serve jointly as a hotel and a clubhouse. The building was of frame construction and contained forty rooms. The enthusiastic builder was aware of the fine appointments that would be required if the hotel were to attract guests and make them comfortable during their visit to the boom town. The hotel served as a popular meeting place for practically all social gatherings in the town. Soon after it was opened, Oscar S. Straus, the United States ambassador to Turkey, visited at Battery Heights.

The first floor of the hotel contained a large ballroom, reception and reading rooms, office, dining room and kitchen. The guest rooms were on the second and third floors. The interior walls throughout the building were finished with native growth gum, oak, walnut and maple paneling. Modern plumbing in all guest rooms, connected to sanitary sewers in the town, eliminated any possibility of unhealthful conditions or epidemics. The building was heated by steam. One of the most popular areas of the hotel was the observatory above the third floor, from which there was a commanding view of the valley to the east.

The Bridgeport Board of Trade advertised:

> Life in Bridgeport has its sunny side, for means of recreation are abundant. Horseback riding is especially enjoyable, and there are innumerable shady roads in valley and over mountain to afford endless variety of scene to add to the interest in the sport. The mountains abound in game and offer many charming bits of scenery to tempt the lover of Nature. Cascades, rocky glens and weird caverns lend objectives for excursion parties. Steamboat excursions on the Tennessee will disclose some of the most impressive sights to be found on any American waterway. The Flora of the country is peculiarly diversified and attractive. No regular boating club has been formed yet, although it is hard to understand why the straight, broad course of the river here should not tempt the athletes to aquatic sports. . . .
>
> All about is historic ground. Chickamauga, Mission Ridge and Lookout Mountain are within an hour's ride by rail. . . . An hour's ride from Bridgeport to the mountain top has the same climate effect as a journey five hundred miles Northward. . . . The climate has beneficial effect upon all throat, lung and catarrhal diseases. Scarlet fever and dyptheria, those dread destroyers of child life, are almost unknown; they have never been epidemic in the present generation. The chalybeate springs of Sand and Cumberland Mountains are highly beneficial for indigestion and stomach troubles. In fact these mountain plateaus are Nature's own sanitarium.

The Panic of 1893-94 ruined the plans of the boom town. As is the usual case during panics, people had little money to invest and Bridgeport suffered accordingly. The Battery Heights Hotel failed to attract patronage and Mr. Kilpatrick and his associates went broke. Keenly disappointed, Mr. Kilpatrick returned to New York, giving up the idea of a "New York in Alabama" which he had anticipated for Bridgeport. In his disappointment, he refused to sell his interest in the Battery Heights Hotel, and it remained closed for several years. He also refused to keep the hotel in repair. Finally, the building was converted into an apartment house. In 1920, after the death of Mr. Kilpatrick, it was torn down and the salvage material was used in the construction of several small homes near the site.

Battle House MOBILE

"The new hotel opposite the custom house has been commenced; for a crowd of workmen were yesterday tearing up the old foundation and digging place for the new," City Editor C. H. B. Fisher wrote in the Mobile *Register* on July 31, 1851.

The "new hotel" was a necessity for Mobile. In 1850 the Mansion House, on the corner of Royal and Conti streets, was destroyed by fire, and a week later the Waverly Hotel, two blocks away on the southeast corner of Royal and St. Francis streets, also burned, leaving the city without adequate hotel accommodations.

The "old foundation" was that of the Waverly and its next-door neighbor on the south, the Franklin House, both sites being needed for the construction of a hotel by a company formed after the 1850 fires under the leadership of James Battle and including Samuel J. Battle, Samuel H. St. John, Thomas St. John, Newton St. John, Sanford Cooley, William D. Dunn and Jonathan Emanuel. It was as a compliment to James Battle's leadership that the new hotel was named the Battle House. It was finished in September, 1852, and opened to the public on Monday, November 13, the same year.

Frederick Law Olmsted, in recording his memorable impressions of the South in the early part of 1853, had this comment to offer: "The Battle House, kept by Boston men, with Irish servants, I found an excellent hotel; but with higher charge than I had ever paid before. Prices, generally, in Mobile, range very high. There are large numbers of foreign merchants in the population; but a great deficiency of tradesmen and mechanics."

The old Battle House was a five-story brick building—although the fifth floor was not added until 1857—with 240 sleeping and living rooms, gas fittings, baths, hot and cold water, and space for twelve storerooms or shops on the ground floor. Paran Stevens, a noted New York hotel man, took the lease on the building and made Henry Chamberlain and A. D. Darling managers. The furnishings, ordered by Mr. Stevens and shipped from Boston on the schooner *Maine,* were the best that money could buy.

Since all the ground floor fronting on the two streets was let for business, the hotel proper began on the second floor. A pair of stairs, curved in a semicircle, entered a tile-paved lobby on that floor. The lobby and hall extended the full width of the building, and other halls ran to the dining rooms and bedrooms on that floor. Stairways led to the upper floors.

The planters from the Black Belt along the deltas of the Alabama and Tombigbee Rivers, and from the upland prairies of Alabama and Mississippi, were regular patrons, especially after the crops were laid away. Their year's work completed, they flocked to Mobile with their families for entertainment, and the Battle House was their principal meeting place. Every notable wedding in the upper country was followed by a honeymoon in the Battle House, and scenes of banquets, dances and other festivities followed closely upon each others' heels as the winter season passed.

The Battle House became the home of romance, and its cuisine and genial hospitality won widespread praise. The Hon. Amelia M. Murray of England, coming directly from the noted St. Charles in New Orleans, said in a letter of May 7, 1855, that in Mobile she found "a hotel, the best managed I have met in the United States."

The social life during the War Between the States, according to Kate Cummings, who had lived in Mobile since childhood, made the city "an abode of wealth and luxury." Thomas Cooper de Leon, a traveler who spent some time in all the important cities of the South, wrote that "the tone of Mobile society is more cosmopolitan than that of any city in the South, save perhaps, New Orleans." Madame Octavia Le Vert, who had enjoyed the rare privilege of foreign travel, maintained a "salon" in her spacious home. Many social and literary gatherings were held there and visitors were eager to join her circle. It is no wonder that the Confederate soldiers on leave flocked to Mobile to be entertained in the fine old homes by the patriotic young women of the city. But William Corson, an English merchant who visited Mobile in 1862, reported that "the absence of wine at hotel tables and of bar drinking kept the city and the troops in excellent order, but was hard on the traveller."

On May 27, 1863, an advertisement appeared in the Mobile *Register*, advising that the Battle House was "for rent," with possession promised on November 1 by Jonathan Emanuel, president of the Battle House Company. The same advertisement appeared simultaneously in the Montgomery *Advertiser,* the Memphis *Appeal,* the Charleston *Courier,* and the Richmond *Dispatch.*

Mobile directly realized the effects of the War Between the States in August, 1864, when Admiral David Farragut's fleet took possession of the entrance to Mobile Bay. The city itself, however, was not taken until April, 1865. A major catastrophe occurred on May 25, 1865. The ammunition surrendered by General Dick Taylor at Meridian had been brought down the river for storage in Mobile. As the powder and shells were being stored in a warehouse near the river, one of the shells apparently ignited accidentally. Frederick G. Bromberg, a merchant, said that "the city was shaken as if by earthquake." The Battle House, blocks away, suffered between $10,000 and $15,000 damage.

Following the war C. D. Barnes, formerly of the Astor House in New York City, became manager of the Battle House. The hotel was advertised extensively as a place of "large corridors, elegantly furnished rooms, and handsome dining rooms. The charges are $2.50 to $4.00 per day, and $50.00 and up per month."

44 BATTLE HOUSE

The following compliment was paid the Battle House by the noted actor, W. J. Florence:

Battle House, Mobile, November 17, 1888.

My dear Mr. Barnes:

I cannot leave your hotel without expressing my sense of obligation for your attentions and the many courtesies extended Mrs. Florence and myself during our stay. You have the best hotel south of New York City, and we are delighted with it. You deserve all the praise we hear so freely bestowed upon its management.

Yours faithfully

W. J. Florence

C. D. Barnes, Esq., Battle House

With the passing of years the hotel became outdated. In 1900 it was given a general overhauling. A large part of the ground floor of the building was taken for hotel purposes, the rooming space was increased, new parlors were furnished and other alterations, including the decoration of the main dining room in rococo style, were made.

Five years later, on the night of Sunday, February 12, 1905, flames were detected in the Battle House. The fire, discovered about 10:45 P.M. by one of the hotel cooks, originated in unoccupied rooms over the kitchen in the north wing of the hotel—rooms temporarily being used for storage purposes. Prompt alarm through the hotel annunciator system brought every one of the 147 guests out of the hotel safely, and a general alarm brought all of Mobile's firefighting apparatus to the scene. Despite the fire department's promptness in getting ten leads of hose into the building, the fire defied all efforts to subdue it. Shortly after midnight the north portion of the roof fell in, cutting off power and communications in the city's downtown section. Within another hour it was apparent that the entire building was doomed, as interior floors began falling in, one after another. Fortunately a heavy rain helped extinguish sparks falling on nearby roofs.

A check of the fire toll revealed a loss of approximately $250,000 in the hotel proper and another $200,000 in other business firms. William and A. Vizard, proprietors of the hotel, carried $150,000 insurance on the building. With the fire the old house passed into history, to be replaced by the present Battle House, which was erected three years later.

Almost every traveler of importance moving through the South had stopped at the old Battle House. They included, among many others, Sir Charles Lyell, the English naturalist; Henry Clay, statesman; William Lowndes Yancey, orator; Jefferson Davis, on his way to be inaugurated President of the Confederacy; General Braxton Bragg, General P. G. T. Beauregard, and Admiral Raphael Semmes, of Confederate fame; General E. R. B. Canby, commander of the land forces which took Mobile during the War Between the States; General Ulysses S. Grant, before he became president of the United States; and Millard Fillmore, after he had held that office.

The old Battle House, as a social center of Mobile, played an important role in the activities of the city. The Grand Ballroom was the scene of the Mardi Gras balls for many years.

In 1906 some of Mobile's leading citizens formed a company, with D. R. Burgess as president, to build a greater Battle House, and the new hotel was opened in 1908 after an expenditure of $1,350,000. The Louis Seize dining room and the Rotunda, with its great glass dome supported on piers of Caen stone and its decoration on the theme of "Mobile Under Five Flags," became major attractions.

On December 1, 1945, the hotel was purchased by the Mobile Battle House, Inc., of which Culver White was president and Leon Waite, Jr., vice president and manager. Work was soon started on what was then the largest modernization program ever undertaken by a hotel, and by late 1949 the program was completed. The Battle House was completely rehabilitated from basement to roof at a cost of more than $1,900,000.

It continues as "One of America's Fine Hotels," emphasizing the Southern hospitality which the Battle House name made famous more than a century ago. In 1958 this fine hostelry became a link in the chain of Sheraton Hotels.

46

Bellevue Hotel GADSDEN

In a valley at the foot of the southern terminus of Lookout Mountain, on the western bank of the Coosa River, lies Gadsden, ninety-two miles south of Chattanooga, fifty-four miles northeast of Birmingham, and fifty-two miles west of Rome, Georgia.

The Gadsden Land and Improvement Company, which was organized in January, 1887, owned three thousand lots in and around the city. Much of the property was situated on an elevated plateau, eighty to one hundred feet above the river, thus assuring beauty and health for those who wished to establish their homes there. The land company also offered sites for manufacturing purposes.

About three miles northwest of the city, where Black Creek hurries to join the Coosa River, is the site of Noccalula (Black Creek) Falls. At that point Noccalula Falls throws the water twisting and tumbling, creating an exquisite aquatic performance that is a fitting finis to the activities of Black Creek on Lookout Mountain. The creek runs along the depression on the top of the mountain for nearly thirty miles until it widens over a vast ledge of rock, falling one hundred feet into a whirlpool below. Half a mile from the falls, at the highest point overlooking the city five hundred feet below, the Gadsden Land and Improvement Company built the Bellevue Hotel, as a part of the company's boom promotion.

The Bellevue Hotel, with its one hundred rooms, was an architectural gem. The structure cost nearly $100,000 and was considered by many to be one of the finest resort hotels in the state. The building was considered a two-story structure; however, there were rooms at the third floor level in one section. An observation tower at a fourth floor height provided a vantage point for observing stretches of mountain scenery, magnificent forests, yawning precipices, and glimpses of a broad, winding river. The hotel was opened in 1889, under the supervision of the Gadsden Land and Improvement Company.

Within five years the Bellevue Hotel suffered the results of the Panic of 1893-94, as did the Gadsden Land and Improvement Company. Colonel R. A. Mitchell, president of the Queen City Bank of Gadsden, was also the president of the Gadsden Land and Improvement Company. During the Panic and the "trying years" that followed, Colonel Mitchell held together the property of the land company. Unfortunately, even before the Panic the hotel had proven a bad investment for the land company and it was closed.

The Bellevue Hotel building was well equipped and Colonel Mitchell solely through his own efforts established Jones College, a junior college for girls, in the building in 1895. The college was named for Dr. Amos B. Jones of Huntsville, who moved to Gadsden to become its president. Previously, Dr. Jones was president and proprietor of the Huntsville Female College until it burned in 1894. For the opening session of Jones College, there was an enrollment of 135 pupils from nine states. Because of the widespread interest in the fine facilities and educational advantages, Captain W. H. Weller brought his family to Gadsden for his children to be educated. While there, he organized the Weller Manufacturing Company, the pioneer of pipe manufacturing in Gadsden.

The Jones College was short-lived, operating for only two years because of the lack of patronage. Dr. Jones had purchased the Bellevue Hotel for $18,000, paying on May 17, 1895, the sum of $5,750, with the balance being secured by notes.

Following the closing of Jones College due to financial problems, the hotel building was used privately for the next few years by the principal stockholders of the Gadsden Land and Improvement Company during the summer months.

In 1901, Loui Hart, a resident of Gadsden, organized the Bellevue Hotel Company, with the following officers: Loui Hart, president, J. B. Cobbs, treasurer, and E. S. Jones, secretary. In July, 1901, the Bellevue Hotel Company purchased the hotel and adjacent unimproved land for $15,000. Loui Hart became manager of the hotel. He brought his "help" from New Orleans, including a chef and his assistants, waiters, and a five piece orchestra, all of whom were employed by New Orleans hotels during the winter months. An advertisement appeared in the Gadsden *Times*, stating the hotel was in need of five hundred spring chickens, large, medium and small, and was willing to pay the top market price for them. Broiled chicken was to be a specialty at the Bellevue.

For the 1904 season, Hart employed Charles S. Daly to manage the hotel. As a summer resort, the Bellevue attracted the social elite from many parts of the South; however, Manager Hart limited the number of guests to 150. Special emphasis was given to conventions and state-wide meetings. Dances were given regularly in the hotel's ballroom, said to be the largest in the state. Golf, tennis, billiards and pool provided additional entertainment for the guests. Music during the meal hours was a feature of the hotel.

A pavilion near the hotel was used as a place for picnics, outdoor dances and public gatherings. A chalybeate spring near the pavilion and two other springs in the vicinity, one of sulphur and the other freestone, were considered useful for their medicinal values.

At the falls, steps were built at an opening in the gorge, and many hotel guests were entertained under the overhanging rocks. Often a brass band was engaged to play at the falls. The falls and the amphitheatre under the cataract were often illuminated with calcium lights. Down in the gorge there were ferns of many varieties which gave forth a hue of green, made fresh by the mist of the falling water.

The Bellevue Hotel Company also developed the land adjacent to the hotel property as a high-class residential section. Lots were surveyed and building sites were offered for sale. One of the disadvantages to the area was the lack of transportation facilities. The road leading up the mountain was nothing more than a moutain pass.

In 1910, Loui Hart reorganized his hotel company as the Mineral Springs Hotel Company, Lookout Mountain, Gadsden, with a capital stock of $100,000. Loui Hart was president of the company and D. Hart was secretary and treasurer. It was advertised that the hotel would be known as the Mineral Springs Hotel.

The Mineral Springs Hotel Company in a brochure stated:

> The hotel is lighted with clusters of electric gems which gleam out and seem to vie with night's diadem of stars in brilliancy, rendering beautiful and bright this noble edifice.
>
> Sulphur, Chalybeate and Lithia-Freestone waters are all here, and situated as it is, 1,500 feet above sea level, with no malaria, no mosquitoes and the purest of air; with a table bountifully supplied with every delicacy that the southern and northern markets afford, farm products, fresh vegetables, chickens, butter, eggs, and milk fresh every day from the truck farms around it; make it by far the leading resort in this southern country.
>
> The hotel has recently put in new plumbing throughout and has added many private bath rooms, single and en-suite. The rooms are large and all of them outside ones, most of them having two or more windows each. The building is almost the shape of a crescent, with a central stem in the rear. Exceedingly picturesque, with many verandas where one can see in all directions as far as the eye can reach.
>
> The Queen & Crescent system is the direct route from New Orleans, Vicksburg, Jackson, Meridian and Birmingham; change for the Electric car at Attalla, and after arrival in Gadsden the hotel bus will take you to the mountain in twenty minutes for 25 cents each way; a charge of 25 cents for each trunk will be made, which is as cheap as you can get it in your home town. There is no charge for hand-baggage.

At the time the Gadsden Land and Improvement Company built the hotel, a franchise was granted by the city of Gadsden for a dummy line to be constructed to the falls. Later Loui Hart used his efforts towards an electric car line in lieu of the dummy line. At the expense of the hotel company, the car line was constructed.

On June 4, 1912, at one o'clock in the morning, a glare in the sky like that of a volcano located on the mountain gave the alarm that the hotel was afire.

It was not in operation at the time, although preparations had been completed to receive thirty guests two days later. Several persons, including two caretakers and a Negro servant, were asleep in the building when the blaze was discovered. Loui Hart was visiting at his mother's home in Gadsden when he received news of the fire. The fire started in the northwest corner of the building but soon spread throughout. At the time the hotel was valued at $55,000, but Mr. Hart carried only $10,000 insurance. The building was a complete loss.

Two days following the destruction of the hotel, the first electric street car made the trip to the mountain. The hotel company was left with much needed transportation facilities but no hotel.

Mr. Hart immediately made plans for another hotel to be built on a site near the one which had burned. He organized a company with the purpose of constructing an eight-story building to be used as a year-round hotel, the construction of which would be of brick, concrete and steel. He envisioned a beautiful, unique, tall building on the edge of the precipice overlooking the area that included Gadsden, East Gadsden, Alabama City and Attalla. He planned for it to be brilliantly lighted at night so it could easily be seen for miles around.

The foundation walls for the new hotel, measuring 65 by 120 feet, were laid. For the lack of sufficient capital paid into the company by the stockholders, no further progress was ever made. The walls remained there for many years until the site was acquired by Lonnie Noojin for his home. The walls were later removed, as were the large trees which had grown to full size within the area of the walls.

The section of the mountain as planned by Loui Hart and his company is still known as Bellevue Highlands, and presently is one of Gadsden's fine residential sections. Mr. Hart's dreams have been realized many years after his original planning.

Noccalula Falls in the vicinity still attract visitors, though the volume of water in the past few years has diminished to such proportions that often during the summer months there is little water to be seen. The picturesque beauty of the rocks continues to make the natural setting one of interest. Bus service to the mountain has replaced the long-abandoned car line.

51

Bladon Springs

In a beautiful valley near the Tombigbee River, in Choctaw County, was located the once-famous watering place, Bladon Springs, named for the original patentee of the land upon which the mineral springs were discovered. S. S. Houston, a member of the House of Representatives from Washington County, reported, "Bladon Springs are eighty-five miles from Mobile, seven from Coffeeville, in Clarke County, eight from Barrytown, in Choctaw County, and three from the Tombigbee River, between which and the Springs are pine lands, with no swamp intervening. The surrounding country is much broken and diversified. The growth is pine, with an admixture of oak, hickory, etc., and it is abundantly supplied with good water. The river up to this place is always navigable for steamboats of some class; and the run from Mobile can be made in from ten to eighteen hours."

By 1838, the curative properties of these springs had become well known and they were opened to the public by the owner, James Conner. In 1845, Professor Richard T. Brumby, state geologist, analyzed the water. He reported that "the constituents of the water were ascertained to be sulphuretted hydrogen, carbonic acid, crenic and hypocrenic acids, muriate of soda, carbonate of soda, carbonate of lime, carbonate of magnesia, and carbonate of protoxide of iron."

The grounds where the springs were located were enclosed in a large park of many acres, where stood row upon row of cottages of quaint design and one of the largest wooden hotels in the state. It was the most important spa in Alabama and comparable to any in the South. Bladon Springs was often referred to as "the Saratoga of the South."

The Bladon Springs Hotel, with its colonnade, great white pillars, spacious rooms, large ballroom, beautiful stairways and mullioned windows, was constructed and ready for occupancy for the summer season of 1846. It was a two-story structure, with a full, useful basement. A front veranda extended the length of the building on the first and second floors. The accommodations of the hotel were sufficient for two hundred guests. The cottages, built before the hotel, housed one hundred guests.

Peter Flint, a master carpenter from Maine, came to Bladon Springs and took charge of the construction of the hotel. The dining room, with a seating capacity of two hundred, used also as the ballroom, had no central columns. The interior walls of the hotel were plastered and beautifully decorated, as were the walls of the cottages. Mr. Flint was skilled in the construction of windows that extended to the floor. These particular windows were used on the first floor of the hotel only.

Madame Octavia Walton Le Vert of Mobile, who later became the glamorous world society leader, wrote in her diary on August 29, 1847, a description of Bladon Springs, as follows:

> I have recently visited a Watering Place, in Western Alabama, called Bladen Springs. I found it a perfect 'Balm in Gilead.' The waters are wonderful, for their health giving qualities. They resemble greatly the far famed waters of Germany. The Seltzer and the Spa. The country around is highly romantic. Tall Pines, with their mysterious whisperings encircle a

spot, like an Oasis, filled with verdant Elms, Walnut, and Hickory. The sparkling Fountain bubbles up! neath the soft shadow of its guardian trees, and it needed but one wave of the wand of Imagination to people the green sward with Fairies. The tranquil scene appeared to be fitted for their haunts and gambols.

In the old romantic steamboat days, the boats on the line of the Alabama Central went leisurely back and forth tri-weekly from Mobile to Demopolis, carrying merry parties to their haven of rest and pleasure. What could intrigue one's fancy more than these stately boats as they drew to the landing while the music of the old calliopes floated over the blue water of the Tombigbee? Then there was the ride for a distance of three miles to the hotel, over the leafy winding road, with the silvery notes of the bugle to herald the coming of the guests.

There were various places of amusement for guests, including a skating rink, bowling alleys, billiard rooms, croquet grounds and swings under the spreading oaks. A latticed summer house was built around the chief spring and from this a flight of steps led to a long pergola, also latticed, where children played or grownups engaged in cards or chatted on warm afternoons. The ballroom in the hotel presented a lively picture each evening with the guests dancing, the invalids watching, and the children dressed in party clothes running about. A bar in the hotel basement, which was open day and night, was stocked with wines and liquors.

Around the estate belonging to the springs and its buildings, clustered the village of permanent residents of Bladon Springs. Their homes were large and beautiful, indicating culture and refinement. Many of these people had visited Bladon Springs as invalids and found the valuable mineral ingredients of the water so beneficial that they chose this place to establish their permanent residences. The local residents frequented the hotel each evening to enjoy the entertainment and to meet friends.

Bladon Springs was famous for its six fountains of water, each differing slightly in their deposits and characteristics. The springs were located in a small area near the hotel, furnishing abundance of water and presenting a striking appearance. The virtues of the waters were fully attested for many years and were confidently recommended for "the cure of gout, rheumatics, scrofula, skin disease, dyspepsia, diseases incident to females, dropsy, and general debility. The waters were especially recommended to all suffering from diseases incident to warm climates, such as liver complaints, affections of the bowels, kidneys, and all diseases arising from impure blood. The water acts as an alterative, restoring the organs affected to their natural healthy functions." The hotel was open during all seasons of the year, thus permitting especially those who were sick to come for the water at any time.

The story is told of the wealthy planter's wife from Demopolis who journeyed to Baden-Baden in Germany to drink of the waters and to consult a specialist there. He told her that her health would be benefited by a prolonged stay but that there was a place in the southern United States of America where the waters were better. When reminded of Bladon, she commented that she resided but five hours carriage drive from it.

The bath houses were picturesque, built over a stream of water fed by the springs. They were kept in orderly fashion by an old Negro, familiarly known as "Uncle Scip," who was always in good spirits. He had a pleasant or witty remark for the passers-by and the bathers, and his pleasantness enlivened the spirits of the invalids.

A letter from Mobile published in the Montgomery *Advertiser,* August 21, 1855, described Mobile as comparatively empty. It reported, "a great many people were away at Bladon's, Freeman's, Point Clear, Pensacola, Pascagoula and Biloxi. Louisiana sugar planters patronize Bladon Springs, and the doctors of Mobile and New Orleans particularly recommended the water. Sometimes there were as many as fifteen hundred people there."

During the War Between the States, Bladon Springs Hotel remained open in a limited way. Indicative of conditions prevailing there at the time, the following advertisement appeared in the Mobile *Evening News* on August 14, 1864:

> BLADON SPRINGS
>
> The proprietor of this watering place takes this method of informing those desirous of visiting this season that they will have to provide their own towels, sheets and pillow cases.

Immediately after the War Between the States a regiment of Negro troops camped at Bladon Springs and, unrestrained by their white officers, overran the town, committing many crimes, burning houses and shooting their occupants. Sometimes the fear of these soldiers was so great that women and small children were hidden in the woods at night. It was difficult for the old southern aristocrats at Bladon to believe that these sinister men in uniforms with their shining guns and fierce scowling faces, eager for pillage and blood, belonged to the same race that they had loved and trusted.

By 1870, the hotel was again in full operation. Manager Conner advertised the facilities and the mineral waters very extensively. Boats were again making regular trips on the Tombigbee. The hotel rates for room and board were $15.00 per week. Children and colored servants were charged half-price and white servants $10.00 per week.

The Old Bladon Spring water was perhaps the most famous of any spring water in the state and it was advertised accordingly. Demijohns, holding about five gallons, were shipped to many parts of the United States. For all practical purposes, it was advised that invalids should come to the springs whenever possible, to obtain the full medicinal effects of the water. Sales agents for the water were Isaacson, Seixas and Company, Grocers, New Orleans; W. F. Martin, Mobile; and Dr. H. A. Howard, Montgomery.

Here are a few testimonials included in a brochure sent out in 1870:

Mobile, March 1870.

I have been acquainted with the medicinal properties of Bladon Springs for twenty years, and during that period have sent many patients to the Springs. I have the highest opinion of the water, and do not hesitate to recommend it to invalids who are suffering with diseases of the skin, the liver, the digestive and the urinary organs.

Wm. H. Anderson, M. D.

New Orleans, March 11, 1870.

Messrs. James Conner & Co.:

I have no hesitation in stating that from my knowledge of the constituents of the Bladon Sulphur Spring, I am convinced it will be found very efficacious in many hepatic diseases, and beneficial in those affections of the urinary organs connected with excess of uric acid.

W. Crawcour, M. D.
New Orleans School of Medicine.

Bladon Springs, Ala., March 31, 1870.

Messrs. James Conner & Co.:

It is with great pleasure that we add our testimony in favor of Bladon water; we have had peculiar advantages, (being the resident physicians of the Springs) of witnessing the wonderful properties of this water, upon invalids afflicted with disease in nearly all of its forms. We have witnessed the rapid improvements almost from the first week of the use of the water, upon those afflicted with diseased digestive organs, liver, kidney, rheumatism, cutaneous diseases, diseases of females, and that troublesome disease syphilis, in all of its forms. We honestly believe no water equals Bladon as a curative agent.

M. Turner, M. D.
J. S. Evans, M. D.

Mr. Conner also advertised, "For the Sportsmen there is abundant amusement during Fall and Winter months. Deer are killed within a mile of the Springs. Foxes are plentiful, and a fine pack of hounds is kept in immediate vicinity. Wild duck and smaller game in abundance."

Advertising was Mr. Conner's successful method of attracting patronage and restoring prosperity to the once-popular resort, which had suffered from the war and Reconstruction days.

Again there came the fashionable clientele from Mobile, New Orleans, and other southern cities, and also literary and musical people found rest and pleasure in this retreat. Its portals welcomed General P. G. T. Beauregard, and again the famous Madame Le Vert of Mobile, whose presence drew so many to whatever abode she selected that the proprietor refused any remuneration. Mrs. Augusta Evans Wilson and Madame Adelaide de Vendel Chaudron, Mobile authors, chose Bladon Springs for their summer residences.

In 1887 James Conner sold the property to Dr. James Whitfield of Demopolis. Upon the close of the sale, Dr. Whitfield leased the hotel, cottages and springs to W. A. Turner of Bladon Springs. Mr. Turner reconditioned the hotel building, provided new furnishings and improved the grounds. Immediately patronage increased. During the summer seasons the hotel and cottages were filled.

Following the War Between the States, Charles Cullum, founder of the Cullum Springs resort nearby, brought to his grounds an old Confederate cannon from Mobile. When he moved from the springs, the cannon was placed in the cemetery. The cemetery, being on a hill, became known as Cannon Hill. It was an established custom of the town people to fire the cannon in celebration of Democratic victories in national elections.

The last time the cannon was used was in 1892, when Grover Cleveland was for the second time elected President of the United States. The town went wild with excitement. A group of demonstrators readied the cannon for action. It was found the only cannon powder in town was at the store of Peter

Flint, a rock-ribbed Republican. Mr. Flint refused to give or sell any explosive material for a Democratic celebration. Undeterred by this obstacle, they gathered together some powder, loaded the cannon and packed in a volume of rocks and Spanish moss. Finally, everything was set and the fuse ignited. The cannon blew to pieces, with no casualties and not much noise for the celebration. A number of the guests from the hotel were on hand.

Unpleasant drama swept down upon Bladon Springs in 1891, an experience which was long remembered by those who were visiting at the resort as well as by the local residents. It was on a balmy summer afternoon that a marshal stopped there on his way to Mobile to deliver his prisoner, Bob Sims, a resident of a small village known as Old Samuel about fourteen miles from Bladon Springs, who had been evading the law for many years. Sims proclaimed himself to be the reincarnation of Jesus Christ, and on this ground he recognized no law but God's. Strange to say, he had quite a following among his relatives and friends.

As it was near nightfall when they reached Bladon, the marshal and his assistants decided to spend the night at Bladon Springs Hotel. Sims, who was handcuffed, was placed in a vacant cottage with one man on guard. The party was to leave for Mobile the following morning by boat.

Later the peaceful night was shattered by the sound of shots, causing the wildest consternation. It was found that a Dr. Pugh, a young and popular physician, in passing the prisoner's room had paused for a moment to speak to the guard. The doctor was killed by a bullet from the gun of an assailant, intended for the guard, and the guard was slightly wounded. All was then confusion and excitement, in the midst of which the prisoner, still handcuffed, made his escape. A few of the hotel guests remembered that several sullen-looking men had been seen about the grounds earlier, two of whom proved to be Sims' brothers, Neil and Jim, and another his son, Bailey, who intended to get Bob Sims released at any expense. Bailey was shot and killed that night, and Jim was wounded and was hanged the next morning. Along with Bob Sims, his brother Neil made his escape also.

By midnight an absolute silence had settled over the town, with persons huddled in frightened groups, afraid to speak or move. The next day the hotel guests departed in large numbers. As the guests were leaving, two young ladies, Laura and Beatrice Sims, the daughters of Bob Sims, arrived in a mule wagon to take charge of the bodies of their uncle and brother. Refusing coffins made at Bladon, the young ladies carried the bodies away in the open wagon. With Bob and Neil Sims at large, the Bladon people feared their return, so the town was guarded for weeks.

Bob Sims made an appearance near his home at Christmas time. Sims had the idea that his neighbor, a Mr. McMillan, had reported him for selling whiskey, and he wanted to settle the matter. He and a few of his followers surrounded the McMillan home, set it on fire, and shot down members of the McMillan family as they ran out. There was only one survivor—a baby two years old found in the yard clinging to his dead sister.

The militia from Mobile was sent to apprehend the fugitive. Bob Sims surrendered on condition that the women and children of his family would not be hurt. All six of the men in the family were hung on one tree. The women and children were given a few hours to leave the state. Then the Sims' house with all of its contents was burned to the ground. This ended the incident remembered by the older residents of Bladon Springs as the "Sims Tragedy."

Mr. Turner managed the hotel until he cancelled his lease in 1913, at which time Sam McClinton took over. After a few years Mr. and Mrs. Andrew Price became managers. Time, with its changes and modern improvements, its hurry and commercialism, gradually left Bladon Springs out of the scheme of things. The hotel management found it harder and harder to attract guests. Northern resorts were again attracting tourists, as were the mountains and the seaside. Because of the lack of patronage, the condition of the hotel fell below standard.

Bladon Springs Hotel did not pass out of existence all at once. After it was closed to guests, a lumber company leased the building for use as sleeping accommodations for their logging crews. In 1934, the State of Alabama bought the property for a state park, and converted the hotel building into an apartment house for state workers. Seven families were living there in 1938, when the structure was destroyed by fire of unknown origin.

The cottages have all been removed. The only building remaining at the present time is the summer house near the springs, stripped of the lattice. The summer house exemplifies the architectural design of other buildings which were once there.

There were no spas in Alabama which surpassed Bladon Springs. Bladon would have never been chosen Madame Le Vert's favorite had there been better resorts in Alabama. As to society, she was Alabama's best judge of her times. As to the mineral waters at Bladon, the analyses and testimonials have spoken.

59

Blount Springs

Blount Springs, one of Alabama's most fashionable spas of yesteryear, lies thirty-five miles north of Birmingham, in Blount County. Today it is but a ghost town, a dim reminder of the prosperous long ago when thousands of people from the Southeast sought joy there, as well as cures from the bubbling lithia and sulphur waters. In few places were fun-lovers and health-seekers thrown together in greater, more brilliant array.

By the end of 1825, Blount Springs had become well known and popular with the social leaders of Huntsville. To meet the increasing demands for transportation, a weekly stage was run between the two places by L. Morgan & Sons.

In 1828, J. H. Harris and J. Perrine purchased the Blount Springs property with the idea of making it a renowned watering place of the "western Country." They built several cottages, cleaned the springs and advertised their establishment as "the most comfortable and pleasant resort to all those who may visit it in pursuit of either health or amusement." Six years later the resort had become famous enough to be listed in the *Accompaniment to Mitchell's Reference and Distance Map of the United States.* The white, red, sweet sulphur, freestone, limestone and chalybeate waters within the vicinity were once considered the greatest natural advantage of Blount County, earning for this Sequatchee Valley site the nickname, "Alabama's Fountain of Youth." The presence of certain minerals in relatively large quantities, not commonly found in Alabama waters, strongly appealed to the sick. The waters were believed especially helpful in the cure of scrofula, rheumatism, dyspepsia and infection of the bladder and urinary organs. One spring, "Red Sulphur," was said to contain more sulphuretted hydrogen and lithium than any other water in the state, and the temperature of all the springs remained fairly constant, never rising above sixty degrees.

In the summer of 1843, a personal friend of Legislator Charles E. B. Strode of Morgan County visited Blount Springs, hoping to improve his health. In a few days Mr. Strode joined him and asked his companion whether baths could be had to refresh oneself after a long, dusty stagecoach journey. He was told that the proprietor of the springs would speedily furnish a bath, either hot, cold or tepid ("tea-pid," he called it). Mr. Strode ordered a warm bath without commenting upon his friend's pronunciation.

Late that night, Mr. Strode suffered a very painful attack of colic. His friend, of course, afforded him all the relief in his power. The patient exclaimed, in great agony, "Oh! What pain; farewell; I cannot survive this attack, I never had such pains before. I am to die in the prime of life. You must pardon my candor in the hour of death. Oh, how sharp the sting! Think not hard of me when I say, you caused my pain, not this infernal colic. Oh, can I have time to tell you what pain you inflicted on my literary taste! Oh, mercy—I shall die, but Milton, you did pronounce that word 'teapid' horribly; I expected better things of you."

With the arrival of the landlord and a doctor with hot baths, mustard plaster, stimulants and anodynes, the conversation was hushed. In the course of an hour, Mr. Strode, entirely relieved, fell into a gentle slumber. His friend watched by his bedside during most of the night, and when he awoke the first remark he made was, "Milton, how kind you are. I thought you were a refined scholar, as your style denotes; but you must mind your pronunciation. It is unworthy of your character. You ought to be a finished gentleman."

Dr. Henry Tutwiler, a professor at LaGrange College, Franklin County, who had been the first professor of ancient languages at the University of Alabama, visited Blount Springs in search of a suitable location for his private academy. His decision finally narrowed down to a choice between Blount and Green Springs, in present-day Hale County, near Havana. In 1847, Dr. Tutwiler chose the latter because it was closer to the homes of the majority of prospective students.

In 1850, Blount Springs property deeds were held in the name of one George Goffe, who lavished an ample fortune in transforming the place into a "Grand Spa." On the highest hill, adjoining the property to the east, a three-story structure of great elegance overlooked the rural landscape. The Goffe House was a colonial-type inn of forty rooms. The exterior walls and foundation were of slate rock, and a porch extended across the front. The basement, known locally as the "Devil's House," was forbidden territory for minors—sulphur water was not the only liquid served at the springs.

Already families from Alabama's Black Belt were finding Blount Springs an ideal place to escape from the chills and fever of the low country. Even sulphur water had a better taste than quinine and "No. 6," a patent medicine, which were regular summer diets. Brett Randolph of Greensboro built the first family cottage at the springs, and John D. Phelan, his wife, and his daughter, Mary, who later became Mrs. Thomas H. Watt, were frequent visitors.

Matthew F. Duffee and his family moved from Tuscaloosa to Blount Springs just prior to the War Between the States. During the summers of 1868 and 1869 Mr. Duffee took over the operation of the Goffe House, changing the name to Duffee House. His daughter acted as his hostess, in charge of the music, dancing and other social affairs. When the Duffee House was destroyed by fire in the fall of 1869, the family moved to their nearby mountain acreage, which they had acquired in 1850.

In 1871, work was renewed on the South & North Alabama Railroad "to complete the sixty-six mile gap that lay unfinished between Birmingham and a point south of Decatur." Colonel J. F. B. Jackson of Chattanooga, a construction engineer on the road, foresaw the possibilities of the springs and bought several thousand acres of land in the area, including Blount Springs. Closely associated with him was G. D. Fitzhugh, another engineer. It was a happy event when the officials and stockholders of the railroad met at Blount on September 29, 1872, to see the last spike driven, completing the line from Decatur to Montgomery.

Soon after the South & North was finished, Jackson built a small new hotel, giving it his name. Erected scarcely a thousand feet from the depot, it served as a "stopover" for passengers as well as a home for vacationers. As before the War Between the States, Blount Springs once again became a mecca for visitors.

After the completion of the railroad, Mr. Fitzhugh made his home at the springs, calling his estate "Glenwood." Here many social events and house parties were enjoyed by his three daughters, Elizabeth (Mrs. Dyer F. Talley of Birmingham), Frances (Mrs. Louis A. Hobart of Birmingham), and Grace Lee (Mrs. Arthur M. Pitts of Selma).

On July 4, 1873, an excursion party of two hundred persons from Birmingham visited Blount Springs, spending the day in fun and games and returning home that evening. By early morning of the next day, seven of the group had died of cholera. Later, however, when the disease was declared epidemic in Birmingham, many people from that stricken city chose Blount Springs as a sheltering place until the cholera subsided. It was claimed that the seven who had died had contracted the disease before coming to the springs.

The possibilities of a health resort at Blount Springs were probably realized more by Dr. Herndon Beverly Robinson than by any other man. Dr. Robinson moved from Forkland, in Greene County, to Birmingham in 1872, rendered valuable aid during the cholera epidemic, and, at its close, moved to Blount Springs, declaring that Birmingham "will never be more than a pest hole." Dr. Robinson immediately established a hospital on the highest peak of the mountain adjacent to the Blount Springs property on the south. His hospital had ten rooms, each opening onto a long porch for the convenience of the patients. He was a firm believer in sulphur water as a healer and he prescribed it with success. Dr. Robinson practiced medicine and surgery there until his death in 1898, although a few years before his death he converted the hospital rooms into guest accommodations. The families of Senators Pettus and Morgan and Governors Jelks and Seay were "regulars" at the Robinsons', as was Hilary Herbert of Greenville, Secretary of the Navy under President Grover Cleveland.

In 1873, upon the invitation of Colonel James R. Powell, mayor of the young city of Birmingham, the New York State Press Association decided to hold its next annual session in Birmingham. In May, 1874, Colonel Powell received word that about seventy members of the association were preparing to accept the invitation, and he went to Louisville to meet and escort them to Alabama.

Before reaching Birmingham, the New York delegation was entertained at Blount Springs. In an address of welcome to the excursionists, a resident of the springs remarked:

> It becomes my pleasant duty, gentlemen of the Press Association of New York, to welcome you to Blount Springs, Ala., long and well known throughout the land as 'the Saratoga of the South,' and, like that famous resort of your own State, situated between two beautiful rivers, surrounded by a combination and variety of landscape as matchless as it is grand and beautiful. Geologically speaking, these Springs are a marvel of Nature; they gush forth, as you will percieve upon examination, in large numbers and with a great variety of mineral waters; their curative virtues and medicinal qualities have won for them a fame that has placed them beside the fountains of Saratoga, and the most noted watering places of Great Britain and the Continent of Europe; and, although Art seemingly has done so little where Nature has done so much, yet at these Springs have gathered, from season to season, for the past fifty years, the most elegant representatives of Southern Society. Here, seeking health and pleasure, came men whose names shine forth brightly from the public record of the nation.
>
> That pure statesman and true patriot, the late Hon. William R. King, of this State, Vice President of the United States, pronounced them, in point of curative qualities and beneficial influences, vastly superior to any mineral waters he had ever tested on the American Continent. The late Hon. John Bell, of Tennessee, regarded them as the most wonderful and effective mineral waters he had ever met with in his travels. President F. A. P. Barnard, of Columbia College, New York City, when Professor of Chemistry in the University of Alabama, considered them without a superior. Dr. L. C. Garland, formerly President of the University of Alabama, and now of Vanderbilt University, Nashville, Tenn., in the most unqualified manner, asserts his belief in their medicinal elements, and their superiority over all other sulphur waters south of Saratoga. The practical test of thousands who have sought and received health and strength from these

> waters, confirms this testimony. In 1835 they were carefully analyzed by Prof. R. T. Brumby, then of the Chair of Chemistry of the University of Alabama. The result of his analysis is too tedious to give you in tabular form; suffice it to say, it placed them in the very first rank of the Mineral Springs of America. And I may here add, that it is the opinion of learned scientific men who have formerly experienced their healing effects, that an analysis at the present time would reveal still greater strength and variety of chemical elements.
>
> It is a matter of fact, also, that where a fair trial has been given them, they never have failed to relieve and permanently cure severe cases of chronic diseases of almost every nature, some of which had baffled the skill of the most eminent physicians; and to-day, all over the land there are healthful and happy men and women whose very existence is a living witness to the truth of this assertion. Nor will this statement seem strange when I tell you that these waters are cathartic, tonic, astringent and diuretic in their operations upon the system; the strong presence of carbonic acid gas gives them a pleasant flavor and a highly stimulating and refreshing effect; indeed, as a mere beverage they are sought by many persons; while the presence of iron in all of them adds to their valuable tonic effects, and the influence of the salts of iodine is plainly visible in their purifying and healing qualities.

On July 12, 1878, Blount Springs' New Jackson House was opened to the public, replacing the temporary hotel which had been constructed six years before. It stood across the road from the depot, adjacent to the railroad right-of-way. The three-story building had porches encircling the first two floors. The ground floor provided space for the office, dining room, ballroom, kitchen and a recreation room for the men. Invitations to the "Grand Ball" were extended to socially prominent people throughout the state.

In 1879, the Blount Springs Natural Sulphur Water Bottling Company had as its general agent D. P. West of Montgomery. Mr. West advertised many new cures for the sulphur water. A few of these included "skin diseases, sore eyes, gout, pimples, blotches and ulcers of every description, restoring lost appetites, and for paralysis, the water has no equal on the continent." It was also well advertised that "Nature, the Great Physician, never intended the sulphur water to be sold on draught. It has to be natural, to be effective."

The 1880's found Blount Springs transformed into a place of particular interest. The hotel grounds were terraced, the spring yard improved, and on an elevated site behind the Jackson House a new two-story hotel building, Mountain House, was completed in 1883. At the same time the name of the Jackson House was changed to the Main Hotel, although both hotels were under the same management and jointly spoken of as the Blount Springs Hotel. Through the use of convict labor, Jackson developed the limestone rock quarries nearby for use in the Birmingham furnaces. He also opened a livery stable, a necessity in every town, and constructed several new cottages. In 1887-88, Blount Springs was recognized to the point of having its business enterprises included in Polk's *Gazetteer* as the community continued to prosper.

The town of Blount Springs was incorporated in 1885. James I. Cox was elected mayor and Thomas Jones justice of the peace, and there were two day and two night marshals. In 1889, the incorporation of the town under the general laws of the state was repealed by the Legislature because of population decline during the off-season.

The Blount Springs *Herald Weekly*, under the editorship of Judge Charles W. Ferguson, is remembered as one of the rarities of the community. Though short-lived, the few issues published in 1887 were received with enthusiasm, since the news dealt mainly with social life at the springs.

Blount Springs had many attracting features, but none surpassed the mineral waters. The most popular among these was the "Red Sulphur," which was bottled in blue glass because, it was thought, glass of that color preserved the strength of the water. Boys representing the bottling company boarded the northbound trains at Warrior and the southbound trains at Hanceville, selling water to the passengers, and bottles were also shipped to many towns in Alabama and Tennessee.

With frivolity on every hand, gambling became a favorite pastime at Blount Springs. Under the Alabama law gambling was legal at the resort, and slot machines and roulette tables were stationed in the hotel. Card games attracted many players. It is claimed that on several occasions over $50,000 changed hands in one evening. A half-mile track on Jackson Mountain, less than a mile from the hotel, provided entertainment for those who enjoyed horse racing.

In 1887, Jackson sold his holdings to J. W. and Mack Sloss, brothers who operated the Sloss furnaces in Birmingham. They set out to make Blount Springs an even more popular resort for weary businessmen, a sanitarium for invalids, and a playground for children, while at the same time retaining and increasing its reputation as the rendezvous of southern society.

Workmen were engaged to repair and redecorate the physical properties, elegant new furnishings were acquired for the hotel, and gas lights were installed. Kitchen equipment large enough to prepare for a thousand guests was purchased and a corps of French chefs were imported from New Orleans to serve dishes comparable to those in the finest foreign restaurants. Joseph F. Lux of Louisville, a noted landscape gardener, was employed to beautify the grounds and spring yard, and a pavilion was constructed. The fountains of old Blount became more sparkling and beautiful than ever. A new bath house with water connections from the sulphur springs afforded convenience to the patrons

and modernized plumbing was installed throughout the hotel. Freestone water was piped into the building for those who were visiting for pleasure rather than due to ailments.

These added improvements attracted social leaders from Birmingham, Montgomery, Mobile, and New Orleans, and the resort took on new life. At the hotel dancing was enjoyed nightly, with special attention to the Saturday night German. A billiard parlor indoors and a bowling alley in the spring yard offered amusement for the men, as did the bar in the hotel. The ladies and children provided their own entertainment typical of a resort.

To celebrate the opening of the 1887 season, the most brilliant social affair ever held at the spring was staged at the new hotel. The ballroom was decorated with hydrangeas and ferns, huge wreaths of cut flowers and two immense horseshoes of roses and carnations, and was lighted by hundreds of Chinese lanterns. Flags and bunting gave a military atmosphere to the occasion, honoring the Birmingham Rifles and the Birmingham Guards. Gay uniforms contrasted pleasantly with conventional dress suits. Many of the women were dressed in gay colorful French court costumes. Waltzes, quadrilles, boccaccios, landers, polkas and gallops were danced until three o'clock in the morning. Satin programmes, souvenirs of this grand spectacle, have remained as mementos of this eventful occasion. At least three hundred people from Birmingham alone attended the affair.

The reputation of the hotel's cooking spread throughout the South. On special occasions the Mobile Brass Band and Gramb's Band of Birmingham were featured in concert, and infrequently plays were presented in the ballroom by stock companies. By 1888 the summer population of Blount Springs had reached more than three thousand.

The often-recalled "Gay 'Nineties" found Blount Springs gay in the full measure. This period in the life of the spa was its brightest. Families from all parts of the state established summer homes there. House parties attracted the young people. Week-end excursions were sponsored by the Louisville & Nashville Railroad, and Birmingham churches found the springs a delightful and popular place for annual picnics. The height of Blount Springs' popularity was realized during this period, as the Sloss brothers flew the banner of "society" above that of the invalids.

On June 26, 1899, the springs took on a festive air in honor of Basil Manly Allen, a Birmingham attorney, who four days before at the annual convention of the Benevolent Protective Order of Elks in St. Louis had been elected Grand Exalted Ruler. A delegation from Birmingham went to Blount on a special train to meet Mr. Allen and his party and to accompany them to Birmingham amid pomp and splendor.

In 1903, the Sloss holdings were sold to Mel Drennen of Birmingham. The first major improvement to the property made by the new owner was the construction of a dam on Cold Creek, which runs along the western edge of the property, to provide a place for swimming and boating. The dam is still in good condition. In season, rhododendrons bloom profusely and colorfully along the high banks of the creek.

John Perkins and Frank Jones, the two colored attendants in the bath house, made the "plug-muckum" bath the most popular in the history of the springs. Taken in extremely hot red sulphur water, this bath, followed by a massage with salt and soda, gave patients pleasure, comfort, and a very red appearance—all for fifty cents. Other baths included the Turkish, Russian, Spray, Vapor, Electric and Mud, all given by Perkins and Jones, who also met all trains, assisted new arrivals with their trunks and valises, and furnished hack service between the hotel and the depot.

Alvin H. Sinclair became manager of the hotel in 1909 and made it a point to uphold the old standards of hospitality. One noticeable characteristic of this era was the influx of youngsters, the second generation of the "oldsters" who had enjoyed many seasons there earlier. "Come and join us" was the tone of the many stories of their activities in the society columns of the Birmingham newspapers.

The Louisville & Nashville operated the old South and North as a section for many years, and in 1914 assumed complete ownership. In November of that year a new route was built, eliminating the tracks through Blount Springs. On June 3, 1915, a fire started in the kitchen of the Main Hotel and spread to the adjoining buildings, bringing a virtual end to the resort. With the destruction of the hotel, the removal of the railroad, the increase in automobile travel and ways of making the summer's heat more endurable in the cities, Blount Springs had little left to offer.

A revival of interest in the community was suggested in 1926-27, when a Birmingham realtor proposed that the property be subdivided into home sites amid beautiful drives, a shopping area, a country club and an eighteen-hole golf course. Another effort was made in 1933, when the property was offered to the United States as a site for a veteran's hospital. Both plans failed.

About thirty families are now living in the vicinity of the springs. The community has a post office, several stores, two churches and the rock quarries. The few summer cottages remaining are scattered among the hills. In 1948, the abandoned depot burned, erasing from the landscape the last reminder of the early railroad days, when the springs were the happy destination of many Alabamians.

In talking with people who frequented Blount Springs in its better days, the chronicler has found that the water, the saloons, the food, the ballroom and, lastly, gambling, in that order, were the greatest attractions of the old resort. Surely, also, many belles who met their beaux there would list another favorite pastime—at least, the results often pleased their ambitious mamas.

In an unkept spring yard the sulphur-laden waters of Blount Springs still gurgle as they did six score years ago when Harris and Perrine dreamt of making the spot the most renowned spa of the "western Country." Today there is no grandeur, certainly nothing to suggest the brilliance of former days. Even so, perhaps more people in Alabama have fonder memories of the resort than of any other in the state. Whether they went in search of fun or health, people loved Blount Springs as they did the companionship of an old friend. A few years ago the Alabama Historical Association erected a highway marker at Blount Springs, telling of its importance as a foremost watering place.

70

Blue Springs

Tourists passing through the drowsy little village of Blue Springs would never imagine that it was once a popular summer resort. Blue Springs is famous for its natural spring and pool, which for many years drew large crowds of visitors to the Blue Springs Hotel and cottages there, seeking the pleasures of a watering place and the curative powers of its water.

Blue Springs is on the west bank of the Choctawhatchee River, seven miles from Clio in Barbour County, thirty-two miles from Eufaula and eighty-five miles southeast of Montgomery. One of the interesting phases of this community's past is "The Great Summer Resort," as it was called. The resort was built around a spring which has been a movable, whimsical one. It poured out its pure water in two other locations before it settled in its present spot.

A few of the oldtimers remember that the spring first appeared north of the highway approximately three hundred yards from its present site. But suddenly this spring dried up and reappeared just south of the highway at the west end of the Choctawhatchee River bridge. Here the spring was improved and made into a small swimming pool.

A Mr. Harrison in 1890 built a small hotel in the village, the population of which was about two dozen families. Mr. Harrison undertook to create a summer resort on the spot, with the water the attracting feature. Visitors from the surrounding area frequented the watering place. It is remembered that when Mr. Harrison closed the gate to the pool in order to raise the water level, something strange occurred in an old lime sink located about two hundred yards away. In the lime sink the water raised itself to the same level as that in Mr. Harrison's spring pool.

J. T. E. Whigham owned the lime sink, the site of the present pool. When the water was ditched from the lime sink to the river nearby, Mr. Harrison's pool promptly dried up and the spring rapidly bubbled up in Mr. Whigham's lime sink. The sink became a pool occupying an area about twenty-five feet in diameter.

In 1900 Mr. Whigham built the Blue Springs Hotel. Two years later additional rooms were added to increase the number to twenty-eight. Frank O. Deese of Ozark, Alabama, managed the hotel during the summer of 1901. Subsequent managers included Hill Pearce of Clayton, Mrs. A. J. Locke of Eufaula, D. B. Easterling, Lawson Whigham of Headland, a Mr. Renfroe of Ariton, J. A. McRae of Louisville, and Mrs. Milligan.

The area around Blue Springs was the home of several prominent Barbour County politicians and always, at election time, there was much excitement and interest there. During campaigns it was a popular place to hold the "speakings," and candidates were always sure of attracting a large number of listeners at Blue Springs.

The Fourth of July each year was known in the section as "Blue Springs Day" and the occasion afforded many pleasurable times—and some not too pleasurable. It was here that family squabbles were often disposed of. Rarely did a Fourth of July pass without some sort of fight, which became accepted as a part of the agenda for the day.

For many years Confederate soldiers held reunions at Blue Springs in the month of July. The people of the community furnished lunch to those who attended. The soldiers came from all parts of the South. Also during July the horse traders in the area annually held three-day meetings to trade horses and enjoy the Blue Springs hospitality. Often the crowd at Blue Springs for a single day was estimated at one thousand.

In the earlier days of the resort, men and women were not permitted to bathe together in the pool. The women, whose bathing garments consisted of long-sleeved all-over bathing suits with long black cotton stockings and bathing shoes, went to the pool but would not enter the water as long as a man was within sight. After the women splashed around awhile in the sixty-seven degree water, they all came out together and returned to the hotel, and then it was time for the men to enjoy the pool. Later Mr. Whigham built a modern bathhouse.

Mr. Whigham's Blue Springs Hotel was a popular retreat during the summer months. A room and three meals a day cost $1.00. Fried chicken was served every day, and the bowl-and-pitcher hotel was full from June first until the middle of September. Because of the limited number of rooms in the hotel, families began pitching their tents near the pool. At times there were as many as fifteen to twenty tents set up under the shade trees. A few families built

small cottages there. The majority of the patronage at Blue Springs were families from the nearby towns of Eufaula, Clayton, Louisville, Clio, Brundidge, Troy, Ozark, Abbeville and Headland.

In 1913 Mr. Whigham installed concrete around the sides of the pool, and opened a small pool for children. The large pool remained in operation until about 1938. Since that time it has fallen into disrepair.

The hotel was closed in 1924. A part of the building still remains, but the dance hall and the bathhouse have been removed. The once-famous resort with its gaiety has almost disappeared, except for the pure blue water which is being piped to homes of the Whigham family.

The property is presently owned by the J. T. E. Whigham estate. It has been in the Whigham family for over one hundred years, having originally been owned by the father of J. T. E. Whigham.

74
Bluff Park Hotel

Atop Shades Mountain, at an altitude of 1,068 feet, centering around the Bluff Park community nine miles southwest of Birmingham, was the original settlement of Spencer Springs, owned by Octavia Spencer. Early in the 1820's his holdings consisted of four hundred acres, on which he built forty single and double log cabins and a pavilion to accommodate guests from Elyton, Selma, Mobile, Montgomery and other parts of Alabama, who came there to enjoy the summer resort. The cabins overlooked Spencer Springs, which were located partly down the mountain and within walking distance of the cabins. There were two springs, one which produced freestone water, and the other chalybeate. The latter was renowned as "the finest chalybeate water."

In 1858, Gardner Hale purchased the property. There were only a few cabins and the pavilion remaining then, and Mr. Hale had no plans for the continuation of a resort. He converted the pavilion into a dwelling, to be used as his home, inasmuch as he selected that site in an effort to regain his health. He was formerly connected with the Daniel Pratt Cotton Gin Factory at Prattville as superintendent. Upon moving to his new home, the Spencer Springs became known as Hale Springs.

The Red Mountain Iron & Coal Company of Alabama was incorporated on November 5, 1862, "a corporation successor to the Alabama Arms Manufacturing Co." The Alabama Arms Manufacturing Company was organized for the purpose of mining ore and manufacturing iron for the Confederate ordnance. The Confederate government advanced money with the stipulation that the advance be repaid in pig iron. The new company began the erection of two stone blast furnaces at Oxmoor, the first of which was put into operation in the fall of 1863. The iron output was destroyed early in 1865 by General Wilson of the federal army.

> The Red Mountain Iron & Coal Company of Alabama announced in 1868 that the North-east and South-west Railroad (hereafter to be known as the Alabama and Chattanooga Railroad), if constructed through Shades Valley, will cross the Nashville and Decatur Railroad at the place which we have named 'Ox Moor,' near the centre of a tract of land containing more than three square miles belonging to this Company. It is a beautiful location for a town, well watered, and convenient to building material of every description. Here, at this crossing, it is expected that the 'Atlanta' of regenerated Alabama will spring up, and some very sanguine persons already look upon it as the future capital of the State. These great expectations of a city as yet uninhabited may never be realized, but a town of some importance at this point must necessarily result from the building of the railroads above mentioned.

Mr. Hale's property adjoined the property of this company, and it is assumed his hopes were high. Unfortunately, the plans never materialized.

Following the death of Gardner Hale in 1885, his daughter, Mrs. H. O. Williams, added several rooms to the home and accepted boarders during the summer months. The rates were $15.00 per month, including room and board. Summer after summer her house was filled with guests. It was the only popular summer retreat in Jefferson County, but it was a hard place to reach because of the lack of roads.

The story is told that on occasions when Mrs. Williams decided to make a trip to Birmingham, she had to go to the brow of the mountain and blow a trumpet to signal Aunt Jane Blackman, who lived in Oxmoor, in Shades Valley below, to hitch her oxen and make the trip up the mountain trail to transport her to Oxmoor station for the train. After a road was built from Oxmoor to Hale Springs in 1892, guests made trips in carriages and buggies from Birmingham. Tallyhos from Birmingham often brought week-end guests to the springs. After Mrs. Williams died in 1905, her brother, George Hale, operated the guest house during the summer of that year.

In 1907, the Bluff Park Hotel Company was organized, with J. A. Yates as president. The company purchased six acres for the site of a hotel, and the Bluff Park Hotel was constructed in the same year.

The hotel was a two-story structure containing twenty rooms. A broad porch on each of the floors encircled three sides of the building, and all of the rooms opened onto the porches. The dining room in the hotel accommodated up to twenty-five guests. To the west of the hotel was the dance pavilion, connected to the main building by a long corridor. Week-end dances were held regularly, with orchestras from Birmingham furnishing the music. To the rear of the hotel, a garden was maintained to supply fresh vegetables for the dining room.

Sunset Rock and Lover's Leap were popular places for the guests to enjoy. These were large boulders overhanging from the ledge of the mountain, which made excellent places to watch the setting sun in the late afternoons and to view the blast furnaces at Oxmoor. The sixteen by sixteen foot observatory, at the third-story level of the hotel, also was a fine place from which to view the surrounding country.

Lover's Leap has historical interest. It was on this rock that Thomas W. Farrar, organizer of the Farrar Lodge No. 8, A. F. & A. M. (Elyton), in 1818, and the first Grand Master in the Grand Lodge of Masons of Alabama, serving in 1821, 1822 and 1824, inscribed the first four lines of Verse XXV, Canto the Second, from *Childe Harold's Pilgrimage* by Lord Byron, as follows:

To sit on rocks, to muse o'er flood and fell,
To slowly trace the forest's shady scene,
Where things that own not man's dominion dwell,
And mortal foot hath ne'er or rarely been.

To Seraphine Farrar

1827 Thomas W. Farrar

The original boulder was removed and placed in Farrar Lodge on the 114th anniversary of that lodge and the Grand Lodge of Alabama. A replica of the inscription was carved on another boulder near the original location in 1935, on a site donated by Jonas Schwab of Birmingham. The work was inspired by George B. Ward, former mayor of Birmingham, who also provided fencing for its protection, and Thomas W. Martin, chairman of the board of the Alabama Power Company.

In 1911 James A. Yates acquired the property from the Bluff Park Hotel Company, and he operated the hotel until it was sold to J. P. Wright in 1913. The following year Mr. Wright sold the property to the Ingram Realty Company. In 1915, the property was deeded from the Ingram Realty Company to R. M. Ingram, individually. Mr. Ingram operated the hotel until about the time of World War I. R. M. Ingram, Jr., son of Mr. Ingram, managed the hotel for one season during this time. After World War I, Mrs. F. D. Gamble and her family, local residents, occupied the hotel building until 1923. The building was then boarded up.

In 1925, William Levi and C. P. Campbell purchased the hotel and grounds, and reconditioned the building throughout. Upon its completion, Mr. Campbell purchased Mr. Levi's interest. When the new owner was prepared to again open the resort to the public, for the season of 1925, the building caught fire and burned to the ground. The fire ended the story of the Bluff Park Hotel.

Several private residences have been constructed on the site of the former hotel. This location on Shades Crest Road is a beautiful setting for homes, and the property values are high. Hale Springs, close by, continues to flow and is the only reminder of the resort which once stood on Shades Mountain. Bluff Park is now an incorporated town with all modern conveniences. It is reached by paved roads from every direction, including the ghost town of Oxmoor. Several descendants of Gardner Hale are residents in the community.

78

Borden-Wheeler Springs

Borden Springs, high in the foothills of the Blue Ridge Mountains, was one of the romantic spots of Alabama. It lies in a valley between mountains that lie unbroken for fourteen miles on either side. Borden Springs is located on the Seaboard Air Line Railroad, ninety-two miles from Birmingham and seventy-five miles from Atlanta, in Cleburne County near the Georgia state line.

Shortly before 1900 the Borden-Wheeler Company, composed of twelve men from Atlanta, Newnan and Carrollton, Georgia, bought the land from the Wheeler family and had assembled on a knoll above the spring a two-story hotel to replace a small twenty-room structure which had been used earlier.

The hotel had been formerly owned by the Fruithurst Company, a corporation which in 1894 secured large holdings of land in the east-central part of Cleburne County as the site for a colony of Swedish vinyardists who came from Minnesota for the purpose of raising grapes for the making of wine. The vineyard colony established the town of Fruithurst, which was incorporated in 1896. The hotel building, established originally as a clubhouse for prospective land buyers, was short-lived, for within a few years the company went defunct. The Borden-Wheeler Company purchased the clubhouse and employed J. C. Bass of Carrollton, Georgia, to dismantle the structure, move it sixteen miles to Borden Springs, and reconstruct it as the Borden-Wheeler Hotel. The moving was accomplished with mules and wagons.

The Borden-Wheeler Hotel, consisting of one hundred rooms, was a marvel of southern architecture, and immense for so small a place. It was a structure with wide porches, and its many windows caught the sunlight from all points. The hotel with its broad wings was surrounded by mountains covered with pine, maple, oak, elm, sweet and black gum trees, ash and the "grandsir graybeard," with his long, snowy locks. Among the trees were great blocks of limestone, with their changing veins of color.

There was soon a village of cottages around the hotel, built of rough lumber and much screening and creosoted in browns and greens to harmonize with the background of the trees. Every cottage had electric lights, running water, and maid service.

So much was said about the magic properties of the spring that the management advertised the water as being "a close second to Ponce de Leon's famed 'Fountain of Youth'."

Near the hotel stood a small cottage built of logs that were hewed and peeled by hand, with a puncheon floor. This was the home of Sarah Alexander Wheeler and C. M. Wheeler, who were among the pioneers of Borden Springs. Often the resort, better known as Borden Springs, was called Borden-Wheeler Springs.

Borden Springs resort grew to such popularity that the Seaboard Railroad issued excursion rates to the resort. A one-way fare from Birmingham was listed at $2.77 and a season ticket at $4.60. The rates from Atlanta were slightly lower.

The earliest settler on the Borden property, soon after Alabama was admitted to the Union, was John A. Borden. He entered his land at Huntsville and became the possessor of one thousand acres west of the spring, lying along wide, lazy Terrapin Creek, a rich lowland which was flooded each year. At a bend in the creek he built a large grist mill to grind his wheat and corn.

Nearby, Mr. Borden built the well-known Borden dwelling. The open hallway extended the length of the structure, with living rooms on each side. With wide fireplaces and many-paned windows, it sat snug and comfortable, facing south, with three sides protected by the mountains which towered above and around it. The Borden dwelling in later years proved to be an interesting feature of the resort because of its location. The long avenue of old cedars, so old that the trunks were divided, which led to the old homestead created as much curiosity and interest as did the house.

After Mr. Borden, Arthur Alexander bought 160 acres which included the spring and the land around it. Mr. Alexander's son, Matthew, purchased four hundred acres surrounding the acreage owned by his father. Matthew Alexander married Annie Borden, daughter of John Borden.

Then came C. M. Wheeler, who bought the spring property, which was increasing in value because the spring was becoming well known for its "magic qualities." Mr. Wheeler married Sarah, the daughter of Arthur Alexander. So from these three — Borden, Alexander, and Wheeler — come most of the families living at Borden Springs.

At one time during the War Between the States, the guerrillas came to the Wheeler home to take the youngest of seven sons, a boy of seventeen, to join their ranks. Mrs. Wheeler had the boy go into the house and fasten it well, and then took her stand on a wide stone stoop in front, with a broadax concealed beneath the folds of her capacious apron. When they rode up and demanded the boy, she said: "If my son were of age to be in the army, he would be there, but he is not of age and he is not going." At a threatening move on the part of the men, the ax came out and was lifted high with both hands. "If any man puts his foot on this step, his head will come off," she warned. Perhaps the men were moved with admiration of such courage, and some fear, too, for they quickly left.

On many occasions fine hospitality prevailed in the community. It was not unusual for six to twelve travelers, waterbound by rising creeks which had no bridges, to be housed until they were able to ford the creeks. When that happened, the hospitable neighborhood turned out to a barn-dance in honor of the visitors.

After the death of C. M. Wheeler, the spring property was sold to the Borden-Wheeler Company, which improved it. The modern hotel had windows everywhere, filling the building with light so that it was like a huge sun room.

Broad galleries, rooms with high ceilings, and wide spaces seemed to beckon with an air of gaiety. From the knoll on which the hotel stood, the terraced lawns, green as emerald and smooth as velvet, dropped down past the wide dancing pavilion to the spring. There were a swimming pool, golf course, and blooded horses for the entertainment of the guests.

The hotel was furnished with every adornment that money could buy, which lent to the happiness and pleasure of the guests, but the resort was unable to attract patronage in numbers sufficient to support such lavishness. The rates were reasonable at $15.00 per week or $50.00 per month, American plan. It became known as a week-end resort and rendezvous. Approximately forty employees were retained through each week, awaiting the large crowds on the week ends. Rates for the week ends were somewhat higher.

Perhaps nowhere in Alabama were there better or more elaborate appoint-

ments and conveniences in a hotel. French cooks were hired to prepare fancy meals which were unequaled in the state. The orchestras which furnished music during the meals and for dancing were the best that could be obtained in Alabama and Georgia. The entertainment was superb but costly. Socially prominent people from all parts of Georgia and Alabama made up the clientele. The hotel was open from May through October, although June 1 through Labor Day was considered the season.

The Borden-Wheeler Company operated the hotel only for a few seasons and then the stockholders sold their holdings to J. C. Bass, who had moved the building from Fruithurst. Mr. Bass operated the hotel until his health failed in 1920. His son, Bernard, then acquired the property and operated the hotel until 1927, when he sold his holdings to a Florida syndicate headed by Leon Prine of Fort Meade. Mr. Prine operated the hotel until 1933, when it closed and was never reopened. During the years of several ownerships, Charles W. Smith held a mortgage on the property, and he ultimately acquired it by foreclosure.

Fire swept the hotel and the twenty cottages in 1935, leaving nothing but ashes. The people of Borden Springs must have felt as Cinderella did when the clock struck twelve, when all her fine clothes vanished and she was left in rags and ashes, her lovely golden chariot only a pumpkin shell, her milk-white steeds only white mice. But, after all, she really was the girl with whom the prince had danced, and in the end she married the prince and was happy ever after. So it was with the Borden-Wheeler enterprise. All of the things that were there at the beginning were untouched; the spring, the trees and the mountains which were provided by nature.

Borden-Wheeler Hotel had the appearance and appointments of an important spa, comparable to the finest in the South, but it was far too elaborate for its location.

83

Butler Springs

It cured people of what ailed them! The Butler Springs water was full of minerals, and people came from far and near to drink the water and enjoy the recreation. Butler Springs is in Butler County, in the southern part of Alabama. The springs were named in honor of Captain William Butler, who was killed by Indians in 1818 about two miles northeast of the springs.

There is a general belief that the springs were discovered by hunters as early as 1830. The medical properties of the water were not entirely established until about 1842, when Jesse Knight of Butler County sent his sick wife and afflicted son, Thomas, to the springs to drink the beneficial waters. Mr. Knight built a rough cabin to be used by his family when they arrived. Mrs. Knight recovered from her illness and the news spread rapidly.

In 1843 John Ubanks built a temporary tavern at Butler Springs and advertised it throughout the surrounding country. He gave a barbecue on the Fourth of July the same year. Frederick W. Crenshaw, who had just graduated at the University of Alabama, delivered an address on the occasion. For the next sixty years or more the Fourth of July picnics were regular events at Butler Springs.

The springs were purchased in 1844 by Nat Sims, a wealthy Lowndes County farmer, who soon erected a "fine" hotel for the accommodation of the crowds that began to frequent this place. However "a large number of persons came here and camped under tents for eight or ten days to recuperate themselves by drinking the water, and to strengthen themselves by the hardships of camping."

Here is a letter from Elizabeth C. Fountain to Hannah L. Coker of Society Hill, South Carolina:

Carlowville (Dallas County) Ala.,
August 25, 1845

My Dearest Aunt: It seems that every body will get away from Carlowville ere long; I presume you heard that about sixty persons left for Pensacola a few weeks since; and several others, about the same time for the Butler Springs, (Cousin Robert, Uncle Joseph, Mr. Rumph and some others). Well, to-morrow Grandma Aunt Mary and Uncle Eli will leave for the Springs to be [absent] about a month or two. Grandpa had made up his mind to go, but he concluded to day to wait until after the Protracted Meeting. Don't you think we shall be quite lonely after they all leave? Uncle Joseph came up on Saturday to stay a few days. He says there are about 150 persons there, and others constantly coming in—says it is a very pleasant place—every one seems to be happy he enjoyed it very much. Uncle Eli has been trying to persuade Mother to go, but I believe, as Grandpa says "We might as well try to move this house down there, as to move her." I should think a change might be beneficial to her health and a little respite from her sewing. . . . Your affectionate niece,

Lizzy

Here are excerpts from a letter from the "Aunt Mary" mentioned in the preceding letter, written after her return from the springs to the same woman in South Carolina:

Carlowville (Dallas County) Ala.,
October 6, 1845.

My Dear Sister: No improvement is made at the Springs except the grogshop and a floor to dance on, it is really amusing to see them dancing (I Mean the inhabitants) I never saw such awkwardness and such confusion before, though they do not consider it so, the ladies or rather women dressed up in dark calico suitable only for winter and gauze shalls that comes down to their waists or a quantity of very gay ribbon twisted twirlled about their necks, and the gayest and largest kind of cotton handkerchief in their hands, others again were dressed very well, a good many of them are rich but they have no improvement and don't know how to use their property. Hannah I thought if you had only been there you could have had so much sport. 8 or 10 families were tenting while we were there but they were coming and going all the while. I did not mingle in society much, became acquainted with a very few, with some I was very much pleased, but must confess that I live in total darkness of the ways of the world, never heard of such wickedness and blasphemy before, did not know that man was capable of such. The water has not been analized yet but is thought to be mostly sulpur. It tastes like parched eggshells, a very disagreeable taste to me, but some are very fond of it. Pa and Ma have been wishing hard for some. Our water is so good I don't want any better. We camped just by the side of steep hill, and just on top is a great many rock which are literally filled with shells of different kinds. I brought a specimen with me, if I have an opportunity I will send some to brother Coker. A Mr. Coker and his daughter camped just by us, we could stand in each others tents and talk together, they are in comfortable circumstances to judge from appearance indeed I know from what Mr. Coker told Pa he has considerable propperty. He is a widower and some where a bout 50 his daughter a bout 25, to see her you would think they were rich, I believe she put on a new dress almost every day. . . .

Mary E. Lide

The two letters give some idea of Butler Springs in its earliest days.

Isaac Keiser opened a store in connection with a billiard saloon in 1846 and John Clark opened a "dram-shop" (the 1846 version of a cocktail bar).

Captain T. A. Knight and Alph Carter purchased the property in 1860 from John Eddy, who had bought it from the widow of Nat Sims in 1855. Messrs.

Knight and Carter improved the property and expended large sums of money in the way of repairs. They built a spring house and curbed in "with costly marble" four distinct springs, the water of each being different from the others. Originally the water from the four springs flowed from one opening in the ground. Often there were over five hundred guests and visitors present at one time after the spring house was constructed.

The property deteriorated during the War Between the States. People had little interest in and no money to spend on watering places. In 1862 Captain Knight sold his interest to James Benson, and Alph Carter sold his to John Carter. William A. Sims bought both interests in 1874.

As other watering places and resort hotels were developed, especially during the 'eighties and 'nineties, most of the local people preferred to visit places more convenient to railroads. As a result, Butler Springs suffered a lack of patronage, which was reflected directly in the general condition of the hotel and grounds.

But, amazingly, about the turn of the century Butler Springs reached its peak in popularity, with the hotel operated by Mr. and Mrs. William Jones and the carriages making daily trips to Greenville to meet the guests who arrived by train.

The hotel was a large two-story wooden building. Practically the entire space was devoted to bedrooms, although there were a small lobby and a large dining room. A recreation hall was a few steps to the east of the hotel, and in front, beyond the picket fence, was a dance pavilion. There were several cabins operated in connection with the hotel.

It was said there were few users of the tin tub in the hotel's bathroom, which was added to the side of the house with its only door opening to the outside. Water for the tub came from a nearby well, but it was a long and hard task to draw sufficient water for much bathing. The water drawn from the well was poured into a trough which carried it through the wall into the tub.

Rest rooms were quaint, old-fashioned outhouses. The ladies' rooms were a short distance to the rear of the hotel. The gentlemen's room was across the creek, somewhat downstream from the hotel.

The stream in front of the hotel had a foot bridge, but no bridge for vehicles. Vehicular traffic forded the wide but shallow creek. This ford was a favorite spot for the children who liked to wade in the cool water.

The hotel burned to the ground in 1913 and was never rebuilt.

87

Caldwell Hotel BIRMINGHAM

THE CALDWELL HOUSE

Opened August 8, 1889. Absolutely Fire-proof. Finest HOTEL BUILDING in the South.
Elegant Appointments and Table Service.
Every room an outside room.
F. W. Jewell & Co. . . . . Proprietors

This advertisement appeared in the *Evening News,* August 31, 1889. In three short hours on Friday night, July 20, 1894, flames completely consumed the "absolutely fire-proof" Caldwell Hotel building, as well as the Johnston-Hawkins building across the street.

The Caldwell Hotel was a six-story building, located on the northeast corner of Twenty-second Street and First Avenue, North, in Birmingham. The Johnston-Hawkins building, located on the northwest corner across the street, housed several establishments, including the Stowers Furniture Company. The fire was detected in the basement of this store shortly after closing time. Soon it had spread to the Perry-Mason Shoe Company, and within minutes the entire building was in flames.

A very strong wind from the west fanned the flames toward the Caldwell. No one thought the fire would endanger any part of the brick-constructed hotel building, but in an incredibly short time the tongues of flame were licking its walls.

The fire caught first in the hotel's gilded dome and observation tower, 165 feet from the ground. The dome, which contained windows, had been the scene of a notorious poker game, reported to have been operated for three years by a stately white-haired "Southern Colonel"-looking man from the North, before the police were able to get evidence enough to close it. The dome was accessible only by climbing out of the top-story windows of the hotel and walking around the ledge of the dome and in through the windows. A special signal system had been devised so that the operator could be warned when the police were coming to make a raid.

By midnight, every window casing on the west side of the hotel was aflame, and soon the entire building was burning. Sparks and pieces of burning debris were blown by the hard wind for over a mile. Every precaution was taken to see that loss of life would be prevented. Not a door was left on its hinges, in insuring that no guests were left within the burning building. Only two people had to use the fire escapes, and not a single guest was injured.

When daylight dawned upon the scene, the wreckage was deplorable to behold. Smoking ruins had replaced the largest and finest hotel in Alabama, said to be matched for elegance only by the Ponce de Leon Hotel in St. Augustine, Florida.

An incident of the fire which attracted universal attention was the discovery of the bust of Dr. H. M. Caldwell, owner and president of the Caldwell Hotel Company. The bust, still upon its pedestal in a niche of the wall in the office, was caked with ashes and plaster, though not cracked by the fire. The bust showed the features of Dr. Caldwell, looking upon the ruins of the once splendid edifice. In sarcastic distinctness above the bust was the coat of arms of Alabama and the motto: "Here We Rest."

The Caldwell Hotel Company was incorporated in 1886 and the construction of the building was started later in the year, with R. P. McDavid of Birmingham breaking the first ground. The Elyton Land Company, of which Dr. Caldwell was also president, contributed $100,000 towards the much-needed hotel for Birmingham. The building, erected on the highest elevation in the downtown area, measured 150 by 150 feet, with open courts, so that each of the one hundred rooms would be airy and comfortable. The windows and cornices were faced with granite. Its rotunda is said to have been magnificent and its elaborate, two-storied dining room, which measured forty-eight by seventy feet, was the scene of many festive occasions, including a luncheon for President Benjamin Harrison when he visited Birmingham in 1891, and the many parties given during the famous Confederate Reunion in April preceding the fire.

During the existence of the hotel, there were only two managers, F. W. Jewell and Edward B. Freeman.

After the fire, there was nothing left except a few bare walls to remind Birmingham that its finest hostelry, valued at $300,000, was gone. The empty walls stood for several years, until Goodall-Brown Dry Goods Company acquired the property in 1906, and were then removed to make way for the building which stands there today.

Birmingham learned a lesson from this fire. It learned that adequate fire protection in the city would be necessary if the city was to grow. It had been caught without the proper equipment, having to call for help from Montgomery and Meridian, Mississippi. "Hard times" in Birmingham had caused the city council to reduce by half the manpower of the fire department. Because of the Caldwell fire, the council took the necessary steps to maintain a proper-size fire department with good equipment.

The Caldwell Hotel lives on in the memory of the oldtimers of Birmingham and Alabama, because of its beauty and grandeur, being the earliest first-class hotel in the city. Birmingham enjoyed it for nearly five years, thinking all the while it was "absolutely fire-proof," as advertised.

90
Cedar Hotel VALHERMOSO SPRINGS

Valhermoso Springs resort, which was begun in 1823, reached high peaks of importance as a pleasure and health resort through the years. Its attractive natural surroundings make it easy to understand the selection of its name, Valhermoso, which means "Vale of Beauty." Approximately twenty miles east of Hartselle, in Morgan County, on Highway 33, this once-famed community is easily accessible to motorists.

The site of the Cedar Hotel, which gave Valhermoso its claim to prominence, is about fifty yards north of a wide gorge which is bordered by the fringe of cedars from which the hotel obtained its name. Given Creek flows peacefully in the bottom of the twenty foot wide gorge, and sixty feet below its edge the rocks are so arranged as to form a natural swimming pool. Oaks, beech and evergreens surround the pool, lending to the beauty of the natural setting.

The resort was popular because of the several springs located near the swimming pool. They were in comparatively small circular arrangement, and each spring produced a different kind of water. The white sulphur water at Valhermoso contained sulphate of magnesia, chloride of magnesium, sodium and calcium, sulphuret of sodium and iodine. It was said that "if the sulphur water is dipped deeply, the sparkling dipper will ignite to the touch of a match."

Many cures were offered in the testimonials of guests. Rheumatism, constipation, diseases of the kidneys, stomach, skin and liver, nervous prostration and sleeplessness, consumption and even the distress of gray hair were said to have been abated here.

Dr. Samuel Cartwright of New Orleans described the unparalleled sanitary conditions of Valhermoso as excellent. It was stated, "the whole country for miles around is partly undermined by natural ventilators and purifiers, a fact which may also account for the proverbial healthfulness of the table-lands of Morgan County."

An advertisement had this to say:

> This celebrated resort, endowed marvelously by nature, is located among the healthy pine regions, where consumption and pulmonary diseases are unknown. The locality is cool and pleasant, and the temperature is much lower than that in the East and West, during the summer months. The nights are always cool and pleasant . . . and there are no mosquitoes. Here, too, the hunting and fishing are good, and lovers of natural beauty will find along the banks of the nearby Tennessee River most magnificent and ever varying scenery. The great tunnel cave of Ittachooma with its Walhalla of God's own sanctuary, the mineral and coal regions, and the many other points of interest are easily accessible from the Springs.

The Cedar Hotel building was a three-story structure, typical of early resorts. It was a rectangular building with front porches on the first and second floors at one end. The eight guest rooms were well-windowed. The first floor included the office, lobby, parlors, bar and dining room, kitchen and pantries. The second floor housed the owner's apartment and guest rooms. An enclosed stairway led from the lobby and bar on the ground floor to the second floor; however, the owner's apartment could be reached by a private stairway. The owner's apartment contained the only fireplace in the building. The third story was floored and plastered and was used as the ballroom.

Several rows of cottages surrounded the hotel. These buildings were long-type with entrances leading to a porch. Each building would accommodate at least six families.

Erected in 1818 by the Mannings, this resort began a period of service that attracted guests from points on the continent as well as the states. Late in the 1820's and during the 1830's, the magnificent balls at Valhermoso attracted notables from all over the Southeast. From the pages of the hotel register, it is found that guests included Miss Julia Tutwiler, William Rufus King, whose name is found several times along with his wife and daughter, and Mrs. Edna Earle De Gray of Scotland. There were guests there from England and Switzerland, and another from the banks of the Rhine, whence came Jean Joseph Giers, the owner of the resort, who acquired the property in 1855.

Much of the success of Valhermoso Springs and the Cedar Hotel centered around his wife, Mary L. Gooch Giers, and himself. Mr. Giers lived in Washington, D. C., each winter and returned to Valhermoso for the summer. He was quite a scholar, being able to speak nine foreign languages and enjoying a keen knowledge of many Indian dialects. He wrote poetry and also composed, played and taught music. As a writer of a column called "The Lady of the Lake" in the Washington *Gazette,* Mr. Giers wrote on many subjects, including his own biography. A close friend of Abraham Lincoln, Mr. Giers did not believe in slavery but he enjoyed being served by slaves. Mrs. Giers was born in Murphreesboro, Tennessee. She is remembered as a "hot-blooded" southerner, and during the War Between the States she had Confederate soldiers in the hidden recesses beneath the eaves on the third floor of the hotel when the federal troops bivouacked in Morgan County.

Valhermoso enjoyed the convenience of a post office in 1859. By 1875, the resort had grown to such popularity that it was listed in *Popular Resorts and How to Reach Them,* and described as follows: "A short distance below Decatur . . . are the beautifully situated Valhermoso Springs."

At the death of Mr. Giers, on December 16, 1880, the property passed to his son, Ernst. The son and his wife operated the hotel until 1920. Perhaps no summer resort in Alabama received the personal supervision of its owners that Valhermoso did.

In 1950 a tornado swept away the third floor and the porches of the hotel. In the same year, the remains of the hotel and many of the cottages burned. The fire that destroyed the buildings left one lone chimney which still stands, like a silent sentinel, to mark the site of this historic resort.

93

Chandler Springs

Chandler Springs, in Talladega County, was a modest resort where one could go for a summer vacation, relax and drink mineral water. It received its name from James Chandler, a tailor, who came there from Texas in 1832. Mr. Chandler settled at this point soon after he discovered three mineral springs. It is told that "Mr. Chandler, as he was walking through the woods, saw some deer scratching around for water. He dug a pit for the springs and they have been flowing ever since."

Soon after the discovery of the springs, a land rush followed. Talladega County was in the Coosa Land District, and the lands, most of which were owned by the government, were subject to entry at the land office, which had been established in Mardisville in January, 1834. In 1842, the land office was removed to Lebanon, in DeKalb County. Before the removal of the office from Mardisville, land entries were very active. Settlers and others were in vigorous competition for entries in the vicinity of Chandler Springs due to fertility and location. On several occasions Mr. Chandler traveled at night to Lebanon and Mardisville to be present when the doors of the land office opened the next morning in order to register his claims and to avoid discovery.

Ultimately Mr. Chandler received several deeds for a total of five hundred acres of land, signed by Presidents Buchanan, Fillmore and Van Buren. This land was the site for the future summer resort to be known as Chandler Springs, located exactly twelve miles from Talladega Court House on the Ashland pike. The springs are located on the northern flank of the Talladega Mountain range.

Very early Mr. Chandler built a two-and-one half story hotel and several log cottages. The cottages were in a quadrangle, in the center of which was a large pavilion used for dances and parties.

The post office was called Mountain Spring when it was established in 1838. The name was changed to Maria Forge in 1844 and to Chandler Springs in 1855. James Chandler was the postmaster for many years. The Talladega *Democratic Watchtower* of April 3, 1840, referred to "the Mineral Springs of Chandler and Grantham."

By 1875, Chandler Springs resort had grown to such importance that it was listed in the national publication, *Popular Resorts, And How To Reach Them,* by John B. Bachelder. The accommodations for visitors were listed as "fair." Talladega Springs, Shelby Springs, Sulphur Springs, and Bladon Springs were the other Alabama resorts listed and each of these also received a "fair" rating.

Chandler Springs water contained potassium, sodium, magnesium, calcium, iron, alumina, chlorine, sulphuric acid, carbonic acid, and silica. Dr. Eugene A. Smith, state geologist, in 1907 reported, "This is an alkaline-saline water which, from the relatively large amounts of iron and the sulphates of potassium and magnesium, should possess some medicinal quality." The Chandler Springs water is derived from the Hillabee schist.

Chandler Springs Hotel attracted families from various parts of Alabama. It was always considered a family resort, and usually family resorts are small. Several families from Talladega built cottages at the springs on the Chandler property. No land was ever sold to anyone. Among those who had cottages there were Major Joseph Hardie, of Talladega, who was at one time the international president of the Y.M.C.A., and James B. McMillan, one of Jefferson Davis' bodyguards at the time of the surrender. Mr. McMillan held in his possession a gold coin given to him as a token of appreciation by Jefferson Davis. Captain John T. Plowman, former congressman, owned a cottage for his family. The Storys, Jemisons, and Elstons also had cottages there.

Chandler Springs was ordinarily reached by horse and buggy travel from Talladega. A horse and buggy could be rented for $5.00. In 1903 the Eastern Railroad of Alabama built a spur line from Ironaton to Pyriton and a mixed train brought guests to the springs.

Recreation at Chandler Springs included bowling on the lawn, gathering at the post office, playing games in the "play house" or listening to the bullfrogs. A story is told that the guests often named the frogs and could tell which of the frogs were "off-key" on certain nights. The resort was operated as a place for relaxation. The Fourth of July celebrations were outstanding events in

the earlier days. General Charles M. Shelly of Talladega often delivered addresses for these occasions.

After the death of owner James Chandler, the resort was leased to several hotel operators, including F. G. Doggett, Miss Carrie Harrel, W. M. McCaffrey, and Emory Horn.

The hotel burned in 1918, and the cottages, with one exception, were later removed. The remaining cottage is owned by Mrs. Nona Doggett of Ashland. Where the hotel once stood, a thicket of pine and cedar trees is appearing. The home of Ed Ponders has been constructed on the old grounds. Mrs. M. F. Chandler, daughter-in-law of James Chandler, is still a resident in the Chandler Springs community. Now very elderly, she is the only woman member of the Talladega County Democratic Executive Committee, a post she cherishes highly.

For the first time in seventy-five years, the summer drought of 1954 temporarily dried up Chandler Springs creek. The water for this creek is supplied by three springs. Ordinarily the springs run freely and many still stop by for a drink of the cool water.

Choctaw Tavern LIVINGSTON

By the Treaty of Dancing Rabbit Creek, signed in Noxubee County, Mississippi, September 28, 1830, the United States acquired the Choctaw Indian Lands east of the Mississippi River. Most of these lands which lay in Alabama were, on December 18, 1832, formed into a new county which the legislature called "Sumter," in honor of General Thomas Sumter of South Carolina, the ninety-eight-year-old patriot who had passed on just five months previously.

Edward Livingston of Louisiana was Secretary of State of the United States, and a few months later, when a county seat was selected for Sumter County, the place was named for him. Livingston is located upon a beautiful sandy plateau, with black, undulating prairies on the north and east, and the Sucarnatchee River on the south and west. Prior to its settlement by the whites it had been an Indian village known as Holeeta, meaning "fence" or "pen."

By 1833, the Choctaw Tavern in Livingston was in operation, bearing the name of the Indian tribe which had formerly occupied the territory. The tavern stood on the corner of Washington and Marshall streets, south of the square. It was first opened by W. B. Ochiltree and Thomas P. Alston. Mr. Ochiltree later moved to Texas because of ill health in his family. The tavern, a two-story frame structure sixty feet long, contained approximately thirty-five rooms in addition to a number of offices, and was beautifully furnished. A wide porch extended the width of the building on both floors. A plantation bell was used by the proprietors to announce the time for meals.

Mr. Ochiltree considered the tavern "the most valuable piece of property in his knowledge, since it fronted on two of the most public ways of approach to the town." The tavern enjoyed good patronage, the proprietors describing it as "thronged with business." Through the years, the tavern was kept at various times by Robert Arrington, Stephen W. Murley, Jim Tucker, William Lockard, E. W. Hooks, W. D. Battle, Jr., Messrs. Hudson, Cowin, Randall, Reynolds, Loftin, and Dave Bell.

To the east of the tavern a stable was connected with it, kept in the early days by William Kirkland. Later it was operated by E. W. Hooks, a Mr. Tisdale, Vice Tutt, and Ben Winslett.

The inn served as a popular place of entertainment even in its early days. One particular social event, the Anniversary Ball, was widely advertised for February 22, 1838, at the Choctaw House. The following signed as "managers who would furnish the Ball" for the occasion: William H. Green, James C. Adams, William B. Ochiltree, Joseph A. Smith, Daniel W. Miller, J. C. McAlpine, Willis Crenshaw, Joseph L. Scruggs, David Lowe, L. F. Whitehead, William M. Inge, Edward J. Williams, E. R. B. Thomas and H. W. Norville.

In 1854, the Choctaw House proprietor "repaired, replenished and enlarged the inn in Pattern Style," and advertised his "ambition to keep pace with the improvements of the age and no traveller shall have reason querulously to complain, 'shall I not take mine ease in mine inn?', but will find at the Choctaw House every comfort a well kept house can supply."

Livingston became a watering resort of widespread reputation. While boring for water with which to supply the town, a saline current was reached, which, upon investigation and analysis, was found to contain wonderful curative properties. Work was begun upon the well on December 13, 1854, and it was not completed until April 1, 1857. The well is 1,062 feet deep, and yields less than a gallon per minute. The water caught at the spout in a clear glass discloses slight effervescent qualities, as the minute bubbles rise to the surface or cleave to the side of the container. The water is saline in taste, and to most persons is slightly unpleasant tasting at first, but it becomes quite palatable in a little time. The temperature of the water is sixty-eight degrees Fahrenheit at all times.

The following is an analysis of the water:

Fixed Ingredients (Troy Grams)	
Silicic Acid and Silicates	1.138
Bi-Carbonate of Iron	0.204
Bi-Carbonate of Magnesia	2.320
Bi-Carbonate of Lime	7.140
Perchloride of Iron	0.190
Chloride of Calcium	2.983
Chloride of Magnesium	1.839
Chloride of Potassium	0.352
Chloride of Sodium	295.435
Strontia	Trace
Bromide of Sodium	0.980

Livingston, being situated on a bed of "sandy draft," has excellent subdrainage. This fact, as well as the complete drainage of all the surrounding country is no doubt the reason for its well-established reputation for healthfulness. The well is located on a corner of the public square and is covered with a carpet of green grass and shaded by broad-branched water oaks. The water has been noted for the cure of dyspepsia and chronic diarrhea, or dysentery. It acts freely upon the kidneys and has a reputation for curing diseases of this organ.

The story is told that a noted Negro character in Livingston, Sam Slick, passed the well while carrying a traveling man's luggage to the hotel. The visitor stopped to sample the water, and then inquired of Sam as to whether the water had been analyzed. Sam's answer is still quoted today in Livingston, as follows: "Yas Suh, hits been scandalized by de best fenologists, an' dey say hits three quarters carbolic acid gas and de other seven eights is hydrophobia; you see Boss dis here is artillery *[artesian]* water and hit will cue everything you got."

Before Livingston had the convenience of railroad facilities, an important west Alabama stage line was run through the town by Jemison, Ficklin, Powell & Company. Four-horse stages ran from Columbus and Aberdeen, Mississippi, via Pickensville, Clinton, Gainesville, Livingston, and Marion, all in Alabama, to Quitman, Mississippi, connecting with the Mobile and Ohio Railroad in twenty-four hours, and thus making the trip to Mobile forty-eight hours. The stage line was cordially recommended as having new and roomy coaches, fine teams, sober, polite and skillful drivers, and plain but excellent fare at the different eating houses enroute. Stage service for Livingston was provided every Tuesday, Thursday and Sunday, and the stage stop there was at the Choctaw Tavern.

In 1871, the Alabama Great Southern Division of the Queen and Crescent Line (now Southern Railway System) linked Livingston with Meridian and Chattanooga, and all connecting points. Soon thereafter, guests arrived in Livingston to use the water. The reputation of the water for its medicinal virtues was soon established. In 1873, *Appleton's Hand Book of American Travel* described Livingston as "a flourishing little place."

A wooden pavilion with an oriental-looking roof was erected over the well, and nearby a hexagonal building was constructed for use as a band stand and the mayor's office. In 1924 the old pavilion was replaced by a brick structure matching the design of the Alabama Inn, which had been completed and opened for guests at the time. All through the years the pavilions have been the assembly place for old and young alike, both visitors and residents.

As a watering resort and education center, Livingston has enjoyed prestige. It has long been noted for its social refinement. The many well-known Livingston educators have included Miss Julia Tutwiler, Dr. Carlos Smith, Mrs. Eleanor C. Gibbs, Dr. B. F. Riley, Professor G. F. Mellen, Professor S. S. Mellen, Miss Eleanor Churchhill Gibbs, Mrs. Mary Champ Short, Professor J. W. A. Wright, Joel C. Dubose, and Joseph G. Baldwin, the author of *Flush Times in Alabama and Mississippi.* Many students through the years have attended school in Livingston because of the social, religious and educational advantages.

The Choctaw Tavern received guests until 1900. Soon thereafter the buildings were partly removed, with much of the salvage material being used by William Larkin to build a cabin on land owned by J. W. Killian. In 1931, the remaining parts of the tavern, called "offices," were acquired by Jenkins Jackson and moved to a location one block further south. They are now being used as his home and law office.

A traditional institution of Livingston since 1840 has been the annual masquerade procession of the D. U. D.'s, an informal organization of men and boys who move by torch light through the streets on New Year's Eve. Its purpose is to mark the end of the old year and the beginning of the new. After the procession, the masqueraders assemble at the well for the judging of costumes. Merchants of the town provide prizes. After unmasking, the crowd remains at the well or individuals visit in the homes of friends, awaiting the ringing of the church bells at midnight. The idea was taken from a similar celebration in England and Scotland, known in the middle ages as the "Feast of Fools." At first the organization in Livingston was known as "The Indomitables," but later D. U. D.'s was adopted. Among the men these letters are taken to mean "Damned Ugly Devils," but to the ladies the explanation is "Dressed Up Dudes." In 1951, the "Maskers," a social club of young married couples, was organized and now holds a costume ball following the procession.

For many years the Choctaw Tavern was a meeting place for the D. U. D.'s on the night of their activities. The story has been told that the first organization, "The Indomitables," was organized at the tavern.

People still visit Livingston to drink the saline water. For dyspepsia, the water is said to be superior to the famous waters of Waukesha. In 1928, an electric pump was installed in the well, replacing the hand pump presented by the late G. B. Fellows in 1904.

The water has been shipped to many parts of the United States. Many who have visited there to get well returned to their homes pleased, and continued the use of the water by having it shipped to them.

The pavilion on the courthouse square continues to be a splendid place to pass away the time, and to sit there without drinking the water appears strange to the older residents of Livingston.

102

Clairmont Springs

"Hospitality House" might well be the name of the sprawling Clairmont Springs Hotel, located between Talladega and Ashland, in the foothills of the Talladega Mountains. The resort is eighteen miles from Talladega, on the Atlantic Coast Line Railroad, in the northwestern part of Clay County. The rambling, unpretentious hotel and a scattering of private cottages are located on the home site of the famous United States Senator, John Tyler Morgan.

A few of the early land owners in the vicinity, dating back as early as 1830, were Thomas Riddle, Gideon Riddle, Richard Grantham, James G. L. Huey,

Richard P. Evans, John M. Pitts, Radney Hobbs, Cyrus W. Cotton, William Peter Cotton, Moses Moore, and the Wesley family.

In 1841, Mr. Huey and the Riddles sold their holdings to William P. Chilton, who later became Chief Justice of the Supreme Court of Alabama. In 1842, Moses Moore sold two hundred acres of land on nearby Talladega Creek to the same man. In 1854 Mr. Chilton's agent, John Tyler Morgan, sold 520 acres of land, on which the springs are located, to Bill Jenkins. The springs became known as Jenkins Springs. The property later was acquired by Mr. Jenkins' oldest son, John. The Jenkins lived in a log house directly in front of the site of the hotel until 1900, when they built a new frame house. Later John Jenkins traded four-fifths interest in the property to W. J. Pearce in exchange for property near Lineville.

In 1906, a partnership consisting of J. W. Jackson, C. B. Allen, E. J. Garrison, and W. R. Pruett, all of Ashland, purchased Pearce's interest and then sold it to Cecil Browne of Talladega, who also acquired the remaining one-fifth from Mrs. Annie McCants of Demopolis. Browne purchased the property for the Title Guarantee and Trust Company of Atlanta. In 1906, the Eastern Railway of Alabama was completed through Jenkins Springs, and the following year this road became a part of the Atlanta, Birmingham & Atlantic Railroad, which connected Brunswick, Georgia, with Birmingham. The Title Guarantee and Trust Company purchased the Jenkins Springs property to develop it. Failing in their plans, they sold the property on March 23, 1909, to the Clairmont Springs Company, a corporation consisting of the following stockholders from Talladega: Cecil Browne, Leon G. Jones, Dr. B. B. Sims, J. M. Thornton, and Captain Thomas S. Plowman, who was named president of the corporation. The name was changed to Clairmont Springs, the word Clairmont meaning "clear (or bright) mountain."

The Clairmont Springs Company erected the first wing of a hotel, surveyed and improved the grounds, and offered lots for summer cottages. The hotel was opened in 1909 under the management of W. R. Buchanan as lessee. A second wing was completed later in the same year, providing a total of fifty bedrooms. The company also built three log houses and a dance pavilion.

On September 29, 1911, J. W. Jackson purchased the hotel, spring property, and 520 acres of land. Under Mr. Jackson's operation the hotel became popular, especially because Mrs. Jackson assumed the management of the kitchen and dining room. "Mrs. Jack," as she has been affectionately known through the years, made the Clairmont Springs Hotel famous for fried chicken, fried ham, hot rolls, and cheese soufflé. Often the dining room has accommodated two hundred guests.

During World War I, trains stopped at the hotel for the passengers to obtain meals, since the railroad had no diners on this route. These arrangements lasted through 1920. Many of the passengers later came back to the resort as guests, never forgetting the meals they enjoyed during their stopover at Clairmont Springs.

As a watering place, the resort can boast of eleven springs. The water from each of the springs has medicinal value and is palatable. The springs produce chalybeate, magnesia, arsenic, black sulphur, white sulphur, alum, and freestone water. Perhaps there is no other place in Alabama with as many varieties of water in a confined bowl. The spot was a mecca for the Creek Indians when they inhabited the territory.

There are countless things to do and see at Clairmont Springs. The Peter Cottontail (of child legend) Rock, measuring ten by twenty by ten feet and weighing over fifty tons, is embedded in Talladega Creek. The legend is that Peter Cottontail, in one of his happier and stronger moments, pushed the rock from a bluff into the creek. Of course, children all want to see this rock.

Present visitors to Clairmont Springs will find amusement in the epitaph of H. L. Horn who wrote for his own marker the following lines:

"Please remember, man, as you pass by,
As you are now, once was I.
As I am now, you must be.
Prepare for death & follow me."

One mile east of the hotel, on Talladega Creek, is the site of an old charcoal furnace used in smelting iron ore. This furnace carries no date, but it is reputed to have been the first in the state. The hammer from the water-driven iron forge has been brought to the hotel grounds. This relic, which weighs over five hundred pounds, interests the Clairmont guests. There is a small ore pit only two hundred yards from the hotel, where ore was obtained for the furnace.

A recreation hall and a swimming pool, facilities for dancing, tennis, and horseback riding, and a five-acre lake for fishing and boating provide entertainment for the hotel guests. For those who enjoy rocking and talking, there is the usual spacious screened porch. Informal dances are held at the dance pavilion on special occasions. The pavilion was enlarged in 1932. Musical concerts have been presented at the hotel from time to time by the State School for the Blind at Talladega. Mrs. I. M. Moore of Talladega, who for many years wrote under the name of Betsy Hamilton, has often given readings from her humorous works. Clairmont Springs has been a favorite place for picnics. The Woodmen of the World on several occasions came by special trains to hold their annual statewide picnics, at which new members were initiated. For several years the railroad ran Sunday excursions from Birmingham to the springs.

After the death of Mr. Jackson in 1943, Mrs. Jackson took over the management of the hotel. She was assisted by her brother, William T. Stephens, and later, in 1946, by her son, Dwight M. Jackson, until she retired in 1949. Dwight Jackson is presently the manager, and at one time was postmaster for the post office which was formerly located in the hotel. He and his wife, Irene, are cordial hosts at the resort.

Clairmont Springs is truly a watering place with an ante-bellum atmosphere. It is a beautiful spot where one may rest and appreciate the beauty of living. It is "off the beaten path," and those who come that way come for a purpose. The purpose could easily be a pleasant week end or a longer visit at this "marvelous-time" place, where simple living reigns and where mountain breezes blow.

The old hotel register shows names from Georgia, Florida, the District of Columbia, Illinois, North Carolina, Missouri, Arkansas, Tennessee, Louisiana, New York, Mississippi, Kentucky, California and from all parts of Alabama. Perhaps the resort's largest clientele has come from Birmingham, Talladega, Ashland, Lineville, Alexander City, Roanoke, Opelika, Montgomery, and Bessemer.

106

Cook's Springs

LaFayette Cooke was an opportunist. He took full advantage of the construction of the Georgia Pacific Railroad (now part of the Southern Railway System)which was begun in 1882. When the work started, he began making plans for a resort, and by the time the railroad was opened between Atlanta and Birmingham in November, 1883, his hotel was completed and ready to receive guests.

Mr. Cooke was the owner of some springs and 1,700 adjoining acres of timber land. For a long time he had envisioned the possibilities of a resort there because of the springs, but due to its isolation it had never been developed previously. Mr. Cooke named the new resort Cook's Springs, omitting the "e" from his name.

The Cook's Springs Hotel, a structure of sixty rooms, replaced a wooden frame building which had accommodated a few guests there for several years, primarily because of the mineral water. The new hotel was located on an elevated site near the railroad tracks, with a wooden walkway connecting it with the railroad station. The resort was situated high up in the mountains in Saint Clair County, twenty-seven miles northeast of Birmingham and thirty-six miles west of Anniston, and was surrounded by beautiful mountain scenery. The exhilarating air assured the guests of the comfort they came to enjoy, especially an escape from the summer heat in the cities.

The hotel was operated on the American plan. The dining room seated approximately two hundred people. Mr. Cooke advertised, "The table will be supplied with fresh vegetables from our own garden every day, fresh milk from our own dairy. Everything will be of the best. Cook's Springs is a cool and quiet place, with a motto, 'HERE WE REST'."

From time to time Mr. Cooke leased the resort. Louie Reese, who had charge during the 1905 season, advertised his rates at $8.00 to $15.00 a week, with eight passenger trains arriving daily. Mr. Reese's favorite expression in his advertising was, "Listen to the katydids and the whippoorwills at Cook's Springs." Apparently too few came to listen, for Mr. Reese lost $5,000 during the season.

There were six fountains in the spring yard. Mr. Cooke advertised the waters extensively:

> The beauty of the waters at Cook's Springs is that one does not have to drink them the entire season before they find out whether they are going to be benefited. Twenty-four hours is usually long enough to tell, as ninety per cent of the people who come here for health and recreation improve from the day they arrive, without any loss of time. Life is too short to lose much time, and especially while regaining one's health away from home at the Springs. And again, the medicinal properties of these waters are so accurately compounded by nature, till they are palatable. The most delicate stomachs have no difficulty in taking them, and the very superior virtue of these waters are vouched for by the thousands of people who have tried them during the past eighty years, and found them to contain exactly the right proportion to the user. A trial will convince every one that the virtues of the waters at Cook's Springs are second to none. No malaria can exist here.

The best known water at Cook's Springs was the sulphur magnesia, which was highly recommended for indigestion, stomach troubles and insomnia of the worst form. The chalybeate water was recommended for chronic intestinal catarrh, lung and kidney troubles, eczema, nervous disorders of all types, seminal weakness, and in any case of convalescence when a tonic was required. The alkaline healing water was used for the cure of constipation, liver, kidney and bladder trouble, and was unsurpassed for dyspepsia, nervous disorders and rheumatism. This water was also recommended to build up the system, give strength and vigor to the entire body, clear the complexion, and set the organs right. The Blue Ridge lithia water, which came direct from under one of the spurs of the Blue Ridge, was recommended as a fine agent in the treatment of dropsy, gastritis, diabetes and Bright's disease. It was supposed to quiet the nerves and act as a fine restringent in cases of chronic diarrhea. A resident physician was in attendance during each season to advise on the use of the waters.

Hot sulphur baths were also available to the guests, and a swimming pool, a bowling alley, and a dance pavilion provided entertainment. A string band played for the dances. One thousand feet of verandas encircled the hotel building, and they were used by those who wished to sit, rock, and talk. Hunting, fishing, boating, and mountain rambling were advertised as additional amusements.

By 1907, the popularity of the resort drew attention from all over the state. The name of the hotel was changed to the Mountain View, but this name was short-lived, since Cook's Springs Hotel was still commonly used. On the grounds there were twenty cottages, each with two, three, or four rooms, used by families who came for the entire season. Each of the cottages contained wood-burning cook stoves, and the young boys in the vicinity were able to make extra spending money by supplying wood for the stoves. The cottage guests in most instances prepared their own meals, buying eggs, milk and produce from farmers in the vicinity.

Weekends at Cook's Springs were popular. On Saturday afternoons during the summer season, there were often as many as two hundred arriving by train. As the passengers disembarked, they were greeted with the music of the string band. On several occasions, organizations in Birmingham chartered special trains to the springs for all-day outings.

LaFayette Cooke, doing business as L. Cooke & Company, operated the hotel until 1919, when Mr. and Mrs. C. M. Cook took over the management as lessees. The Cooks managed the resort for six years. P. H. Lewis, of Birmingham, then leased the property for one year. The third and final manager was Thomas Ballard of Birmingham, who also was in charge for one season. Finally the hotel building was converted into a rooming house. It was used for this purpose until LaFayette Cooke deeded the property to the American School of Evangelism, to be used for religious purposes.

Serving on the board of trustees for the school were D. W. Moody and J. E. Griffin of Cook's Springs; I. W. Inzer of Ashville; and H. B. Woodward, J. L. Aders, H. L. Anderton and J. A. Mitchell, all of Birmingham. The hotel, springs property and 1,700 acres of land were deeded to the trustees on June 10, 1936. Improvements were made to the hotel and grounds and several new buildings, including an assembly hall, were constructed. During the following summer, religious activities were instituted at the resort.

COOK'S SPRINGS

In 1941 the summer assembly of the Baptist Training Union in Alabama was held at Cook's Springs under the direction of Davis Woolley of Montgomery. Shocco Springs, near Talladega, had been the assembly grounds previously, but because of defense demands in the vicinity of Shocco Springs, Cook's Springs was chosen. The trustees provided certain improvements and additions to the property to accommodate the Baptist young people. Again in 1942 and 1943, the Baptist Training Union assemblies were held at the springs under the direction of R. Maines Rawls, who succeeded Davis Woolley in 1942.

For several years the American School of Evangelism used the facilities as a school of missions and for religious assemblies. With construction of the new highway from Birmingham to Atlanta, it was necessary for the hotel building to be removed in 1954 when the site of the hotel, pavilion, and several cottages became part of the right-of-way. Because of the condition of the buildings, as well as the desirability of the new assembly site, the trustees have established a modern new camp a mile north of the old hotel. The new Cook's Spring camp is frequented by hundreds each summer.

Cullom Springs

One mile west of the town of Bladon Springs, in Choctaw County, is the site of the once-famous Cullom Hotel and mineral springs, developed by Charles Cullum, formerly of Mobile. In 1853 Mr. Cullum purchased the property and immediately had analyses made of the various springs by J. B. Avequin of New Orleans.

The first spring to be tested was Healing Spring. The water was particularly rich in bicarbonate of soda, and since it was very similar in composition to the celebrated Vichy Springs in Auvergne, France, Mr. Avequin designated it Alabama Vichy Spring. This water was advertised as being unequaled. Flowing from a depth of two hundred feet at nine hundred gallons an hour, there was a sufficient quantity for baths. It was reported, "This water is marvelously useful in curing cutaneous disorders, also for removing freckles and tan from the skin, leaving the flesh as soft as a little child's."

Another spring near Vichy Spring contained the same ingredients but in different proportions. It became known as Alabama Vichy Spring Number 2, but was often spoken of as Soda Spring.

About one hundred yards from Vichy Spring were two sulphur springs, one known as Point Spring and the other as Bridge Spring. These two sulphur springs, situated ten or twelve feet apart, were strikingly alike in their waters. They contained the same elements, nearly in the same proportions. It was reported, "The water from these two springs contained 50 per-cent more bicarbonate of soda and one-third more sulphuretted hydrogen than existed in any mineral spring in Alabama, Mississippi or Louisiana. This water is very similar in composition to that of Aix-la-Chappelle, in Europe."

Ferruginous Spring, near the hotel building, was another popular spring. It was reported, "Few ferruginous springs either in Europe or in America can be compared with it, either for abundance of carbonate or iron or for the paucity of other mineral products." Mr. Cullum was known for his technic in telling of the benefits of the mineral waters at his resort.

Mr. Cullum built a two-story hotel building, which he named the Cullum Hotel, later called the Cullom Hotel. It contained twenty-four bedrooms, two parlors, a clerk's office and room, a dining room 100 by 150 feet, and a kitchen connected to the main building which included a pantry, dish room, and a large double cooking area. In addition to the accommodations in the hotel, there were thirty double and single cabins.

The hotel and grounds were located five miles from the Tombigbee River. Transportation to and from the springs was supplied by steamboats running from Mobile to Demopolis, the same vessels which served Bladon Springs resort. The guests were met at Moore's Landing and taken to the springs in "excellent carriages."

In 1853 Mr. Cullum published for distribution brochures written in French to attract the French-speaking population of New Orleans and Louisiana to Cullum Springs. The brochures carried a complete analysis of the mineral waters and testimonials, and an invitation to visit the springs and enjoy the hotel. J. Waterman & Brother, corner of Common and Magazine Streets, New Orleans, was the distributing agent for the Cullum Springs water in that area.

In 1859 a brochure advertised, "The proprietor who is a gentleman of long experience in the management and administration of an extensive hotel, offers every possible inducement to those who may desire to repair thither during the summer season for the benefit of their health. They will be provided with horses and carriages for pleasant riding, the finest and choicest fare, and the most unwearied attention. In a word, Mr. Cullum's establishment is eminently adapted to the comfort and pleasure of visitors, and does not require any recommendations."

On February 6, 1873, T. W. Coleman, the surviving partner of Glover and Coleman, who lent money on the property, advertised that he would sell at public auction to the highest bidder, for cash, the Cullum Springs property, including the hotel, cottages and mineral springs. The sale was to satisfy the debt secured in a mortgage made on May 5, 1869, by Elizabeth Cullum. Mr. Cullum was able to weather the storm of the foreclosure sale, for he retained the property either by redemption or purchase, and continued operating the hotel.

Mr. Cullum's resort attracted a clientele from Mobile and New Orleans, especially during the summer months. On week ends the resort was filled to capacity, as was its neighbor, Bladon Springs. The continued fear of yellow fever and malaria, especially in the low coastal areas, caused many to visit watering places for the summer months.

In 1884 a Captain Trowbridge purchased the Cullum Springs property and bored for petroleum. The whole depth of the boring was 1,345 feet. At eighty feet water was struck, but it did not overflow. At two hundred feet there was a bold stream of vichy water which did overflow. At four hundred feet another strong stream of mineral water was struck. At one thousand feet a stream of salt water with inflammable gas was struck. The flow of water combined the streams at two hundred, four hundred and one thousand feet.

The water was decidedly salty, with a temperature of eighty-three degrees. The gas collected in bubbles or in a foam on the surface of the water in the tank into which the stream flowed. A lighted match touched to the foam ignited the gas, which burned over the surface of the water for some minutes unless extinguished by an accidental splash. The gas could be ignited at the spout, where it burned with a flame six to eight inches high. The estimated flow of the water was from ten to fifteen gallons a minute. Bath houses were constructed for warm salt baths. These were extensively advertised and many invalids visited Cullum Springs to take advantage of them.

Sam and John O'Hara were managers of the resort prior to the time in 1890 when Mrs. A. C. Dahlberg became proprietress of the hotel. Mrs. Dahlberg operated the hotel until the property was sold to John Cochran of the Alabama, Tennessee and Northern Railroad.

For the season which opened May 15, 1908, the hotel was reconditioned, electric lights and electric fans were installed, and all furniture and equipment was replaced, including carpets and matting on the floors. Conveniences included long distance telephone connections and daily mail service like that of city hotels. In addition, for the pleasure and entertainment of the guests the resort provided a large swimming pool filled by a natural flow of salt water, running continuously then at the rate of about one hundred gallons a minute, an eighteen-hole golf course, lawn tennis courts, a children's playhouse, lawn swings and hammocks.

The grounds, which covered 560 acres, were picturesque and featured shady walks, lovers' lanes, and cozy corners provided with rustic benches and resting places. Guests also enjoyed fishing in the clear creek that flowed across the grounds.

Everything was new or rehabilitated, including the management and the name of the resort, which through a typographical error in a railroad brochure, and subsequent common usage, was changed to Cullom Springs. F. T. P. Allison,

the new manager, advertised rates from $8.00 to $12.00 a week. Perhaps the most convenient addition to the resort was the line of the Tombigbee Valley Railroad, which had been constructed to Cullom, Alabama, leaving only an hour's ride by bus to the hotel. The distance from Mobile to the springs was seventy-five miles, and the time required for the trip was four hours. The springs remained a popular resort until the hotel building was destroyed by fire in 1938.

It may be said that Cullom Springs, so near the famous Bladon Springs, grew up as a reaction to its neighbor. It was popular in its own right, however, and was the first resort in the state to offer its clientele warm salt-water baths.

Presently, most of the springs have dried up and only a small amount of salt water comes from the deep well. It is almost impossible to find signs of the hotel and cabins. In the annals of the Bladon Springs district, Cullom is but a memory.

116

DeKalb Hotel FORT PAYNE

The Fort Payne Coal and Iron Company, organized in the fall of 1888, had two purposes. One was to develop mining and iron manufacturing; the other, to build a manufacturing city in Wills Valley. At a meeting held in Birmingham in November, 1888, the organization was completed, officers and directors were elected, and the capital of the company was fixed at $5,000,000. Four million dollars of the stock was afterwards offered to the public, and most of it was subscribed to by people from the New England states within one month. Ten thousand shares, reserved as treasury stock, were offered to the original stockholders a few months after the company was organized and were soon taken.

The company purchased 32,000 acres of land in and around Fort Payne in DeKalb County. On February 4, 1889, the pioneers of the new city arrived and began laying its foundations. The work of surveying, grading and building was started, and in eighteen months a model city stood on acreage which had been planted in cotton just two years before.

The mountains — Lookout to the east and Sand to the west — created a romantic setting for Fort Payne. The location, 800 to 1,200 feet above tide-water, "tempers the sun's heat even on the hottest days, and the nights are cool and restful," the company boasted. Property was developed and sold for residences and for business and manufacturing purposes.

One of the first important buildings erected in Fort Payne was the DeKalb Hotel, which was built in 1889 and occupied an entire square in the center of the city. The hotel was sold to the DeKalb Hotel Company, Inc. for $100,000. Twenty-five bonds were issued at $1,000 each, fifty at $500, 100 at $300, and 100 at $200 each. The Fort Payne Coal and Iron Company guaranteed payment of the bonds upon maturity and semi-annual interest payments at six per cent. The bonds were dated October 1, 1890, and were to mature in ten years.

Upon completion of the hotel, the company declared that "it ranks among the best hotels in the Union." It was built with the express purpose of making the visits of guests from the North to Fort Payne pleasant and agreeable, especially important since in the city's formative days visitors often came to inspect the progress and to make investments.

The three-story frame building, which contained 125 rooms, was lighted by electricity but lacked elevators. Every room had wall-to-wall carpeting and running water and was heated by fireplaces. There were adequate bathroom facilities on each floor. The company advertised, "The hotel is a favorite resort of the entire country within one hundred miles, on account of its cuisine and admirable management."

The hotel grounds were landscaped with grass and shrubbery, and walkways extended throughout them, especially toward the front of the building. In front of each of the two wings of the hotel an encircled area contained a beautifully designed water fountain. The two fountains, which were identical, were made of iron and cast in France. The fountains were eight feet in diameter and ten feet high, and the bowls were fifteen inches deep. At their base, designs of frogs, snails, shells, lizards, and calla lilies with leaves were molded in iron.

Perhaps the most outstanding social event held in the hotel was the first annual ball of the Thalian Club, a social organization composed of young men in Fort Payne. The ball was staged on Thursday evening, September 15, 1889. The order of dances for the evening was March and Circle, Waltz, Plain Quadrille, Galop, Schottisch, Landers Quadrille, Virginia Reel, German (figure), Quadrille, Galop, Portland Fancy, Waltz, Saratoga Landers, and Waltz (Home Sweet Home). This dance was attended by the social elite of Fort Payne.

In the Panic of 1893-94 the Northern capitalists who had come to speculate in Fort Payne evacuated in fast order, taking with them what could be realized on their investments. Within the short span of three years, no less than $5,000,000 had been spent there in establishing industries, buildings, homes and a hotel.

Following the Panic, practically everything of importance in Fort Payne had either disappeared entirely or decreased drastically in value. The major industries of the district, including the rolling mill, the brick plant, and the Fort Payne & Eastern Railroad, were among the first to suffer the effects of the Panic. The vast majority of the capital invested in the city had come from New England. It is said that, some time after the Fort Payne failure, two veterans of the War Between the States were reminiscing about the war, and the Yankee said, "We sure gave you rebels hell at Gettysburg!" "Yes," the Confederate agreed, "but we sure got even at Fort Payne."

The full significance of Fort Payne as a manufacturing city, as pictured in the vivid imagination of its promoters, was never realized, for all too soon the "busted boom" had its effect. A few of the citizens with hardier spirits stood by and looked to the future. Those who held on, through faith and nerve, perhaps fared better than those who evacuated. This, however, cannot be said of the holders of the hotel bonds, for the bonds became permanently worthless after three interest payments had been made.

As a result of court action brought by A. S. Gayle and the Old Colony Trust Company of Boston against the Fort Payne Coal and Iron Company, N. W. Trimble, then called Master of the Court in Fort Payne, sold the assets of the company to E. N. Cullom of Birmingham, holder of 1,200 shares of capital stock in the company, H. C. Yeaton and E. J. Fletcher. The sale took place in January, 1894, and in May Mr. Cullom and his associates sold the assets to the DeKalb Company, a corporation which Mr. Cullom was to head. The hotel was included in the transaction.

Mr. Cullom disposed of all assets which could be liquidated. He salvaged the machinery and equipment from the two-story laundry building at the rear of the hotel, and also sold the equipment from the barber shop in the hotel itself. Much to the surprise of the people of Fort Payne, he removed much of the furniture and all of the Botsai wall-to-wall carpeting from the building. Because of the adverse conditions in the city, there was little need for a well-equipped hotel.

In 1900 Professor Edwin R. Eldridge, former president of the State Normal School at Troy, opened an institution of learning at Fort Payne. The school, which he called Tri-State Normal, burned during its second year of operation. The students were removed to the DeKalb Hotel, where the proprietor placed them in a separate wing, and here they boarded for the remainder of the school term. They took their meals in one of the large private dining rooms, and classrooms were provided in the nearby Opera House. Professor Eldridge and his family lived with the students at the hotel until the term ended, and then they moved to Birmingham.

In February, 1903, the DeKalb Company was sold to William Schall, Jr. In January of the next year Mr. Schall sold his holdings to the Fort Payne Company, accepting as consideration 395 shares of stock in the company. The Fort Payne Company had A. W. Smith as president and C. M. Hayes as secretary.

In 1911 the Fort Payne Company converted the DeKalb Hotel into an apartment and boarding house, although reserving a few rooms for overnight guests. Walter B. Raymond became president of the company in 1916.

On the night of February 5, 1918, the building was destroyed by a fire resulting from the explosion of an oil heater or a mishap while a chimney was being "burned out." It was a windy night, and the sparks from the fire spread to several nearby buildings and they also burned.

During the time that the DeKalb Hotel was being operated as a regular hostelry, the various owners were fortunate in selecting efficient proprietors. Among them were Colonel A. A. Mabson, Mr. and Mrs. Sam Killian, Mr. and Mrs. Sam Rainey, Mr. and Mrs. Charles H. McCartney, and John Hill. At one period Jim Malone and his wife, Emma, mulatto citizens of Fort Payne who were well liked and highly respected, leased the hotel, but they were never connected with its direct management.

On June 21, 1919, C. A. Wolfes of Fort Payne purchased the block on which the hotel had been located. He also is the present owner of the two water fountains which once graced the hotel grounds.

120 DeKALB HOTEL

The experiences of the Fort Payne Coal and Iron Company, and subsequent companies and individuals, in the operation of a large hotel in a "busted town" were somewhat similar. The DeKalb Hotel had a bad beginning, and its conditions improved little.

Mrs. Walter B. Raymond was made president of the Fort Payne Company in 1934. Since that time she has dissolved the corporation and personally owns its remaining assets.

East Lake Hotel BIRMINGHAM

By the end of 1886 Birmingham could boast of twenty-five land companies, each engaged in developing sites for homes or industries. While "magic" is a much abused word, it doubtless is applied properly to the Magic City, at that time only fifteen years old and already with a population of more than thirty thousand. Birmingham, out of nothing but its earth-wealth, had attracted to itself aggressive capitalists who had faith and nerve enough to invest their funds in land development.

The East Lake Land Company, with capital stock of $200,000, was organized July 6, 1886, by James A. Van Hoose, Robert Jemison, Sr., and Rufus H.

Hagood. The company owned two thousand acres of land in East Lake, now a suburb of Birmingham. At the time the firm was founded, an announcement was made that a large park would be established in the area. The park was to include a lake, the water for which was to be supplied from the Roebuck Springs.

Through an arrangement with the East Lake Land Company, C. M. Boulden built a hotel in 1889 on the border of the lake at the eastern end of the park, at the terminus of the dummy line of First Avenue and Eighty-third Street, North. The building was two hundred feet long and contained 150 rooms. It was a two-story structure that cost about $20,000. Each story had a porch covering three sides. A large dining room was adjacent to the main lobby.

The hotel was built to attract guests especially from Birmingham. Since the East Lake area was elevated, many thought it was an ideal location to avoid the summer heat. The hotel was reached by means of dummy transportation, the land being owned by the land company.

Perhaps the most important gathering to be held at the East Lake Hotel was the third annual ball of the Jefferson Volunteers on the evening of May 15, 1890. The success of the occasion gave Mr. Boulden the idea that the hotel could best be used by organizations, inasmuch as individual guests were not using his facilities. A man about thirty-five years old, Mr. Boulden was inexperienced in the operation of a hotel, and so he offered his venture for sale, first as a Confederate soldiers' home and at another time as a woman's college.

The hotel was located too far from Birmingham to attract commercial guests. Competition with the Lakeview Hotel for summer business was too keen, and Mr. Boulden closed his East Lake Hotel after one year of operation. He disposed of all the furnishings with the exception of one room, which he occupied himself.

On June 10, 1891, at about daybreak, neighbors saw a bright light. Some thought at first that it was the sun rising, but the glare was in the wrong direction. A few minutes later a roar was heard and soon a fire was seen. The flames became so high and hot that trees were scorched five hundred yards away. The hotel building, constructed of heart pine lumber, burned completely down within three-quarters of an hour. It was thought that the fire was started by lightning striking the building.

The room which Mr. Boulden occupied was near the place where the fire started, but he was not in the building. He had left the premises the evening before after telling his neighbors that he was leaving for Pensacola, Florida, where he had interest in the street railroad.

The building was insured for $15,000 and full damages were collected. The cause of the fire was never determined.

The site of the hotel is now a playground, a part of the municipally owned East Lake Park. The man-made lake throughout the years has provided recreation for thousands. It bears the name of the land company which developed the area and provided the site for the almost forgotten ill-fated East Lake Hotel.

124

Exchange Hotel MONTGOMERY

The City of Montgomery is known as "The Cradle of the Confederacy," and here was made and unfurled the first flag of the Confederate States. The capitol of Alabama boasts a unique distinction, for within its walls a nation was born.

After the completion of the capitol building in 1847, Montgomery began to share the responsibility of the political storms that swept over the nation. No other place took a more vivid interest in the heated debates in Congress over the fatal territorial problems thrust upon this section by the Mexican War. General Quitman and General Shields, fresh from the conquests of this war, were given a public reception in the capitol.

Two conventions assembled between May, 1847, and February, 1848. The conventions bore a common relation to one purpose. They inaugurated the popular movement in the southern states against the doctrine of the Wilmot Proviso. In the secession events, Alabama retained the leadership she then assumed and made herself the pivotal state of the Confederate cause.

Coming into existence at approximately the same time that the capitol building on Goat Hill made its appearance was the Exchange Hotel, at the corner of Montgomery and Commerce streets. The hotel was erected by a company composed of Charles T. Pollard, Charles Crommelin, Francis M. Gilmer, Jr., William Taylor and others. The contractors were Robinson and Bardwell, who were also employed to erect the capitol building. The architect was Samuel Holt. The work on the hotel was begun in the summer of 1846, and the building was ready for use just prior to the meeting of the General Assembly in the capitol building in November, 1847.

The Exchange Hotel was a four-story building, measuring three hundred by one hundred feet, fronting on Court Square in the center of the city. The exterior walls were constructed of brick. At the center of the building, on both street sides, there were balconies at each floor level in the open court. In the front of the courts there were too large columns, extending upward from the second floor to the architrave above the fourth floor, which were in line with the exterior walls.

The hotel contained 124 sleeping rooms, each well furnished, light and airy. The billiard and bar rooms were "models of elegance and taste, with hardwood finish, in early English style, panelled with plate glass." The gentlemen's reading room was on the second floor. The ladies' parlor was "particularly noticeable, being handsomely furnished and arranged." An artesian well supplied water.

The hotel was opened by J. J. Stewart, who, in September, 1850, associated himself with Joseph G. Field. In September, 1852, Washington Tilley took charge of the hotel, upon the retirement of Manager Stewart because of ill health.

The destruction of the state capitol on Friday, December 14, 1849, was a great calamity, and produced universal gloom among the citizens. The fire was discovered about 1:30 P. M., while the two houses of the General Assembly were in session. The flames were issuing from the roof, and within a few hours nothing of the beautiful and costly structure was left but the walls. The furniture, in a damaged condition, and most of the archives were rescued and saved. Suitable rooms were provided at the Exchange Hotel, so that there was scarcely any interruption to legislative business. From that year to the present, the Exchange Hotel has been the gathering place for the politicians of Alabama.

The Macon *Republican* on May 1, 1851, cordially recommended the Exchange Hotel to the "traveler, the man of business or of leisure, the valetudinarian and the brief sojourner." Other hotels in Montgomery at the time were the Montgomery Hall, the Madison, the American Hotel, and the Rialto House. On one occasion, the editor of the Claiborne *Southerner* complained that the Montgomery hotels were great in size, but their tables would not tempt even a hungry man's appetite and did no credit to the capital of the State. Of course, the Montgomery *Advertiser* came to the defense of the Montgomery hostelries.

A dinner at the Exchange Hotel was described in the *Advertiser* of January 20, 1855, with evident appreciation: " . . . . oysters of rare quality, turkeys, assaulted though not consumed, lobster salad such as epicureans stare at, cakes, fruits, nuts, candies, confectionery and sparkling exhilarating champagne of the best brands." During 1855, Messrs. St. Lanier and Son succeeded Washington Tilley as proprietor of the hotel.

Frederick Law Olmsted, in his *Journey in the Seaboard States, 1853-54,* says: "Montgomery is an important town of six thousand inhabitants, four thousand whites and two thousand blacks. There are large grocery establishments, hardware stores, an elegant 'Exchange Hotel', a new splendid 'Commercial Hall', the cotton warehouses of Gilmer and Company, and John H. Murphy and Company . . . ."

From 1852 to 1859 the capitol shook to its foundations. William Yancey, Henry W. Hilliard, Jeremiah Clemens, C. C. Clay, and many other forceful speakers threshed out in the state the vital issues that Henry Clay and John C. Calhoun were debating in the national capitol. Tenseness increased as the debates stirred the nation with respect to the issues of States' Rights.

January, 1861, saw Alabama's famous Secession Convention. To this convention went William Yancey—a young man of great oratorical powers and sweeping convictions for States' Rights—with a platform which was adopted. This, the famous Alabama Platform, was the first formal resolution stating the views which southern men were beginning to hold, that neither Congress nor the territorial legislature had any right to prohibit slavery in the territories, but on the contrary should protect it.

It was a time of tremendous excitement. State after state was seceding, Alabama being the fourth, and all were sending delegates to Montgomery to form a new Confederacy. On February 4, 1861, these delegates organized the Confederate States of America, of which Alabama became a member. A provisional constitution was adopted. Jefferson Davis of Mississippi was elected president and Alexander Stephens of Georgia was elected vice president.

President Davis reached Montgomery on February 17, 1861, and made the Exchange his headquarters, including living accommodations and office. From the Commerce Street balcony of the hotel, President Davis was introduced to the people of Montgomery and welcomed by William Yancey, who had been appointed by the mayor and council of Montgomery to deliver the address of formal welcome, in which he declared, "The man and the occasion have met."

On February 18, Mr. Davis was inaugurated as president before a gathering of more than ten thousand people. The procession to the capitol formed at the Exchange Hotel. President Davis occupied a carriage drawn by six grey horses and in the vehicle with him rode Vice President Stephens, Reverend Basil Manly, and Captain George Jones, personal aide of the President. Colonel H. P. Watson was marshal of the parade. The military escort consisted of the Columbus Guards, the Barbour Rifles, the Perote Guards, the Independent Rifles, and the Alabama Fusiliers. The inaugural parade was led by Herman F. Arnold's Montgomery Theatre Band, and at the suggestion of Mrs. Arnold, "Dixie" was selected as the music. On the front portico of the capitol, the new officers and cabinet members were sworn into office by Howell Cobb of Georgia, president of the Provisional Congress.

The members of the Confederate cabinet were quartered temporarily in the Exchange Hotel, where they held informal conferences. It was from the President's office in the hotel on April 11 that the telegraphic orders were given to fire on Fort Sumter. This message was carried by Phil Gayle to the telegraph office in the Winter Building, across the street from the hotel.

On May 16, J. B. Jones, clerk in the War Department, described the conditions in Montgomery as follows: "The principal hotel is the Exchange, as in Richmond; the entrance to the bar, reading room, etc. is by a flight of stairs from the street to the second story, with stores underneath. Here there is an incessant influx of strangers coming from all directions on business with the new government. But the prevalent belief is that the government itself will soon travel to Richmond. The buildings here will be insufficient in magnitude for the transaction of the rapidly increasing business."

By vote of the Congress on May 24, Richmond was chosen the permanent seat of government. Though President Davis did not favor the change of cities, the Congress over his veto passed the resolution to remove the seat of government to Richmond. On May 29 President Davis departed for Richmond, officially bringing to a conclusion the affairs of the Confederate government in Montgomery.

Miss Kate Cumming, who served the Confederacy as a nurse and hospital organizer, visited Montgomery in 1862 while traveling through the South. Her observations regarding the Exchange Hotel are as follows: "We arrived at Montgomery the morning of August 29th, and put up at a fine hotel, the Exchange, and paid one dollar each for an excellent breakfast." After visiting Montgomery again on February 8, 1863, Miss Cumming reported: "On missing the West Point train at Montgomery, we put up at the Exchange Hotel, which is a very fine house. We had a splendid dinner, for which we paid three dollars each. Everything was there, the same as in peace times."

During the latter half of the war, the Exchange Hotel was under the proprietorship of Messrs. Bulger, Hukill & Company. After the war, A. P. Watt & Company took over the management. In 1869 the company advertised: "This old and well-known Hotel, which has so long enjoyed the patronage of the Southern people and of visitors, has been thoroughly refitted, and is prepared to extend the best accommodations to guests."

The Lanier brothers, Sidney and Clifford, nephews of Mr. St. Lanier, found employment at the Exchange Hotel in 1866. Sidney had contracted tuberculosis, which was first noticed at Point Lookout, near Chattanooga, while he was serving the Confederate cause. For over a year, he served as night clerk at the hotel where "a growing impulse towards a literary career moved him." Also, tradition has persisted that as night clerk he often played softly upon his flute, and guests opened their doors and windows to welcome the notes which interrupted their sleep. During the first summer at Montgomery, Sidney completed his first novel, *Tiger Lilies.* In 1867 he left Montgomery to begin a teaching and writing career, which included the essays, poems and novels, for which he became so famous.

During the post-war era, the Exchange Hotel received national attention. In *Appletons' Hand-Book of American Travel, Southern Tours,* of 1873, the following listing is noted: "Montgomery—The Exchange is the Best."

When the people of Alabama were ready to dedicate the spot on which the monumental tribute to the dead soldiers and sailors of the Confederacy would be placed, they called upon ex-President Davis to make the trip from Beauvoir to Montgomery to join in the ceremonies. The exercises took place on the Capitol Hill on April 29, 1886. President Davis stopped at the Exchange Hotel, where he had stayed in 1861. A procession was formed with General Edmund W. Pettus as grand marshal of the day. Preceded by several military companies as an escort, President Davis, ex-Governor Thomas H. Watts, Governor Edward A. O'Neal and Mayor Warren S. Reese, in an open carriage drawn by four white horses and followed by carriages containing other distinguished visitors, moved up Dexter Avenue to the state capitol. President Davis was deeply moved by the reception he received and he expressed his appreciation by constantly bowing to the enthusiastic crowds.

At the capitol he took his place on the front portico, on which he had sworn to defend the Confederacy years before, and again spoke to his beloved people. He mentioned the fact that the demonstration of 1861 did not exceed that which was accorded him now. Referring to the reception given him on the evening in February, 1861, when he was introduced by Mr. Yancey in the Exchange Hotel, he said: "I felt last night as I approached the Exchange Hotel, from the galleries of which your orator, William Lowndes Yancey, introduced me to the citizens of Montgomery in language which only his eloquence could yield, and which far exceeded my merit, I felt, I say again, that I was coming to my home—coming to the land where liberty dies not, and heroic sentiment lives forever."

Many famous statesmen, actors and musicians have been guests of the historic old and new Exchange Hotel. Among them were President Grover Cleveland, Stephen Douglas, Millard Fillmore, Wilkes Booth, Lawrence Barrett and Joseph Jefferson.

Several historic markers have been placed in the hotel. A bronze tablet at the entrance has been erected commemorating the Old Exchange Hotel, which was for more than fifty years the social and political center of the town. A bronze plaque on the second floor is in memory of Jefferson Davis, who occupied a suite of rooms there. Another tablet is in memory of Sidney Lanier, who served as clerk during 1867. The Lanier family has held an interest in the Exchange for four generations, and it is still maintained.

In 1904 the old hotel building was removed to make room for a new building. In 1906 the New Exchange Hotel was completed, and has been in operation since.

Florence Hotel

In 1831 William S. Mudd, still in his boyhood, came to the town of Elyton, where later he became a prominent attorney and a law partner of Walter K. Baylor. At the age of twenty-three he was elected to the state legislature, where he served with such men as William L. Yancey, Leroy Pope Walker and Jere Clements. Later he became solicitor for Jefferson County and in 1856 he was elected a circuit judge, an office he held consecutively until 1883, when ill health forced him to retire.

In 1841 Judge Mudd married Miss Florence Earle, the daughter of Dr. Samuel S. Earle, one of the earliest physicians of Jefferson County. Shortly after they were married they chose a wooded knoll in the vicinity of Elyton as the site of their new home. Here they built the large colonial type home which today is known as Arlington. Arlington, now owned by the City of Birmingham, is of much historic interest to visitors.

Judge Mudd was eminently a businessman. For many years he was a prosperous merchant, and he accumulated a good fortune in the mercantile business, with J. B. Earle as his partner. In 1880 Judge Mudd, in co-operation with T. L. Hudgins and Josiah Morris of Montgomery, established a private bank, the City Bank of Birmingham. Four years later this bank, together with the National Bank of Birmingham, became the First National Bank of Birmingham. Judge Mudd was a charter member and director of the Elyton Land Company, the company which established Birmingham. He was a director in the South and North Railroad, and a holder of many parcels of real estate in Birmingham.

In 1883 Judge Mudd built the Florence Hotel, Birmingham's first large public inn. The four-story structure was situated on a lot measuring 100 by 140 feet, on the northwest corner of Second Avenue and Nineteenth Street, North, and was "a neat and tasteful brick structure; the first building of the kind in the city." The hotel was named Florence in memory of his wife, who died in 1867.

The hotel was opened to the public in April, 1884, with Campbell & Yeates as managers, but it passed into the hands of J. T. Nixon, of the Nixon House in Birmingham, four months later. Judge Mudd died on September 22, 1884, and the hotel property was willed to three of his daughters, Florence Earle (Mrs. Mortimer H. Jordan), Virginia Taylor (Mrs. William A. Walker), and Susie Emmett (Mrs. Pette Basil Clarke and later Mrs. John Rivers Carter).

The Florence Hotel was beautifully lighted with electric lights. The rooms were well ventilated and heated and would accommodate 170 guests. The sanitary arrangements were as good as men could make them. Ventilating and plumbing systems were designed so that nothing was to be feared from sewer gas and foul air. The office was a delightful room, with fine lofty ceilings. Besides this, the elegant lobby and writing rooms, the fine dining hall capable of seating ninety-six people, and other business establishments were on the first floor. Elevator service was provided the patrons. It was advertised as "one of the finest fitted-up houses in the South."

The cuisine of the Florence was not surpassed in the city. The dining room, known as the Indian Room, was the gathering-place for many formal dinners. A portion of the dining room was a bar.

From the time the hotel was opened it was the pride of Birmingham. Three years of the city's history embrace what in many respects was its most eventful period. The big land boom of 1885, 1886 and 1887 was brought on by intense real estate speculation, when men bought lots from the Elyton Land Company and resold them at fabulous profits. The land company paid its stockholders ninety-five per cent dividends in 1884 and forty-five per cent in 1885. The company's stock which had once sold down to $6.00, now rose to an all-time high of $4,000 per share. The Florence Hotel and the other smaller hotels were crowded to capacity by speculators who were there to get in the trading. The story is related that barber chairs in the hotel's barbershop brought a rental of $1.00 per night when no other accommodations could be had.

A very notorious incident occurred at the Florence Hotel on March 20, 1887, when a "race issue" prohibited Senator John Sherman of Ohio from receiving a group of Negro gentlemen. Senator Sherman was registered at the Florence Hotel and during the day was handed a letter signed by A. L. Scott, a real estate man, and W. R. Pettiford, J. M. Goodloe, A. J. Headon, A. D. Jemison and R. Donald, pastors of Negro churches in Birmingham, seeking an appointment for ten o'clock the following morning. At the given hour, Senator Sherman received a note from the hotel proprietor that the delegation would not be permitted to visit his room. Thereupon, the senator checked out of the hotel and went to the Metropolitan Hotel, where he was permitted to see the delegation. The mission of the group was to deliver an official welcome to Birmingham to Senator Sherman in behalf of the Negro citizenry. It is needless to state that Birmingham and the Florence Hotel received wide publicity and criticism throughout the nation. "The incident was condemned and deplored by the leading Democrats of Birmingham," according to Senator Sherman.

The annual meeting of the Southern Baptist Convention was held in Birmingham in 1891. It was in the Florence Hotel that a very important question was settled by a committee of the convention. For several years there had been discussion of whether the convention should publish a series of Sunday School "helps," and then as the issue became more definite and concrete, as to whether the convention should have a separate and co-ordinate board to take care of these several interests. A committee of the convention met in an "upper room" in the Florence and prepared a report which was accepted by the convention in session, thus creating a Sunday School Board and ending an agitation which had lasted for six years. The Sunday School Board was made responsible for promotional and educational work of the Baptists, with headquarters in Nashville. Now, as publisher of denominational pamphlets and books, it is one of the most important boards of the Southern Baptist Convention.

The Florence Hotel suffered the effects of the Panic of 1893 and 1894. The lessees of the hotel were hardly able to pay the rental. During these severe times, members of the Walker and Jordan families took their meals in the Indian Room, for the purpose of "eating-out-the-rent."

The Florence Hotel was in close proximity to the retail and wholesale trade centers, and accessible by street railroads and horse cars. When the Caldwell Hotel was opened for business in July, 1889, the new hotel had severe effects on the Florence. The Florence remained a good hotel, but it was not considered the most popular. Five years later, when the Caldwell Hotel burned, the Florence regained its popularity, although sharing it with the Morris Hotel which had opened in 1889. The Florence and the Morris shared these honors until the Hillman Hotel was opened in 1900 and surpassed them both.

In 1905 R. D. Burnett, Sr., took a lease for a period of ten years on the Florence Hotel. He remodeled the entire building in an effort to attract the patronage from the Hillman and the Morris. He managed the hotel until January 1, 1916, after which it was torn down to make room for a new building to be constructed for the Louis Saks Clothing Company. The property is presently occupied by the Newberry store.

Following the demolition of the hotel building, the Birmingham Hotel building on the northwest corner of Eighteenth Street and Second Avenue, North, was reconditioned and the name Florence Hotel was attached to it, but there was no connection with the one formerly owned by Judge Mudd or his heirs.

Truly the Florence Hotel was a venture illustrating Judge Mudd's abiding faith in the Magic City, where he had invested much of his hard-won earnings. Unfortunately he died too soon to see his hotel in its prime. His descendants still own the property.

Grand Hotel POINT CLEAR

"Christopher Columbus had scarcely been in his grave fourteen years when Pineda discovered Mobile Bay and gave it the most sacred name in his vocabulary — the Bay of the Holy Spirit," wrote Colonel David Holt, Mobile historian. "He must have witnessed such a sunset as we often have beheld, when the clouds of evening were banked in purple splendor like the pictured throne of a reigning deity, with shafts of light flecked with webs of gold across streamers of tender blue radiating from a scarlet sun. He must have seen the evening star appear as a pale, silver ornament in a canopy of blue, pale rose and gold, and watched it grow in brilliancy as the reflected sunlight would fade from the sky."

A deed in the old Mobile records shows the conveyance in 1800 of "forty arpens by the usual depth at Punta Clara" to Eugenio Lavalle of Pensacola. This is the first mention of the famous resort site.

Point Clear is located halfway down the bay on the eastern shore, in what is now Baldwin County. It appears on the H. S. Tanner map of Georgia and Alabama in 1823 as Big Point Clear (the printing being in the bay proper), and the bayshore community at the point is called Williamsburg. The L. T. Hinton map of Alabama and Georgia in 1831 shows Point Clear on the land side of the point. Other maps show the point and use such names as Red Bluff, Alabama City, Williamsburg, Mullet Point, and Great Point Clear.

In 1820, a few immigrants crossed Mobile Bay in a sailing craft and began converting a pine forest into what was to become a noted resort. The original settlers were Caleb Dana and Joe Nelson. The Dana House was the first constructed. Early Point Clear village was separated from another village, Battles (named for John and James Battle), by Point Clear Creek, just above the Old North Wharf, reportedly built by A. D. Darling and F. H. Chamberlain.

Mr. Chamberlain, who owned extensive lands in Baldwin County, built the first Point Clear Hotel in 1847, with lumber brought from Mobile. The hotel was a rambling building about one hundred feet long. The two-story structure had shedded front galleries extending the length of the building. Outside stairs at each end of the building led to the second floor. There were about forty rooms in the hotel.

For the convenience of the guests, the proprietor provided two wharves, one for the male guests and the other for the women, since mixed bathing in the bay was frowned upon.

The dining room was in a separate adjacent building. Next in the line of buildings was the bar, called the Texas. The name "Texas" was customarily applied to such buildings in those days, meaning that the building was "set apart" and "distinct" like the state of Texas from the rest of the nation. Another interpretation of the name is attributed to that part of a steamboat called the texas deck, meaning "above other decks." The bar was a two-storied affair with outside steps at one end leading upstairs. Though the original building was demolished in the 1893 hurricane, it was rebuilt and used until 1940, serving for almost a century as a gathering place for resort guests and local residents alike to meet and pass away the hours with storytelling, to the accompaniment of clinking glasses.

Near the hotel was the two-story frame mansion known as the Gunnison House, in its early days almost as colorful as the Texas. John A. M. Battle built the house in the early 'fifties and occupied it for several years as his summer home. It was one of the greatest gathering places in this area during the ante-bellum period. As tradition has it, "they rode 'em high at Gunnison's." Here cognac passed freely, staggering sums changed hands at cards, and sumptuous feasts were served in the old southern manner.

An inscription on a metal plate on the Gunnison House bears the legend, "Compliments of Admiral Farragut, August 5, 1864." The plate was placed there by Major James K. Glennon, Confederate soldier and prominent Mobile citizen, as a reminder of a shell hole made by Farragut's guns when he damned the torpedoes and ordered his ships "full speed ahead!" in the Battle of Mobile Bay. The Point Clear Hotel also received a shell from the federals. John D. Cain was the caretaker of the hotel during the war years, and his sister, Lucy, who also lived at the hotel, was ill at the time and later died from the shock of the shelling. During the War Between the States the Gunnison House was used as a hospital, and in the last year of the struggle the 21st Alabama Regiment was encamped immediately to the rear of the house, near the hotel.

General Dabney H. Maury, in his *Recollections of a Virginian,* writes:

> Soon after assuming command of the Department of the Gulf, I was notified that a steamer, under flag of truce, would arrive in Mobile Bay with the sick and wounded Confederate soldiers from Vicksburg. This was one of the many considerate and kindly acts of General Grant, who never made war upon women or other unfortunates who might fall in his power. . . . We cordially welcomed our weary and wounded comrades, and went down in steamers to meet them and escort them to that charming bay-shore resort at Point Clear, where the hotel and cottages awaited their reception, and no soldiers of the Confederacy ever enjoyed a happier destiny than these, in exchanging the damp and soggy climate of Vicksburg for the fresh salt breezes and sparkling waters of Mobile Bay, with its fishing and bathing and famous oysters, and now and then a boat load of limes and bananas and other tropical luxuries brought in by the blockade runners.

The Point Clear Hotel, famous for its hospitality and good cheer long before the war, served southern soldiers well after it was converted into a hospital. Following the war, it was again used as a resort.

On the night of July 14, 1869, the Point Clear Hotel was destroyed by a fire which began in the bake-room of the kitchen. With the lack of firefighting equipment and the stimulus of a powerful northwest breeze, the flames spread rapidly and the main building was leveled. At the time of the fire there were approximately 150 guests, but no lives were lost. All of the personal effects of the guests were saved, as was the linen of the hotel and most of the furniture. The hotel building was insured for $15,000. The cottage to the east of the main building was also destroyed, but the Texas bar, billiard room, tenpin alley, one cottage, and the wharves survived undamaged.

Ten days after the fire the Mobile *Weekly Register* announced:

> There is some reason to hope that despite the late disastrous destruction of the main hotel building at the Point, the denizens of the hot city will not be deprived of the relief of a puff of the salt air and a plunge into the salt water at that place. There is talk (and we hope it will result in reality) of keeping what is left of the hotel open. The building that escaped the fire, with some little improvements, will enable the proprietor to accommodate one hundred guests, and we understand that some families have already engaged rooms. It will not take much energy and capital to enlarge the accommodations, by building cabins after the fashion of interior watering places.

On a hill not far from Point Clear is an old cemetery called Confederate Rest. The original tract was seven acres, and although more than three hundred Confederate soldiers are buried there, the plot was neglected for many years. In 1927, the Eastern Shore Memorial Association enclosed a small portion of this tract, cleaned the grounds, and erected a granite marker to the Unknown Confederate Dead. The records of the soldiers were kept in the hotel at the time of the 1869 fire, when the identities of those buried in Confederate Rest were lost.

In the Mobile *Daily Register* of June 10, 1871, an advertisement signed by J. A. Sample, proprietor, stated that first-class accommodations were available for seventy-five to one hundred guests at the Point Clear Hotel. The Point Clear Hop, well advertised in the *Register* of July 24, attracted considerable attention from Mobile dancers. During the 1871 season, Captain H. C. Baldwin, master of the steamer *Annie,* used the newspaper to keep Mobilians informed of his fine services to the Point.

While a crowd of excursionists clambered aboard the twenty-seven-ton steamer *Ocean Wave* as she prepared to leave from the Point Clear pier on the afternoon of August 27, 1871, an explosion wrecked the steamer, killing more than a score of her two hundred passengers and injuring many others. The following is part of an eyewitness account of the tragedy as given the

Mobile *Register* by Ben Lane, who was sitting on the porch of the Point Clear Hotel at the time of the explosion.

> It was my ill fortune to witness the saddest scenes I ever beheld. The report *[was]* followed by a rumbling, hissing sound. . . . Fragments of timber and metals flew in all directions. The fore part of the boat and cabin was completely carried away. . . . The guests of the hotel and the residents turned out in a body and rendered every possible assistance. Large numbers of boats were hurried to the scene, but they arrived too late to save the drowning. All was over with them in less than five minutes. How many were lost, it is impossible to know. The system of inspections everywhere is loose, careless and reckless, and officers who give an official safety certificate to use old shells of boilers, ought to lose their official heads, if not their necks.

The Texas bar, following the explosion, was used as an emergency hospital for the injured. Parts of the wrecked steamer were seen for many years on the bay shore when the tide was low.

Captain H. C. Baldwin of Mobile, the well-known steamboat captain on the Alabama and Tombigbee Rivers and Mobile Bay, acquired the property on

which the remains of the Point Clear Hotel stood. On the same site, and using parts of the same foundation, Captain Baldwin built the Grand Hotel at a cost of $75,000. The new hotel, completed in 1875, resembled the former except that it was longer. Like the first, it was a two-story building. It measured nearly three hundred feet in length and contained sixty suites of rooms. On both floors, front and rear, arched, columned galleries with overhanging roofs extended around the building. All sleeping rooms opened onto the galleries. Through the center of the rectangular building, both upstairs and downstairs, a large hall extended to connect the front gallery with the rear one.

A long pier was built for the convenience of the steamers that brought guests to the resort. On the pier there were rails on which a small flatcar, drawn by a horse, carried guests, baggage, and hotel supplies. Under the direction of Captain Baldwin, the Grand Hotel enjoyed a successful beginning. Following his death, in 1878, Burton Adams became the manager.

In 1882 Dr. William H. Anderson, professor of physiology in the Medical College of Alabama, then located in Mobile, edited a brochure entitled, *The City of Mobile and the Contiguous Country about the Gulf Coast as a Winter Resort for Health and Pleasure of Invalids and others from the North and Northwest,* in which he described the eastern shore of the bay as follows:

> On the eastern shore of Mobile Bay are several delightful watering-places, much frequented in summer, and serving also as winter residences for some of the inhabitants. The climate on this shore is delightful all the year round, and parties are now contemplating the building of a sanitarium for invalids in the winter as well as in the summer season. At Point Clear, a watering-place about twenty miles from the city of Mobile, there is a large and elegant hotel, filled in summer with visitors from Alabama, Mississippi and Louisiana. It is also open in winter to all who may desire to take advantage of the salt air from the Gulf. This watering-place is the finest, most healthy and most commodious in the South.
>
> The bathing-houses are within fifty yards of the hotel. In the rear and at the eastern end of the building may be found the magnolia, growing, in many instances, to an enormous size, and filling the surrounding air, in spring, with its agreeable perfume. Some orange groves, in full bearing, already exist, and others on a large scale are coming to maturity. The whole shore, for twenty miles, is studded with cottages and handsome residences, which are filled to their utmost capacity during four or five

> months of the year. The Gulf breeze on this side of the bay must be felt to be appreciated. The Atlantic coast has no wind that can be compared with it for health or for agreeability. Its temperature is the same whether it rises into a gale, or blows lightly enough only to ruffle the quiet waters of the bay. For this reason it is allowed to blow night and day through the cottages, where the doors and windows are left open continually to receive it.

A circular of the Mobile Board of Trade, dated June, 1882, declared, "The Point Clear Hotel will be kept open for the winter. Terms: $2.00 per day, $10.00 per week, $40.00 per month. Communication by steamer three (3) times a week. . . . Telegraph office in the hotel. . . . Good hunting and fishing all along the coast."

When the Vine and Olive Society, composed mostly of persons exiled from France upon the fall of Napoleon, failed to gain a foothold in Marengo County, many of its members drifted down to Mobile, and followed the fashion of seeking summer homes upon the hill (Spring Hill). The last to leave Marengo was Frederic P. Ravesies, president of the society, who "was the first to cultivate the azaleas on Spring Hill, which brought the 'hill' into notice because of these flowers."

In 1884, Ravesies wrote:

> After twenty-five years' absence I was trotted up the long north wharf in a horse car to Grand Hotel at Point Clear, and realized the gulf of changes since that time, the greatest of which, to me, was myself—from a youth then I stood there now an old man.
>
> The huge masses of white buildings, erected after the fire upon the same original plan and upon the same sandy spit, hung upon their foundations, roof over roof, turret over turret, pure, clear and light as banked clouds in a summer day's sky. The long, extending double-shedded passages and galleries in front towards the south, echoed and re-echoed the tread and voices of a goodly number of boarders. Pretty children, round limbed and strong, picturesquely attired, skipped and chattered around; courted in front of the same doors of the same rooms of the old building, or were alike unto them in construction. The halls, windows, and all the inanimate things, were the same apparently as twenty-five years ago . . . .
>
> The hotel is well kept, because that old-time and experienced gentleman, George B. Clitherall, is helmsman, and I don't care who disputes it, I shall

> always believe that only a gentleman can keep a hotel. The servants are attentive and have been taught by the present generation not to expect *douceurs*. Cooks and material are both good and clean, and of course well served and serving 'te duce, Major.' The beds, bathing and sleeping are 'chic', as the French say; but the music of champagne corks popping were heard no more at meals. No servant brings round the iced Chateau y'Quem, with the compliments of Col. Blank, of Mississippi Bottom! . . . The tall, broad-brimmed hat and swarthy face of the free-handed planter have vanished as a dream. They have gone never to come back again, and have been succeeded by another generation of different manners, ideas and appearances—a generation of people who toiled and drudged while the former amused themselves with horse races, cock fights and draw poker and war, and a generation who now amuse themselves with long bank accounts and so much per-cent per month. Who is the wiser? You pay your money, you have your choice.
>
> But in spite of all these changes of manners and people, Point Clear still remains the most attractive watering place of the South. The best people of the adjoining states flock there in summer to enjoy salt bathing right at their chamber door. The society, fishing, sailing and eating, are unexcelled by any other summer resort in the United States, and the place is perfectly free from malaria or epedemics.

In the publication, *Mobile, Ala., The Gulf Coast Winter Resort,* written by Erwin Craighead in 1889, the following passage appeared:

> The Eastern Shore, with Point Clear, Howard's Montrose, Battle's, and many other places along that shore, are delightful in summer and equally so in winter, although, as yet, Grand Hotel, at Point Clear, is the only place open for visitors during the winter season. The hotel there is excellent and delightfully situated. The winter rates are $35.00 to $40.00 per month. HOW DO YOU GET THERE? By the steamboat, which makes daily trips. Besides, excursions can be arranged to the Eastern Shore, to Blakely, and Spanish Fort, the scene of the late battle of the civil war, to Howard's beautiful spring, to Point Clear and to Fort Morgan, at the mouth of the bay where Farragut fought his great naval battle. The ladies often go also on the fishing excursions to the gulf, although, if apt to be sufferers from sea-sickness, they will do well to avoid anything like rough water.

In 1889 two Montgomery men, J. R. Dowdell and Charles Joseph, became managers of the Grand Hotel. The same year, because of the large patronage the hotel enjoyed and the requirement for a resident physician, the services of Dr. Samuel K. Reynolds, who for nearly thirty years had practiced his profession in Mobile, were obtained and Dr. Reynolds moved to nearby Battles.

On October 2, 1893, Mobile and the bay were swept by the severest storm recorded to that date. A southeast gale, rising at its height to seventy-two miles an hour, did severe property damage and wrecked many buildings and ships. Point Clear resort suffered the loss of the dining room building, which was adjacent to the hotel, and of the Texas bar. Both structures were leveled. Another dining room was soon built at right angles to the rear of the hotel.

In the spring of 1895, a "cruising party" was organized in Montgomery. Approximately twenty-five young couples made the trip down the Alabama River to Mobile Bay in the *Tinsie Moore* and enjoyed a brief visit at the Grand Hotel. They returned to Montgomery on the same river steamer.

A partnership, Styles and Brown, operated the hotel in 1898, remaining there until 1901 when Major James K. Glennon of Mobile purchased the hotel, the Gunnison House, and 250 acres of land in the Troost Survey, running eastward to Lily Lake. Clifton Clarke was Glennon's associate. At the time of the purchase, Point Clear was known as the "Queen of Southern Resorts." Frank A. Hervey and Sons managed the hotel during the 1903 season and Harry Wachenhusen was manager in 1904. Major Glennon then took over the management himself and operated the hotel for several years.

From 1890 to 1906, James A. Carney, now of Fairhope, was the owner of four steamboats which carried throngs of visitors from Mobile to the eastern shore. These were the *Heroine,* a former blockade runner which was built in 1863 on the River Clyde in Scotland; the *Jas. A. Carney,* named for his father; the *Caloosa,* which made trips from Mobile up Fish River; and the *Louis Dolive,* named for his grandfather and great-grandfather.

Other vessels used on the bay during the boat era included the ill-fated *Ocean Wave,* the *Old Apollo, Annie, Abita, Junior, Southern Star, Captain Miller, Josie, Daphne, Relief, Daisy, Silver Star, Crescent City, Fairhope, Fountain, Pleasure Bay* and *Bay Queen.*

The water at Point Clear has a blue-green appearance, and the gently sloping white sand beach was always considered beautiful. For nearly forty years, under the ownership of Major Glennon, Point Clear's Grand Hotel served as a favorite vacation place for Mobilians. It suffered its "ups and downs" under several managers, and even before the depression days of the 'thirties the hotel was rather rundown.

It was advertised as a place of "Every Creature Comfort," although comfort was usually obtained by the guests through their own efforts. Because of the lack of plumbing, it was necessary to send for water for the bowls and pitchers. Bathroom facilities were located at the end of each hall. Water for the shower baths often failed. Despite these inconveniences, the guests evidently enjoyed themselves, for the majority returned year after year. The bandstand in front of the hotel, where afternoon teas and band concerts were held, was the most popular place for the ladies and children. The bar usually attracted the men.

In 1939, Major Glennon sold the hotel and surrounding properties to the Waterman Steamship Company. The next year the dilapidated hotel building was demolished. On the exact site of the two former ones, the third Grand Hotel was constructed. Some of the old lumber was used in the new building, particularly heart pine flooring and framing. The modern air-conditioned hotel, which has approximately ninety rooms and is in operation the year round, is divided into three wings, with guest rooms and suites in the wings. The hotel spreads long and low, with giant picture windows and plate-glassed porches making the beautiful outdoors an intrinsic part of the interior scene.

The hotel maintains an eighteen-hole golf course, a yacht basin where guests may anchor their boats, a stable of horses for riding enthusiasts, a private beach, a fresh water swimming pool, a playground for children, and shopping facilities for the guests. A unique feature is the Directors' Room, where board meetings of corporations and organizations may be held in privacy and comfort.

In 1955, the Grand Hotel was acquired by the McLean Industries, Inc., the company which purchased the holdings of the Waterman Steamship Company. In the same year, Edward A. Roberts, the former chairman of the board of Waterman and now chairman of the board of the Southern Industries Corporation, negotiated for the purchase of the hotel.

On the hotel grounds, near a stately row of cedar trees which once lined the old walk to the wharf, the Mobile chapter of the United Daughters of the Confederacy has erected a handsome granite boulder bearing a bronze tablet as a reminder to future generations that wounded Confederate soldiers were cared for here.

For more than a hundred years the Grand Hotels at Point Clear have played "mine hosts" to guests. Each of these, in its days, has been the pride of the eastern shore, a pride in which all Alabamians have shared.

Green Bottom Inn HUNTSVILLE

Tourists coming south into Alabama on Highway 231 may pause three miles north of Huntsville to examine a reconstructed building on the campus of the Alabama Agricultural and Mechanical College at Normal. Materials for this reconstructed building came from a mass of stone ruins, once the Green Bottom Inn.

Green Bottom Inn, one of the first hostelries in Alabama, was built in 1815 by John Connelly, a lover of race horses. Stone blocks from nearby mountain-sides formed its three-foot walls, enclosing a space thirty-five by sixty feet. The floors were of wide pine clapboards, the doors of paneled oak, and the hand-made hinges of wrought iron. A knocker called for the host's attention, and thumb latches were used to open the door.

Entrance could be made from the approach to the inn by way of the front porch, on a level with the roadway, or from the kitchen door below, reached by means of a series of stone steps. No visitor could accuse the host of omitting a single feature that would have added to the enjoyment and comfort of his guests. Seven porches were to be found on the four sides of the building, several being at different levels. These have view to a roadway bounded, opposite the building, by a wooded rise that continues gently up for several hundred feet, before it begins as equally gradual a descent. On the other sides, the visitor looked out upon a green valley bordered in every direction by mountains.

The driveway into the grounds of the inn, leading off the turnpike, formed a horseshoe and extended to both sides of the building. In its circuit, it reached all adjoining buildings, including the stables and slave cottages.

Past these outer buildings, a small spring of almost icy cold water flowed from beneath a large rock jutting from the hillside. Benches around this spring afforded an excellent place to relax and spend leisure time. It was also an ideal spot for single couples to idle away the time.

While patrons sat beneath shade trees around this spring conversing, drinking mint juleps or smoking long cheroots of Tennessee tobacco, light wood smoke hung in filmy clouds around the bottom land just below, where a race track, with all accouterments, was located.

This ring of beaten sod, scene of more than one mad gallop of horse flesh, was the main attraction for General Andrew Jackson, who was a guest of "mine host," Mr. Connelly, on several occasions. Several times General Jackson brought along his prize steed and raced it to the envy of other sportsmen. It was his ambition to find some horse that could out-race that of the innkeeper, Gray Gander, the champion thoroughbred stallion of the South. Horsemen from New Orleans to Louisville had the same wish, but their wishes were never realized. This champion carried off many purses, the chief of which amounted to $20,000, a fabulous sum in those days.

General Jackson was in Huntsville on December 13, 1819, attending a meeting of the legislature. He was invited to the session and accorded the "privileges of the floor" as he sat "inside the bar" of the legislative hall. On this trip he brought along "some of his horses and roosters for a few days rest." He made his headquarters at the Green Bottom Inn.

President James Monroe's lone trip to the hostelry was made on June 1, 1819. To give Alabama more confidence in its political governmental life, the executive, accompanied by two cabinet officers, arrived in Huntsville, causing a flurry of excitement. He recognized the town with a visit because of its designation as the meeting place for the constitutional convention. He had given no notice of his intended trip and consequently had caught Huntsville unprepared. Huntsville chose the Green Bottom Inn as the place where President Monroe was to be entertained with an elaborate banquet. James K. Polk also visited the inn.

Inside the inn, below the main reception room, a fireplace sufficiently large to roast a whole oxen at one time sent up aromas that invited the traveler to stop and rest, enjoy a meal or spend the night. Around this huge fireplace many guests compared notes on the merits of the sleek and well-bred horses that had been raced at the Green Bottom Race Track, which was also operated by John Connelly.

In 1891 the Green Bottom Inn property became a part of the campus of the Huntsville State Colored Normal and Industrial School, and was called Normal. For many years the inn was used as the president's home.

On February 11, 1930, the Garden Club of Huntsville unveiled a historical marker on the front of the old inn as a memorial. The following year the inn burned, but the marker was saved from the fire.

Several years later the inn was reconstructed in the exact location. Much of the material of the old building was used in the walls. The building is now used as a snack shop for the college students. The historic marker has again been placed on an outer wall of the building.

148
Healing Springs

Washington County, the oldest county in the state, has considerable historic interest. Within its limits is located the town of St. Stephens, the seat of government for the Alabama Territory. It was in this county that Aaron Burr was arrested in 1807. "It is alike noted for the quiet tone of its people, its forests of timber, its health, and its Healing Springs," wrote B. F. Riley.

The Grand Gulf formation in Mississippi and Alabama is the source of numerous mineral springs, especially those charged with the salts of magnesium and with iron.

In the northwestern part of Washington County, near the inland margin of the formation, are the Healing Springs, on a branch of Santa Bogue Creek. The springs, seventeen in number, occur in the low grounds and marshy spots along the stream. The water is under a slight hydrostatic pressure which causes it to rise a few feet above the general level of the stream when confined by boxing or by pipes. Remarkably clear and pleasant to the taste, the water contains a small proportion of dissolved solids, but these are in combinations which probably give them their therapeutic value. The location of the springs, in the midst of a forest of yellow pine, was deemed a distinct advantage and was looked upon with favor by those in search of health.

Healing Springs as early as 1872 was known as a place where the water was very valuable in many diseases. The springs were owned and improved by William Wooten, who advertised Healing Springs as a "place for health and pleasure." He built a small hotel and several cottages for the entertainment of guests, with board at $10.00 a week. Visitors were permitted to pitch their tents. Beginning with the 1878 season, A. B. Jones took over the management of the resort and was proprietor until Will Moseley, who later became sheriff of Washington County, purchased the property from William Wooten in 1885.

The property changed hands again in 1886. H. J. Pettus of Nauvilla, Alabama, purchased 215 acres of land, including the spring property, for the purpose of settling there in an effort to regain his health. Having recovered so rapidly and satisfactorily, Mr. Pettus recognized the possibilities of restoring the resort. In 1900 he built a hotel, consisting of sixteen rooms, and later he built eleven cabins for the accommodation of families that visited there during the summer months.

Soon after Mr. Pettus re-established the resort, the Reverend John B. Hamberlin, pastor of the Palmetto Street Baptist Church of Mobile, visited Healing Springs to drink the healing water and to bathe his one eye, which was dangerously inflamed. His visit to the springs restored his health and improved his eyesight. While there, the Reverend Mr. Hamberlin envisioned the locality as an ideal place for a school. He resigned the Mobile pastorate and moved to the Healing Springs community, purchasing land and inducing the Antioch Baptist Association to undertake the establishment of "The Healing Springs Industrial Academy." The academy property was adjacent to the springs property and the school was built approximately one-third of a mile from the resort. The word "industrial" in its name indicated that the students were permitted to pay a part of their tuition by working on the farm or doing odd jobs.

After struggling along for many years, the academy was given to the Alabama Baptist State Convention and placed under its Mission Board to operate. Parents often sent their children to the school because of the nearby health-giving water and salubrious climate.

Because of financial conditions, the academy was closed in 1914. At the time of its closing, it was the only accredited high school in Washington County. Three years later the buildings burned. In the meanwhile, the Reverend Mr. Hamberlin had died and the property was deeded back to his widow.

The nearest railroad station to Healing Springs was Buckatunna, Mississippi, on the Mobile & Ohio Railroad. A hack from the springs met all trains during the summer seasons to carry the guests over the fourteen miles of rough road to the resort. For many years Mobile, Meridian, and Laurel, Mississippi, were the places from which the majority of the guests came. In 1908, the line of the Tombigbee Valley Railroad Company was extended northward to Silas, in Choctaw County. This line made a connection at Nannahubba with the Alabama, Tennessee & Northern Railroad, providing easy accessibility for Mobilians to Healing Springs. The Tombigbee Valley Railroad went through Millry, a town one mile east of Healing Springs.

The curative powers of Healing Springs water attracted more people who were ill than perhaps any other health spot in Alabama. The resort was selected by many who wished to regain their health in the atmosphere and influence of beautiful scenery and quietude. It did not have the reputation of a fashionable resort where society reigned, but one of simplicity where health reigned. The reputation of the water has been far reaching, with demijohns being shipped as far as California.

The Mound Spring water, known as the woman's friend, was particularly recommended for female diseases. In addition, it was considered unequaled as a cure of dyspepsia, indigestion, stomach troubles, eczema, old sores and all skin diseases.

The famous Creek Spring water contains properties which prove effective in the treatment of kidney, bladder, and all urinary ailments, and Bright's disease. The Iron Spring water is advertised as an almost instantaneous relief for chronic constipation, piles, chills, malarial fevers and as a blood builder.

In 1924 Dr. W. S. Knight purchased one hundred acres of land, including the springs, from Mr. Pettus. Dr. Knight added a second floor to the hotel building and converted the downstairs into a dining room. A swimming pool was built, the water supplied by the springs. The grounds were landscaped, and with the white sand and the long leaf pines, said to be at least three hundred years old, Healing Springs was made beautiful. For over thirty years the resort has been operated under close supervision of the Knight family. Since the death of Dr. Knight, Mrs. Knight continues with the management.

Mrs. Knight advertises, "Due to the wonderful climatic conditions, Healing Springs is a delightful all-year health resort. The waters from these springs undoubtedly possess more health-restoring properties than those of any other known springs of today. Water from these springs will be shipped to any address. In five gallon carboys, $2.00 for the carboy and $1.25 for the water. Carboys are returnable."

Today Healing Springs is reached by good roads. Hotel and cottage accommodations are available for guests. It is one of the few watering places in Alabama, now operating, which ships water on order. There are those who still carry their illnesses there to test the healing qualities of the mineral waters. The hundreds who have been cured of their ailments at Healing Springs during the last seventy-five years or more attest to the fact that the health-giving waters at this place have been correctly named.

152

Huntsville Hotel

One of Huntsville's proudest structures for many years, both before and after the War Between the States, was the Huntsville Hotel, located on the corner of Jefferson and Randolph streets, on the site now occupied by the Henderson National Bank.

On December 14, 1855, by the authority of the state legislature, S. W. Harris, Thomas S. McCalley, George W. Neal, John W. Scruggs, and Septimus D. Cabaniss were appointed commissioners to open books on subscription to the capital stock of the Huntsville Hotel Company, in the amount of $100,000, to be divided into shares of $50 each. It was not until 1858, however, that the hotel was built, under a contract with Matt W. Steele, with only $70,000 having been raised. The building was "bonded for the balance of the cost, in all about $150,000." The hotel was located on the site originally occupied by the historic old Bell Tavern, which burned.

At the time of construction, the Huntsville Hotel was owned by a corporation consisting of Governor Reuben Chapman, Joseph C. Bradley, W. T. Blount, Dr. Thomas Fearn, Chief Justice Robert C. Brickell, Mr. Scruggs, Mr. McCalley, Mr. Neil, Jemison Ward and M. W. Steele. The hotel, which had sixty rooms, was designed to attract an elite clientele. The first manager, one Mr. Lee, attempted to operate the hotel in a manner of luxury comparable to the design of the building. He lost $20,000 the first year.

During the War Between the States, Huntsville was captured by the federal forces on April 11, 1862, when General O. M. Mitchell raided north Alabama. The people of Huntsville suffered severe losses because of the vandalism and pillage by the federal raiders and deserters from the Confederate ranks. Following the withdrawal of the raiders, a federal army post was established at Huntsville. In 1862 Clement Comer Clay stated, "Huntsville is the center of disaffection." The federal troops remained in Huntsville until August 31, 1862. They returned again in July of 1863, and remained until the war ended.

During the federal occupation, an order was issued requiring the stockholders of the Huntsville Hotel to take an oath of allegiance to the United States, the penalty for non-compliance being confiscation of the hotel.

Among the many unfortunate things done by the Union troops in Huntsville was their treatment of former governors C. C. Clay and Reuben Chapman, the latter being the holder of a substantial block of stock in the Huntsville Hotel. These men were old and physically unable to take part in the war, but their sentiments were completely with the Confederacy. They were constantly brought in for questioning, and Governor Chapman's home was burned. He was finally forced to leave Huntsville for safety.

Following the war, Huntsville was overrun with scalawags, carpetbaggers and abolitionists. Often the streets of the city were crowded with drunken soldiers, known as Volunteers, who replaced the federal troops, lewd women, and uncontrolled Negroes. Because of the economic conditions, laborers could be hired only under the supervision of the Freedman's Bureau, with the wage scales being established and enforced by the bureau. Work was almost impossible to obtain. The situation was deplorable.

But in the midst of chaos, the social elite of Huntsville enjoyed the Grand Fancy Dress Ball at the Huntsville Hotel, presented by Professor G. F. McDonald's Dancing Academy on the evening of July 26, 1866. The ball, presented as a "close of the season affair," included a recital by Professor McDonald's pupils for the first part of the program. The recital especially featured Miss Minnie Frye. All present were invited to participate in the second part of the program, the order of dances being Quadrille, Redowa Waltz, Lancers, Schottische, Quadrille, Varsoviane, Quadrille, Polka Redowa, Lancers, Spanish Dance, Circle Reel and Home Sweet Home. This ball, the conclusion to Professor McDonald's third season in Huntsville, was also his final one. In the printed program for the occasion he expressed his appreciation for the many kindnesses which had been extended him, before bidding his patrons and pupils farewell. The pupils of the Dancing Academy were from the most prominent families in Huntsville.

In addition to its commercial value to the town, the Huntsville Hotel was constructed with the idea of attracting people from other towns, who feared the yellow fever epidemics. Huntsville, being located on the Memphis & Charleston Railroad, attracted large crowds from Memphis during the summer months. Dr. J. J. Dement, then health officer for Huntsville made the following report:

> Yellow fever, the great scourge of Southern cities, appeared in Huntsville in 1873, with one case from Memphis; Approximately thirty cases from Memphis, Brownsville, Grand Junction, Tuscumbia and Decatur were received as refugees in 1878, yet no case occurred among the Huntsville citizens; and again, 1879, a lady refugee from Memphis sickened and died at Huntsville Hotel, which was then crowded with boarders, and no other was affected by it. Refugees were treated from time to time, in the lowest of homes to the finest hotels in Huntsville. At no time was Huntsville under quarantine. The absence of yellow fever in Huntsville is attributed to the sanitary condition of the place.

After completing the summer season in 1880 at the Alabama White Sulphur Springs in DeKalb County, Major W. R. Davol moved to Huntsville and became proprietor of the Huntsville Hotel. He was formerly the popular manager of the Stanton House in Chattanooga. Major Davol, while in Huntsville, was elected vice president of the Hotelkeeper's Association, a national organization. He evidently was not too pleased with his lease on the Huntsville Hotel, for he advertised that his interest in the hotel was available on or before January 1, 1883.

The North Alabama Improvement Company was organized in Huntsville on January 17, 1886, to provide sites for homes and industry and to promote the area generally. The company started the construction of the Hotel Monte Sano as one of its first major building projects. On October 4, 1886, the company purchased the Huntsville Hotel from the Reuben Chapman estate, with the estate taking in return a mortgage as part of the consideration. Governor Chapman, prior to his death, had acquired the hotel "after varied vicissitudes of war, pestilence, famine and lawsuits." Later, the North Alabama Improvement Company defaulted on the mortgage, and Reuben Chapman, Jr., purchased the property for $25,000, reselling it to James F. O'Shaughnessy on January 3, 1887, for the same amount. Mr. O'Shaughnessy was aprincipal stockholder and director of the North Alabama Improvement Company; however, he purchased the hotel in his own name, and became the sole owner.

Upon the purchase of the Huntsville Hotel property, which included a vacant lot adjacent to the hotel, the new owner began the construction of an annex to the main building. The exterior walls of the annex were of brick, and they had the same appearance and were the same height as the walls of the main hotel. The only other building in the block was the Opera House, also owned by Mr. O'Shaughnessy. In 1888, the North Alabama Improvement Company issued the following statement: "It can now be justly claimed that Huntsville has a hotel the equal of any city in its elegance, appointments and cuisine, the superior to that of any city of 25,000 in the South." At that time the population of Huntsville was 8,000.

Including the annex, the Huntsville Hotel had 125 rooms. It was furnished from cellar to garret in "the most tasty and elegant style." An elevator was connected with the rotunda and with the ladies' entrance. Each room was lighted by gas and heated by steam. Steam radiators were also placed in the halls, thus making the halls in cold weather as warm and comfortable as the rooms. Each room had an electric bell which was connected with the hotel office.

The rotunda, stairways and dining room were finished with a wainscoting of oak paneling in dark finish. The frescoing was flat relief compo and Queen Anne style of decorative fresco art. The parlor was finished in white maple, with fresco of the French renaissance of the time of Louis XIV, and the furnishings were elegant. The reception room was finished in modern Moorish design of fresco work and furnished accordingly. The ladies' reading room was finished in Italian stucco compo and the furnishings were in keeping with the room's architecture. These rooms were all on the second floor and commanded a splendid view of the courthouse square and courtyard park, and from the dining room one of the "most inviting and picturesque views of mountain and vale seen in nature, was before the guest's eyes."

All bedrooms in the hotel were large outside rooms. Into each room came the clear sunlight. The building was constructed from plans and specifications by L. B. Wheeler, a celebrated Atlanta architect, who had earlier designed the Kimball House in that city. Mr. Wheeler designed the Huntsville Hotel bedrooms so they could be used as single rooms or in suites, especially adapted for families who should desire to spend the winters in Huntsville.

The North Alabama Improvement Company, in co-operation with the railroads which entered Huntsville, worked out an arrangement for the benefit of travelers spending winters in Florida, as well as southerners returning from the North in September and October, enabling them to stop in Huntsville to enjoy the mild climate. The hotel owners advertised:

> For many years it has been a serious question with visitors from the North to Florida where they could pleasantly and comfortably stay after it had become too cold at home, and yet it was too warm in Florida, making the change too abrupt and sudden; and the people from the extreme South, who spend their summers North, where they could go after it had become too cold to remain North, and yet was still unsafe to return to the extreme portion of the South before frost. A medium point was desired where travelers from both sections could spend the months of September, October and November as pleasantly as they had respectively the summer months. Fortunately for this class of tourists, Huntsville, Alabama, is a point that can now meet every demand.

In 1900, the Huntsville Hotel block, the Opera House, the Monte Sano Railway and Turnpike Drive with 1,800 acres of land in the suburbs of Huntsville was sold to a group of capitalists, who formed themselves into a company. W. S. Wells was president; T. W. Pratt, vice president; W. I. Wellman, secretary; and James A. Ward, treasurer, all of Pierre, South Dakota. The directors, besides the officers, included James F. O'Shaughnessy, P. C. Fisk, of Cedar Rapids, Iowa, and R. F. Pettigrew, of Sioux Falls, North Dakota.

In connection with the sale, the following statement was issued:

> Nothing could be more significant of a changing South than the sale of this block to a group of Yankees. The building had been owned by the late Reuben Chapman, sometime Congressman, sometime Governor of Alabama, emissary of the Confederacy to France, one of those who could not be an officeholder after the war. The hotel had housed many Confederates. Its parlors had echoed their wit, its mirrors had reflected the images of crinoline-skirted belles and their beaux, when it was the life to be gay. In the old Opera House at the next corner, the politics and drama of the old school had had their day. The old house must have been out of place with its new masters.

W. R. Steele & Company had charge of the management of the hotel in 1900. In connection with the hotel, the bar was considered "not only to be the handsomest one in Huntsville, but the neatest and best equipped to be found in this part of the State." W. E. Everett, the manager of the bar, was respected by friends and customers throughout the Huntsville area as a good business man. His stock of whiskey, brandies, wines, beers, and cigars was perhaps the most extensive and best selected in north Alabama. Mr. Everett boasted: "Employed assistants are selected with great care to the end that they shall be skillful in the concocting of the latest of mixed beverages, shall be steady, true, and always studiously polite."

The Huntsville Hotel was popular among the drummers. It was advertised: "The drummers—that shrewd element of the business society which always picks the winner—make it a point to rush their trips when they reach this territory with especial reference to being at home in one of these [Huntsville] fine hotels 'over Sunday.' The Hotel is conducted as much as ever possible in such case as a home to the numbers who sojourn the year round, of which there is a goodly number. Mrs. Steel, the very charming and gracious wife of the host, gives her personal attention to the comforts of their family of guests."

G. I. Finnell was proprietor of the Huntsville Hotel in 1905, and Burr Finnell was manager. About this time an advertisement appeared in *Illustrated City of Huntsville, Alabama, Resources and Progress,* which read:

> This Hotel, an old pioneer institution, has been constantly renovated and improved with each recurring decade, is today a model in its interior arrangements, equipments and fittings. The Hotel presents a very imposing appearance, is four stories in height, and is conducted according to the most advanced ideas of modern up-to-date hotel keeping. The Hotel rooms, all of which are fitted up in modern style, with the most comfortable beds, and it is a saying among traveling men that it is a positive pleasure to spend a night here, especially over Sunday, where there is ideal rest and plenty of good things to eat. The bill of fare contains all the delicacies and substantials of the season, prepared by a skilled chef, served by polite waiters, and taking all in all, there is positively nothing lacking to please. Mr. Finnell is a hotel man of vast experience, makes himself popular with the public, and does all he can for his guest's welfare.

On January 23, 1909, the hotel and the Opera House were sold to James E. Penney. Mr. Penney paid $100,000 for the hotel alone. Under the new ownership, the hotel was leased to H. B. May & Co.

The Huntsville Hotel is remembered not only as the smartest building in Huntsville, but also as the site of one of the most disastrous fires in the history of the city. Soon after midnight, on the morning of November 4, 1910, a fire was discovered in the kitchen, located to the rear of the building across a court and connected with the rest of the building by an "el." Fires in the two kitchen ranges were extinguished several hours before, and Manager May stated, "There is small probability that the blaze could have started from either of them." Bad electric wiring in the building was responsible for the fire, it was generally believed. The fire in the kitchen worked around the "el" into the main building.

Many of the guests took their time to dress while others rushed to the exits in night clothes, leaving their possessions. Only a few saved their personal effects. Two guests among the forty-five who were registered used the fire escape. There were seventeen permanent boarders in the hotel.

Another hotel may well have risen from the ashes of the main building had it not been for another fire, one year later. On November 12, 1911, the second fire swept the balance of the block on Jefferson Street, wiping out the hotel annex and the Opera House, buildings which had been undamaged in the earlier fire. Mr. Penney, who came to Huntsville from Birmingham the day after the fire, had announced plans to rebuild the old hotel on the original site, using the annex and the Opera House as collateral for a loan to pay the cost. The second fire changed his plans.

The New Huntsville Hotel, the vision of the North Alabama Improvement Company and James F. O'Shaughnessy, was a reality which assisted in the development of the town.

160

Hygeia Hotel CITRONELLE

As early as 1842, Mobile was a winter resort for consumptives from the northern states. People thought that the mild climate would check the disease, and, in time, restore the patient to health. At any rate, it was reasonable to suppose that the disease would be mitigated, since outdoor exercise, always so important, could be indulged in much oftener than in the North. As a consequence, many patients annually came to Mobile to pass the winter months.

Dr. William H. Anderson wrote in a Mobile Board of Trade publication in 1882:

> But at that time, the fatigue of traveling was so great that numbers who would have come had to seek resorts nearer to their homes. There were no retreats in the vicinity of Mobile where accommodations could be found, if the occasional fogs from the Gulf should for a day or so be disagreeable to

the patients. There were no railroads to transport the invalids to a location above the influence of the Gulf fogs. Nor was there any inhabited country to receive them, if they could have been moved off temporarily.

Rail service from Mobile to Citronelle was established in 1882. The Mobile and Ohio Railroad trains, in less than two hours, were able to take sick patients from Mobile to Citronelle, thirty-three miles away in the beautiful northern part of Mobile County, 352 feet above tidewater. Tubercular patients could remain in Mobile and enjoy the comforts, amusements and elegances of city life at least three weeks in every winter month. Should a short damp season come on, a sufferer could get away to the pine hills to avoid the oppressive weather.

Dr. Jacob G. Michael, a prominent Mobile physician, saw the need for a hotel to serve as a refuge up in the pine country. In 1882 Dr. Michael and his family moved to Citronelle. There he constructed the Hygeia Hotel, using virgin pine timbers throughout the building and finishing the interior walls with pine paneling. By the summer of 1882, the hotel was ready for guests.

Much to the surprise of Dr. Michael, guests who were not invalids filled the hotel. There were sixteen rooms, and these were occupied during the entire summer by Mobile families. A few of the guests remained through the winter season. Within a short time it was necessary for Dr. Michael to erect three two-bedroom cottages and a two-story eight-bedroom annex to accommodate the large number of guests. The winter patronage in the hotel consisted primarily of consumptive patients.

The Hygeia was a commodious and substantial hotel, which offered a good bill-of-fare. The hotel advertisement stated, "After spending a few days in this dry and healthy region, where the time may be occupied, if desired, in hunting and fishing, they can return to Mobile to meet again the sunshine and the numerous enjoyments of city life. Some consumptives prefer this region to the immediate coast, on account of the numerous turpentine distilleries scattered through it, the odor from which is considered wholesome in chronic lung diseases."

Water from Beaumont Springs was pumped to the hotel by a hydraulic ram. For entertainment, the guests could enjoy bowling, tennis, billiards, croquet, dancing, amateur theatricals, and a variety of parlor games. Religious services were held in the dining room each Sunday, and the singing of hymns was heard often. The Mobile and Ohio Railroad provided an attractive open pavilion near the hotel for the pleasure of the Hygeia patrons.

All passenger trains stopped at Citronelle on flag. Railroad fare from any direction to Citronelle, with the purchase of ten to fifty trip tickets, was two cents a mile.

Erwin Craighead, a prominent Mobile writer, wrote in 1889, "Dr. Michael has received hundreds of testimonials, praising the climate and health-giving atmosphere of Citronelle, and thanking him for the warm reception and courteous treatment extended to the visitors. The terms of the hotel are $2.00 per day, $10.00 per week, and $40.00 per month."

Though he was a very active and energetic man, Dr. Michael was not physically strong, having suffered for years from asthma. In 1890 he retired from the hotel business and the practice of medicine.

Miss Minnie J. Michael, daughter of Dr. Michael, tells of the largest social event ever staged at the hotel while her father and mother were managers. She relates, "Mr. E. D. Mann, of Town Topics fame [New York] took up residence in Citronelle and used the Hygeia one evening, enclosing the porches with canvas to make room for a large number. A special train from Mobile brought a crowd of the '400's' and all had a merry time. A luscious meal was served and champagne flowed like water. The Hygeia guests—some of them—were asked to participate. This is the most outstanding affair which I recall ever held at the Hygeia."

The hotel was taken over by Dr. Means Blewett, who acquired it from the Hygeia Hotel and Improvement Company. John Raff Michael, son of Dr. Michael, was secretary of the Hygeia company. Dr. Blewett did not continue the operation of the hotel, but leased the main building to a family as a home. He moved the cottages to a point facing the railroad and leased these to tenants. After a few years, Dr. Blewett sold the property to Roy Moyers, who occupied the main building as his home. In 1912, the old hotel building burned.

It may be said that no other town in the vicinity of Mobile was advertised more extensively than Citronelle. The Hygeia Hotel benefited from this advertising. Though the hotel operation was short-lived, Citronelle and its earliest hotel built a reputation as a health resort in the piney hill country which is still remembered.

In recent years, many have emigrated to Citronelle to "get well" from the benefits of the oil discoveries. The oil wells at Citronelle are Alabama's best producers.

Ingram Wells

Ingram Wells, located one-and-a-half miles south of Ohatchee in Calhoun County, was the site of a spectacular well which produced a lithia water from a depth of twenty-eight feet in Devonian black shale. No water in the state contained a larger number of minerals or was better known than the Ingram water, described as the "king of lithia waters."

In 1841, Richard A. Ingram moved from Georgia to Alabama and settled in Benton County, now Calhoun. In his early manhood, Mr. Ingram was engaged in farming, wagon manufacturing and merchandising. Later, he settled on a one thousand-acre plantation which he had purchased from the Indians.

In the early 1890's Flora Pippin, an overweight young girl who lived near the Ingram plantation, suddenly and unexplainably lost considerable weight and reached normalcy. A doctor, upon examination, found that the girl had been suffering from dropsy and had been cured by the water she had been drinking from the Ingram well. The Ingram family immediately had the water analyzed. It was found to contain minerals in such component parts as to make it very beneficial.

In 1897 the Ingram Lithia Water Company was formed by four of Richard Ingram's sons, John B., A. B., R. M., and S. A., all of Anniston, for the purpose of distributing the water commercially. The water was first sold in Anniston.

The Ingram sons built a rambling "L"-shaped hotel building near the well in 1909 to attract guests. The building measured one hundred fifty feet across the front, and a right-angle wing at one end was one hundred feet long. There were two floors, the first containing the office, sitting room and guest rooms, with the entire second floor containing guest rooms. In the living quarters of the hotel, a hall extended the length of each floor, with rooms on both sides. The building had running water and bath facilities. The interior walls of the hotel throughout were wood paneling, with natural finish, which presented a rustic appearance. The entire forty-room building was lighted by electricity, generated on the grounds. The dining room, which accommodated two hundred, was in a separate structure to the rear of the hotel and was connected to the main building by an enclosed corridor. John B. and A. B. Ingram were the operators of the hotel.

There were eight cottages on the grounds and these surrounded the hotel. Several, reserved for the members of the Ingram families, were painted in various shining colors. Two annex hotel buildings were later constructed, providing thirty-two additional rooms.

Entertainment available for the guests included facilities for bowling, tennis, horseback riding, dancing and hunting. A nearby lake provided swimming, boating and fishing. For many years James A. Van Hoose, a former mayor of Birmingham, visited the resort, and at his request a bugle was blown each morning at eleven o'clock to remind the guests that it was time for their morning swim. Another signal was given each night at eleven by the blinking of lights throughout the buildings and grounds, indicating that it was time to retire. This was not done, however, on nights when dancing was being enjoyed by the guests.

The popularity of the lithia water grew in such proportions that the Seaboard Air Line Railroad built a spur line from Ohatchee to Ingram Wells, principally for the water shipments. This spur line also served excursions which were run from Birmingham on weekends. Excursion rates from Birmingham were $1.73 for a round trip and $2.90 for a season ticket. Often, on the Fourth of July and Labor Day, there were two thousand or more people at the resort.

The management of Ingram Wells advertised: "Why not Summer Here? Ingram Lithia Water is unsurpassed as a remedy for Stomach, Kidney and Bladder Troubles. Enjoy the Shade of a 100-Acred Park. Dancing, Bowling, Pool, Tennis and other Amusements, Coosa River and several Creeks afford Excellent Fishing. Comfortable Rooms and Good Board $8.00 per week or $30.00 for a month. Buy tickets to Ohatchie on Seaboard Air Line R. R.. Hacks meet all trains. A delightful Sunday trip. Resort managed by Ingram Realty Company. Phone 1197 Main, 13th Floor Empire Bldg., Birmingham, Ala."

After first distributing the lithia water in Anniston, the bottling plant moved to Birmingham in 1898. The water was delivered in Birmingham in glass bottles

containing one, five or twelve gallons. The five-gallon bottles sold for $1.00. Patients who purchased the water for medicinal purposes usually bought it by the case; the case containing six half-gallon bottles. The company shipped water to New York, Washington, and to many points in Alabama. The Ingram Lithia Water Company in Birmingham was operated by John B., A. B., and R. M. Ingram. For several years J. A. Van Hoose was connected with the company and from 1904 to 1907 served as its president. Later, the owners manufactured a high-grade ginger ale, which was distributed throughout the state. After the death of John B. Ingram, in 1941, the business operated for a brief period and then it was closed.

Ingram Wells continued as a resort until 1922. By then, good roads and resorts elsewhere attracted the clientele, and this Calhoun resort suffered. A. B. Ingram continued to run the hotel on a limited scale, although his main interest was in farming, and he became well known as a gentleman-farmer.

The resort buildings gradually deteriorated until they became unusable, and the property was sold. Now in the middle of a corn patch, the place would hardly impress a visitor as the site of a once-popular summer resort.

Lakeview Hotel BIRMINGHAM

Situated in the center of the most fashionable suburb of Birmingham, Lakeview was the greatest and crowning development of the aristocracy of the Highlands. Lakeview Hotel, together with the magnificent park and grounds, was known far and wide for its hospitality. The entire development was the property of the Elyton Land Company.

In 1870, Josiah Morris, a Montgomery banker, purchased 4,150 acres of land around the intersection of the Alabama and Chattanooga Railroad (now Southern Railway System) and the South and North Alabama Railroad (now Louisville and Nashville Railroad) in Jefferson County.

On December 20, 1870, a group of corporators headed by Mr. Morris filed a declaration in the Probate Office of Jefferson County that an association had been formed to buy lands and sell lots near Elyton. They proposed to lay off and build a city, and applied for a charter to be incorporated as the Elyton Land Company.

LAKEVIEW HOTEL

On January 26, 1871, the corporators held a meeting at the office of Josiah Morris and Company in Montgomery and officially organized the Elyton Land Company, elected directors and officers, and formally acquired the acreage previously purchased by Mr. Morris. The board of directors adopted by-laws, among which was the following: "The city to be built by the Elyton Land Company, near Elyton, in the County of Jefferson, State of Alabama, shall be called Birmingham."

Among the improvements by the Elyton Land Company, after the city was established, were Highland Avenue and Lakeview Park. Lakeview was located on the east end of Highland Avenue and was reached by two dummy lines. As a part of the Lakeview Park development, the company built the Lakeview Hotel.

The hotel was opened to the public on July 12, 1887, under the management of Linscott and Davids. The building was an imposing frame structure measuring 60 by 250 feet. The site on which the hotel was located was elevated, overlooking the beautiful park and lake.

The hotel was a rendezvous, especially during the summer months, for the elite of the city and of all parts of the South. It was as cool in the summer as any place in the region. The two-story building at first contained seventy-two rooms. Sixty additional rooms were added in 1888, in order to accommodate the crowds. The rooms on the front, both upstairs and downstairs, faced a porch which extended the length of the hotel. Three hundred and twenty guests could be accommodated, 180 in the main building and 140 in the new wing.

The interior arrangements were splendid. The dining hall was capacious and the parlors were elaborate and beautiful. A large ballroom and billiard rooms were provided for the entertainment of the guests. The entire building was lighted by electric lights, and each room had running water and an electric bell. The building throughout was heated by steam.

The cuisine of the Lakeview Hotel was known for its excellence. French cooks were employed and all meats served were purchased in New York.

The park consisted of one hundred acres and had delightful conservatories. A casino with refreshment rooms, bowling alleys, a skating rink, and a huge swimming bath occupied a prominent place by the shore of the lake. The lake was well supplied with boats. The management of the hotel operated the amusement center.

Overlooking the lake on one of the surrounding heights were a number of ornate cottages, also owned by the Elyton Land Company and handled by the management of the hotel.

The pages of the hotel register indicate that guests were first received on July 12, 1887, with H. S. Dawson the first to register. Many names appear in the register, among which are Rufus N. Rhodes, founder and publisher of the Birmingham *News,* who lived nearby; Governor W. D. Jelks; Governor Thomas Seay; Judge J. M. Banks, one-time circuit judge and father of Dr. Frazer Banks, superintendent of Birmingham schools; John H. Bankhead; W. J. Banks, president of the First National Bank of Birmingham; H. R. Shorter, president of the Alabama Railroad Commission; H. D. Clayton, president of the University of Alabama, brigadier general in the War Between the States, and a former circuit judge in Barbour County; T. Tomlinson, owner of the land on which Tate Springs in Tennessee was built; Edward Sidel, architect of the Caldwell Hotel and the Morris Building, Birmingham, who appeared as a guest of Mr. Rhodes; James T. Woodward, president of the Hanover National Bank, New York City, which was interested in the Elyton Land Company; James Speyer, New York banker; Milton H. Smith, former president of the Louisville and Nashville Railroad; Thomas Seden, former president of the Sloss-Sheffield Steel & Iron Company; and Samuel Thomas of Pennsylvania, who operated the Sayreton Mines, and who built the furnace at East Thomas.

Among other Birmingham people who registered at the hotel were: Governor B. B. Comer, Mr. and Mrs. Basil Clark, Morgan Smith, Mrs. J. Rivers Carter, Judge Haughton, Colonel J. A. Montgomery and Robert Jemison.

The Highland Avenue and Belt dummy lines, owned by the land company, furnished transportation to Lakeview, the "Short Route" by lower Highland Avenue and the "Long Route" by Five Points and then on around Highland Avenue. On Sundays the dummy line transportation was overtaxed, for the crowds that frequented Lakeview were tremendous.

But week-end crowds were unable to support the operation of the hotel, and on August 21, 1891, the Lakeview Hotel officially closed its doors. It was unable to compete with other resort hotels in the state. There were no mineral waters to interest the sick. In fact, the Lakeview Hotel and park were intended to serve only as a pleasure resort during the summer months.

In 1891, Dr. H. M. Caldwell, president of the Elyton Land Company, invited

Hawthorne College of Florence, Alabama, to move to Birmingham and occupy the Lakeview Hotel building. The invitation was accepted and in the fall of the same year the college moved. When members of the faculty and many of the students arrived at the Union Station in Birmingham, it was said that no sight like it had ever been witnessed in Birmingham before, for ten thousand people met the train which "brought in the school." Dr. J. B. Hawthorne, noted Baptist minister who founded the college, did not follow it to Birmingham. Professor Henry G. Lamar was made president following Dr. Hawthorne's resignation.

The school became a ladies' seminary under the name of the Southern Female University, with Misses Eliza and Corinne Janes as principals. On December 6, 1893, the building burned. A tragedy occurred during the fire when a student returned to her room to get her watch. She lost her life. The following year the school opened in Anniston.

After the destruction of the Lakeview Hotel building, the casino near the lake was operated as a popular rendezvous and theater, where many fine stage productions of that era were presented at popular prices.

In 1903, Lakeview Park was leased to the Country Club of Birmingham and a clubhouse was constructed. The Country Club remained at this site for twenty-three years, increasing the size of the clubhouse from time to time. Later the property passed into the hands of the City of Birmingham, to be operated as a municipal golf course under the name of the Highland Park Club.

McLester Hotel TUSCALOOSA

Following the War Between the States, perhaps no town in Alabama suffered more or was slower in re-establishing itself than Tuscaloosa. In an agricultural area, the lack of farm labor and low prices of farm products resulted in slow recovery. It was six years before the University of Alabama opened again, and the terrible days of Reconstruction delayed for a long time any renewal of trade or industry.

McLESTER HOTEL

The Tuskaloosa Coal, Iron and Land Company was organized January 15, 1887, with the purpose of "developing 4,600 acres of land and to use every means at its command to build up a great manufacturing city at this point." The company was composed of approximately twenty-five Tuscaloosa citizens, all of whom were owners of lands lying in and around the city.

The stockholders elected the following directors: W. C. Jemison, George A. Searcy, Robert Jemison, J. W. Castleman, J. J. Harris, John R. Kennedy and H. H. Peck. The directors elected W. C. Jemison, President; B. Friedman, vice president; J. W. Castleman, secretary, and George A. Searcy, treasurer. The company announced that "engineers will be put to work at once surveying and mapping out the company's proposed extension to the City of Tuscaloosa, and the character of the officers for energy and business capacity is such as to guarantee an able and vigorous policy of general improvement."

A prospectus issued by the Tuskaloosa Coal, Iron and Land Company in 1887 listed among the successful industries in the city two cotton mills employing 420 "hands" and turning out cotton yarn, plaids, and "checks and stripes" in quantity; two brick yards; two foundry and machine companies; a suspender factory; a grist mill; a cottonseed oil company; and a wool carding plant. Under contract for construction were three railroads, Friedman Furnace, Merchants National Bank, electric light and ice company, the Allen & Jemison Hardware company, a lumber yard and planing mill, a building and loan association, a new four-story hotel which was nearing completion, and many residences.

Although the hotel was not sponsored by the land company, it was greatly encouraged by the organization. The hotel, to be known as the McLester, was an outgrowth of a plan entered into by three sisters, Mrs. E. N. C. Snow, Mrs. William Leland, and Mrs. John R. Kennedy, granddaughters of Richard C. McLester, to invest funds in a building company. The three, with the Old Merchants Bank as the fourth subscriber, formed the McLester Building Company, with each investing $15,000. The company was named for Mr. McLester, who died in 1881.

The company purchased the vacant northeast corner of Greensboro Avenue and Sixth Street, and on that site constructed the McLester Hotel. It was known as a "bowl and pitcher" hotel and each of its thirty-three rooms had a fireplace. Jones and Daniel, a partnership, were the first proprietors. L. G. Daniel served as manager. The partnership also operated a saloon in the corner store of the hotel building. Often, it has been said, the partners were more interested in the saloon than in the hotel.

On May 1, 1892, the Birmingham Cycle Club gave a gala "riding bee" and visited the McLester, a visit which left its mark. With the passage of the years, a few of the antiquarians of the Birmingham district are going around with bent backs as the result of this jaunt from Birmingham to Tuscaloosa and return. The club in Birmingham often sponsored "century rides," which indicated the distance traveled in one single day was one hundred miles or more. Naturally, the group had their picture taken in front of the hotel which, at the time, had a front shed over the sidewalk.

In 1897, the hotel was leased to Mr. and Mrs. H. S. Royal, who operated it without the saloon until 1907. By 1907, all of the stock in the McLester Building Company had been acquired by Mr. and Mrs. E. N. C. Snow.

In 1904, the hotel was enlarged by the addition of twenty-eight more rooms at the rear of the building. Within the next two years, bathrooms were installed in the nine larger rooms. In 1907, E. N. C. Snow, Henry A. Snow, and E. C. Snow formed a partnership and leased the hotel, with E. C. Snow serving as manager. Because of ill health, in 1909 he moved from Tuscaloosa. Henry A. Snow then sold his shoe business and took over the management of the hotel.

The Snow partnership between 1908 and 1913 was engaged in an enlargement and improvement program for the hotel. Forty-two additional rooms were added, twelve of which had private baths, an elevator was installed, telephones were placed in each room, steam heat was installed, and the lobby was doubled in size. As a part of the improvement program, the bays and balconies were removed from the upper floors on the front and the front shed removed from over the sidewalk. The old pot-bellied stove in the small lobby was a traditional part of the McLester Hotel, but it was pushed aside by the improvements.

Henry A. Snow died in 1915, and another brother, Lester Snow, took over the management of the hotel. At the outbreak of World War I, he went into Naval Aviation and did not return to Tuscaloosa.

After World War I, Alden H. Snow returned from France and, in 1919, entered the partnership with E. N. C. and E. C. Snow, and became the hotel manager. The following year, he added fourteen additional bathrooms in the hotel and redecorated the entire building. Year after year, improvements have been added to the one hundred-room building, including new wiring, automatic sprinkler system, an automatic elevator, modernized kitchen and new furniture in sixty of the rooms.

Through the years the McLester served as a gathering place for many organizations at the University of Alabama. Homecoming events centered around the McLester. The hotel has often advertised as follows: "Headquarters for University students and friends. Be sure to stop at the McLester when you come for Commencement."

The dining room has been a popular part of the McLester. The lobby displayed emblems of all the important civic clubs in Tuscaloosa, indicating that these clubs held their weekly meetings there. Organizations have found the facilities of the hotel conveniently arranged for meetings and conventions.

Upon a visit to the hotel, one is likely to meet Dr. George Lang, Presbyterian minister and retired faculty member of the University of Alabama. He registered at the hotel on October 6, 1933, and has been assigned to Room 323 ever since.

The McLester Hotel is a "family hotel," both as to ownership and patronage. One family has been interested, as an owner, since its erection. The friendly family atmosphere by which guests are made to feel at home has been the contributing factor towards its success. Alden H. Snow is still its genial manager.

Mentone

Lookout Mountain, a part of the Cumberland range, runs eighty-three miles north and south between Chattanooga and Gadsden. From the northern extremity at Point Lookout, where the summit is narrowest, the mountain gradually widens, reaching a maximum width of nine miles between Cloudland, Georgia, on the east and Mentone, Alabama, on the west, then narrows again to three miles at its southern terminus near Gadsden.

About halfway between Chattanooga and Gadsden, overlooking Valley Head, Mentone's cool atmosphere and flowing springs have been the source of pleasure to visitors since 1872. In that year one of the first persons was attracted to the area in hopes of regaining his good health. John Mason of Iowa took board and lodging with the Leavitt family on Lookout Mountain, to be near the healthful spring water, until his health improved, then returned to his home. When his condition worsened again he returned to the mountain, this time moving his entire family, and built a home near Valley Head. The family were so happy with their new home that Mr. Mason's son, Ed, was also attracted southward. Ed Mason bought a tract of land at Vernon's Gap and laid out a town which he advertised extensively, calling attention to the pure water and exquisite scenery. Soon homeseekers began to arrive.

In 1884 Dr. Frank Caldwell of Pennsylvania arrived at the top of the mountain with a faith in its future so strong that he built an inn. Dr. Caldwell was boarding with John Mason's family, and when the hotel was finished he was still puzzling over the selection of a suitable name. At the breakfast table one morning, he mentioned the problem to the Mason family and asked Alice, John Mason's daughter, to suggest a name. Miss Mason had recently read press reports of Queen Victoria's stopping at a place in France called Mentone, and the news item said that the meaning of the word was "a musical mountain spring." She declared that since the water from the spring on top of the mountain flowed with a ripple, she believed that Mentone would be a most fitting name. At that moment, Mentone came into existence on top of Lookout Mountain, and Dr. Caldwell's inn became the Mentone Springs Hotel. No mushroom growth can be attached to Mentone, but it became favorably known and people from all over the South visited there.

Among the people coming from abroad was Dr. John E. Purdon, who had served as a surgeon in the British army in India. Dr. Purdon conceived the idea of founding an English colony at Mentone, and advertised widely in English newspapers. He offered to teach farming to any person desiring to learn. Several young Englishmen responded, but after remaining awhile they drifted away.

The Mentone Springs Hotel was a two-story frame structure containing fifty-seven rooms, with hot and cold water in each. An extra wide porch on the first floor reached across the front and the two sides of the building. The dining room was located at one end and was connected with the reading room and lobby by a hall. Water for the hotel was supplied by deep wells.

In 1892 Dr. Caldwell sold the hotel and property to Charles Loring of New Orleans, who took over the operation in the name of the Loring Springs Hotel

Company. By 1898, an analysis of the spring water on the grounds was made and the report was submitted in the name of Loring Springs. The name of the hotel was not changed, but the resort was often advertised as Loring Springs. Under Mr. Loring's management, the hotel became very popular and offered competition to the Lookout Mountain hotels overlooking Chattanooga.

In 1914 the hotel and property changed hands again, with A. A. Chapman and Dr. J. N. Chaney, both of Rome, Georgia, the purchasers. The new owners, in an effort to attract additional patronage, remodeled the hotel and constructed an annex, a two-story building with twenty-four rooms, each with a private bath.

The Mentone Springs resort was widely known as one of the most healthful and attractive spots in the South, with the season extending from June 1 to October 1. It was advertised as "the most beautiful, most remarkable nature-endowed spot in the entire South. A strange 'Mountain Land of Rivers' more than 2,000 feet above the sea." A comparison of the average temperatures from 1910 to 1914 at Asheville, North Carolina, and Mentone indicated the latter place offered a very favorable climate, being from two to four degrees cooler on the average for each season. The management boasted, "A delightfully cool place—my blanket felt fine last night—this will be your expression after the first night at Mentone."

There were many places nearby to visit. Eagles' Nest is one of the highest points on Lookout Mountain. It is a short distance from the rear of the hotel. From Eagles' Nest there is an extensive view of beautiful Wills Valley. Sightseers and nature lovers have also found the famous DeSoto Falls, named after their discoverer, Hernando DeSoto, very interesting. The rock breastworks, the rock houses, and many other formations in DeSoto Park present rare natural treasures. May's Gulf in this park is a tremendous gorge which in places is five hundred feet deep, with a width varying from one hundred yards to a half-mile. The gorge is followed by Little River for a distance of fifteen miles.

Recreation offered at the Mentone Springs resort included swimming and fishing in the river about one mile from the hotel. Tennis, bowling, croquet, billiards, box golf, dancing, and a playground for children entertained the guests. Mineral Springs and Beauty Springs on the hotel grounds were never-failing in their strengthening and curative properties. Beauty Springs was reached by a shaded pathway along the mountain's brink for a distance of two hundred yards. Nearby Mineral Springs (sometimes called Loring Springs) was sheltered by a two-story pavilion which made a splendid observatory for Wills Valley, two thousand feet below.

In 1918 the hotel and property were sold to two brothers, John B. and Bert A. Ingram of Birmingham, who organized the Mentone Hotel and Realty Company. For two seasons this company operated the hotel, with Frank A. Robertson, a professional hotel operator, as manager. During the 1919 season Miss Jessica Ingram of Birmingham, sister of the owners, served as hostess.

In 1920 the Mentone Hotel and Realty Company, in co-operation with the Leeper Real Estate Company, proposed to sell the hotel, improvements, and two hundred acres of land to the Alabama Baptist State Convention for summer activities, at a price of $60,000. A corporation to purchase the property was planned, but upon investigating it was found the state convention could not participate in a corporation of this nature because of charter limitations. Ultimately a private corporation, the Mentone Springs Company, consisting of eight Baptist leaders, acquired the hotel and property and agreed with the convention to provide assembly privileges for a period of ten years. The Mentone Springs Company directors were W. R. Hilliard, A. D. Smith, James H. Chapman, William H. Smith, John B. Ingram, James E. Greene, and Frank A. Robertson, all of Birmingham, and Emmett Moore of Montgomery. The new company erected a dormitory with forty-four rooms, an auditorium with a seating capacity of six hundred, and six classrooms.

The first Baptist assembly to be held at Mentone was the Baptist Young Peoples' Union in August, 1921, with approximately one hundred attending. Beginning in 1922, the summer assemblies were held in June each year. The hotel facilities were then made available to the public for the remainder of the summer season. Assemblies at Mentone grew in such proportions that often there were over one thousand in attendance for the B.Y.P.U. week. Speakers from all over the South were invited there for assemblies. Mobile Baptists often chartered a special train to bring their members. Dr. L. O. Dawson, J. E. Lambdin, James H. Chapman, Henry C. Rogers, R. Elton Johnson, Emmett Moore and Davis Cooper, Jr., were the leaders from time to time who established Mentone as one of the outstanding inspirational summer assembly grounds in the South.

Because of economic conditions in the early 'thirties, the owners of the Mentone properties were unable to maintain the hotel in a satisfactory condition to accommodate the large crowds. The Baptist assembly in 1932 was the last one for Mentone. The Mentone Springs Company leased the facilities to several operators, but with limited success. For several seasons the hotel remained closed.

Ed H. Moore of Birmingham acquired the stock of the company and in 1950 sold the property, including the hotel, to the J. L. Todd Auction Company of Rome, Georgia. On July 4, 1950, an auction sale was held on the grounds and the buildings and many of the lots were sold to the highest bidders. Ben Hammond of Rome purchased the hotel and is presently using it as his summer home. The annex was bought by H. L. Murphy of Summerville, Georgia. It has been reconditioned and is being operated as the Sunset Hotel.

The modern DeSoto Hotel, owned and operated by Hal Howe, is located across the road from the Mentone Springs Hotel. The DeSoto is in operation the year round, and is especially renowned for fine meals.

Mentone continues to be a popular place for vacationers. There are several other hotels and guest houses in the locality to care for the crowds of visitors. The many attributes detected by the early settlers in selecting Lookout Mountain, in Alabama, as a healthful and recreational place are realized by those who have built their homes there. To view the valley below and Sand Mountain to the west from Sunset Rock is worth a visit there at any time of the year.

Mineral Springs is in the possession of Miles C. Allgood, formerly of Birmingham, who now makes his home at Mentone.

180

Monte Sano Hotel HUNTSVILLE

Three-and-a-half miles from Huntsville, on the southern terminus of the Cumberland range of mountains, is the site on which the Hotel Monte Sano was located. Over 1,700 feet above sea level, it offers a panorama of landscape, interspersed with hill and vale, of striking beauty. The mountain's name, Monte Sano, means "Mountain of Health."

When the Monte Sano Female Academy was established in 1830 by the Reverend James Rowe, a Methodist minister in the Tennessee Conference, the following description appeared in a communication: "For the information of our friends abroad, I would say, 'This location [Monte Sano] combines peculiar and numerous advantages.' It is highly elevated, perhaps 1,800 feet above the surrounding plain, and affords one of the most delightful prospects in the western country. The air is salubrious. There is a chalybeate spring within one mile of the institution, to which many resort in the summer season for the benefit of their health. The purest of fresh water is in abundance. Experience evinces that this situation is very healthy, indeed."

As early as 1878, newspapers in Huntsville advocated the development of Monte Sano Mountain, and especially the construction of a hotel. The Huntsville *Advocate* of August 14, 1878, tells that Monte Sano was becoming popular with the local citizens. "There are now located for the summer on the mountain the following gentlemen and their families: R. E. Coxe, C. H. Halsey, I. D. Sibley, Robert Herstein, S. Irwin, Judge William Richardson, James Weil, M. Sanford, and Mrs. Acklin and her family.

On September 12, 1883, the Huntsville *Democrat* added its boost to the prospect of a hotel, saying, "On Monday last, in order to protect a title to the Monte Sano turnpike, it was sold and purchased at $150 by the new company consisting of John L. Rison, W. H. Echols, J. R. Stevens, O. B. Patton and W. B. Newman." The company employed B. W. Blake to repair the pike for a first rate road. The *Democrat* urged construction of a hotel strongly, mentioning the healthy climate and the beautiful view, and commenting that it was an ideal place for a hotel.

In 1884, a promotion drive was launched in Huntsville to build a hotel on the mountain. However, little was done until an epidemic of yellow fever provided the impetus to put over the hotel plan.

On January 17, 1886, the North Alabama Improvement Company was organized to promote the sale of real estate and to induce business and industry of every description to locate in Huntsville. Michael J. O'Shaugnessy, formerly of New York City, was made president of the company. He came to Huntsville following the War Between the States and purchased the machine shops of the Memphis & Charleston Railroad (now the Southern Railway System), and converted them into a cotton-seed oil factory which he conducted with great success. Through his influence his brother, James F. O'Shaughnessy of New York, became interested in Alabama and began plans for the development of Huntsville on a large scale. James O'Shaughnessy established an elegant residence on Monte Sano Mountain for himself and the guests who came from all parts of the United States to visit him. It was through the efforts of the

O'Shaughnessy brothers that the North Alabama Improvement Company established the Hotel Monte Sano on the mountain. Construction work on the hotel was begun on February 23, 1886.

The hotel was a three-story wooden structure of Queen Anne architecture. On the ground floor, a continuous porch circled the building on all but a part of the back side. The 233 rooms were heated by steam and lighted by gas, and into each room entered the clear sunlight. There were no back or inside rooms. The rooms were furnished with all modern conveniences. Double-decked observation towers extended above the third story.

The manager of the hotel, S. E. Bates, arrived in Huntsville several weeks before the building was completed, just after closing the seasonal Continental Hotel in Pensacola, Florida, and the Hotel Monte Sano was formally opened to the public on June 1, 1887.

A grand ball was held on June 2 to celebrate the opening. On July 1, a concert was given and a few days later there was a second ball, at which four hundred guests appeared. The spacious ballroom could not hold all the dancers, and some couples were crowded onto the porches. The dancing floor was covered with canvas, laid over the carpeting underneath. By August 24, the hotel had already registered more than one thousand guests. At the time there were three hundred soldiers stationed on the mountain. They came from Fort Barancas in Florida because of a yellow fever epidemic, and they remained on the mountain until cold weather arrived.

From the first, Monte Sano was a place of style. Everything was handled on a grand scale from the minute a guest arrived at the Monte Sano railroad station, near Huntsville. A tallyho met the guests, with two men in colorful attire in the front seat to waft their whips over the horses, while a similarly dressed coachman sat in a seat in the upper rear of the carriage, his only duty being to bow to the ladies and to open the carriage doors for them. The tallyho would drive up to the *porte-cochere*, the great marquee jutting out from the rear entrance of the hotel, and there the carriage was soon surrounded by other regally bedecked persons who came to bow and get the baggage.

Amusements at the resort included riding horses, buggy and carriage trips, bowling, billiards, croquet, and lawn tennis. The grounds were beautiful with beds of natural flowers and shrubbery trees, and delightful boardwalks for promenading. Elegant drives were built around the mountain, about fourteen miles, to take full advantage of the scenery. Markers pointed out several natural features on the mountain, including Shelter Rock, Wildcat Glen, Brigand's Cavern, Vanishing Falls, Hell's Half Acre, Chalybeate Springs, Alum Spring, Magnesia Spring, Shelter Spring, Cold Spring, and Inspiration Point.

Tallyho service to the mountain soon proved too costly and generally unsatisfactory. Adequate transportation became a dire need when it was realized that the resort could not attract the crowds without it. The hotel closed its first season in October, declaring a profit and promising new features when it reopened. The weather prevented year-round operation.

Immediately following the first season, a handsome two-story cottage was erected on the edge of the bluff a short distance from the hotel. It was named Memphis Row in honor of the city from which more guests had come than any other during the first season. It was intended for use as a dance hall and pool room, but because of crowded conditions it was used to accommodate adult guests. Memphis Row contained thitry-six rooms, with furniture similar to that of the hotel rooms.

By February, 1888, plans were made for a railroad to the mountain. On May 14 a right-of-way was granted to the Huntsville Belt Line and Monte Sano Railroad, and on August 7, the line was completed and began operation.

Shortly after the completion of the railroad, the train had a wreck. Engineer Belue was idling the engine along on its return trip from the hotel. As he started down the steep grade on the far side of the mountain, he applied the brakes to check the natural speed of the train. They held, but the sand pipes were choked, and the wheels slid along the rails with almost as much speed as if they were revolving. The train and three coaches came down the mountain, with the whistle tied down to warn passengers of the danger. Near the point where the railroad crossed the highway, the wheels left the rail and the train stopped without damage or injury to the passengers.

The wreck proved costly, however. The following article by the railroad company appeared in the Huntsville *Mercury* after the hotel had been closed in September:

> The closing of Hotel Monte Sano is no reason why you should desert the mountain in such lovely weather. Our trains will run on schedule until Oct. 1st—longer if you wish. The railway has been built for you to go to the top of the mountain. It has been equipped with a train costing $15,000

> and not a citizen of the town has been asked to contribute a dollar to its cost. Some say the road is dangerous; we do not find a single passenger hurt, though a good deal has been said when an odd truck left the rails a time or two. There have been 'crowns' broken and fair ladies bruised on the pike through faulty harness, bad driving and balky horses, but nothing has been said about that.

Had it not been for patronage resulting from the fear of yellow fever epidemics, the hotel would have found operation difficult for the next few years, for the number of local people vacationing on the mountain dwindled to just a few.

The 1892 season was one of the best the hotel ever had. During August, and before it closed in October, the manager had to make additions to accommodate all the guests. On June 7, 1893, an announcement was made that the railway would not be operated that year because of the World's Fair in Chicago, which was expected to attract most of the pleasure seekers. In 1894, the hotel was opened early in June and attracted during August one of the largest crowds in its existence. Because of litigations among the stockholders, the resort was not opened in 1895, and as a result the railway was not operated.

Though already abandoned, in 1896 the railroad to the mountain was sold by the creditors under a court order, and during the following year the steel rails were scrapped. On June 16, 1897, when the hotel reopened, the crowds were larger than ever. Despite the absence of rail service, it proved to be the best season the hotel ever enjoyed.

Spanish-American War soldiers camped on the mountain in 1898, and were largely responsible for activities there that year. One military ball attracted 250 persons. In the same year, the hotel grounds were lighted by electricity for the first time. The hotel was opened for the last full season in 1900. Transportation and financial problems, along with the lack of patronage, resulted in its closing.

Many dignitaries and elegantly-dressed ladies from various parts of the nation came to Monte Sano during its few seasons of operation. Seldom was the hotel without guests from Tennessee, Kentucky, Missouri, Georgia, Ohio and New York. Names taken from the register of the hotel include William H. Vanderbilt, Newport, R. I.; Walter Damrosch, New York City; Jay Gould and wife, New York City; William Waldorf Astor, New York City; Newton Baker, later Secretary of War in the Wilson administration; and Helen Keller.

Horace E. Garth, a resident of Huntsville and formerly of New York, was an invalid who felt he needed a large place in which to obtain the best attention. In 1909 Miss Lena Garth purchased for her father the abandoned hotel, fully equipped, along with twenty-seven acres of land, for $20,000. The Garth family occupied the hotel as their private residence for several years.

For more than three decades, the old hotel remained alone to its memories under the watchful eye of the caretaker, fondly known as Uncle Dave. The story is told that Uncle Dave, as a railroad man in the 'nineties, stopped over at Huntsville once each week. Of course he never felt he could afford accommodations at the Hotel Monte Sano, but he visited there to watch the young aristocrats frolic. He recalled that, on one occasion, a group of gallants in the observation tower ordered their liquor in a bucket and drank out of dippers. He believed they slept in the town for the remainder of the night.

In the ghost building the barber's chair, which was plush and elegant, attracted much attention. In the kitchen there was a potato mashing machine which was so large that it had to be operated by a man in a standing position. Throughout the years, the furniture in the rooms remained intact, and its once-lush carpets remained on the floors. The principal attraction for curiosity seekers was the remains of the famous tallyho.

The hotel building, with its dust and cobwebs, was sold in 1944 by the executors of the Garth estate for salvage purposes at $9,000. Later the land was sold as a part of the Monte Sano Development Subdivision for building sites for modern homes. The site of the hotel remains vacant.

The hotel is but a memory. The North Alabama Improvement Company, while operating it, was determined "to keep the hotel up to a high standard." The policy was fulfilled as long as it remained open. For the elegance of the resort, however, the rates were too low to operate it profitably. Many reports were circulated that certain rooms were priced at $100 per week, when in reality the rates were as follows: "Parlor and first sleeping floor—one person in room, $21 per week; two in a room, $35 a week. Second sleeping floor—one person in room, $14 a week; two in room, $25 a week. Memphis Row, for adults only—one person in room, $16 a week; two in room, $28 per week. Children, under 10 years, and nurse in ordinary room, $7 a week."

186

Montezuma Hotel BESSEMER

The Bessemer Land and Improvement Company, with a capital stock of $2,500,000, founded Bessemer in 1886. A close companion to the founding company was the DeBardeleben Coal & Iron Company, with a capital stock of $4,000,000. Each of these companies was organized by H. F. DeBardeleben, and he served both companies as president. A. M. Adger, of Charleston, South Carolina, served the land company as secretary and William Berney was treasurer. It was Mr. DeBardeleben who, in tribute to Sir Henry Bessemer, inventor of the steel-making system that revolutionized the industry, gave the new town the name of Bessemer.

Following the surveying of streets and lots, the land company bought from the American Exposition in New Orleans the Mexican building which had been used during the exposition in 1885. The structure was dismantled and moved in freight cars to Bessemer, where it was rebuilt as the Montezuma Hotel. It had been known as the Montezuma Building at the exposition. The building, Queen Anne style characterized by modified classic ornament, was located in Bessemer between Carolina and Berkley avenues and between Twenty-second and Twenty-fourth streets, near the tracks of the Alabama Great Southern Railroad. The general idea of establishing a hotel in the early development of Bessemer was in keeping with the general practice of all land companies in Alabama, especially during the 'eighties.

The Montezuma Hotel, having fifty rooms, was completed at a cost of $35,000. Mr. and Mrs. Michael Clifford were its first operators. The hotel, though open to the general public, served especially a clientele that came to Bessemer to inquire of the town's prospects and to make investments. The hotel was furnished in keeping with the Queen Anne period. The spacious dining room was used for entertainments and parties as well as for dining purposes. The managers were experienced hotel operators who were able to create a home-like atmosphere for the guests.

Fifteen months from April 12, 1887, the day of the first sale of lots, Bessemer had grown into a city, with a regular municipal government and a population of three thousand. Over 250 houses and buildings had been constructed, and work was in progress on a complete system of water works. Industrially, Bessemer had become a boom town, with Bessemer No. 1 and No. 2 blast furnaces in operation, and a rolling mill and fire brick works under construction. The Berney Brothers Bank was in operation under the presidency of William Berney. In 1888 Mr. Berney became president of the Bessemer Land and Improvement Company, serving for two years.

Several other large buildings were constructed in Bessemer at the same time, among which were the Charleston Block, costing $125,000; the Nabers and Morrow three-story building; the Adler Block; the Jenkins Block; and the Berney Brothers National Bank building, all of brick, cutstone and terra cotta. The Bessemer dummy line connected Bessemer with Birmingham, a round trip costing forty cents. The construction, or the promise of construction, of seven major railroads made the prospects for transportation a highlight for the "Marvel City."

Among the pioneer settlers of Bessemer who lived at the Montezuma were H. F. DeBardeleben; David Roberts, the vice president and general manager of the DeBardeleben Coal & Iron Company; A. M. Adger; and the Michael Cliffords.

Perhaps the most enjoyed social occasion in the hotel was the party celebrating the first anniversary of the founding of Bessemer. The hotel was decorated and a fine dinner was served to a large number of enthusiastic Bessemer boosters. Ethel Clifford (now Mrs. Ted Joy of Birmingham), then a small child, and her friend, Grace Judson (now Mrs. Dan Davis of Bessemer), enjoyed themselves by dropping objects from the second floor through a ventilation grill in the ceiling of the dining room, annoying some of the guests below. Whether or not the children were scolded or punished is not told as part of the story.

When the Grand Hotel in downtown Bessemer was completed in 1888, with its accommodations for one hundred guests, the Montezuma attracted less attention and less patronage because of its distance from town. After operating the Montezuma for two years, Mr. Clifford gave up his lease and moved to Birmingham, where he took over the management of the Opera Hotel during 1889 and the Lakeview Hotel in 1890. Later he was connected with the Florence and Morris hotels in that city.

In 1896, the Montezuma University Medical College was incorporated to offer a three-year course in medical training. The college opened under the direction of Dr. J. A. B. Lovett, the president, with an enrollment of fifteen students. By the fall of 1897, the college had become a member of the Southern Association of Medical Colleges. The hotel building was converted into classrooms, laboratories, and rooms for boarding students. Five students, all of whom had studied previously in other schools, were graduated in the class of 1898. The college remained in operation until the building was destroyed by fire in 1900.

Morris Hotel BIRMINGHAM

In addition to the large financial interest Josiah Morris of Montgomery had in the Elyton Land Company in Birmingham, he also acquired and invested in extensive property in his own name. In 1886 Mr. Morris purchased the southeast corner of First Avenue and Nineteenth Street, North, a lot 105 by 185 feet, as the site for an office building to be called the Morris Block.

190 MORRIS HOTEL

The five-story building was designed by a French architect, Edward Sidell, after the Renaissance style. Construction was begun in 1888, but was delayed because of the marshy land and the lack of cement for a firm foundation. The foundation was excavated to a depth of fifteen feet and footings were poured with cement made of lime and sand, but the cement failed to harden. A second pouring of this material brought the same results. Mr. Morris then sent to Vermont for granite. Blocks of this material, three feet square, were used as footings on bed rock. It is said this foundation would support the Empire State Building.

Based on the granite blocks were brick pilasters, four feet wide with twelve-inch projections, reaching to the top of the first floor where the cornice extended over them. On the Nineteenth Street side there were seven bays up to the second floor, with double wood doors glazed with sidelights and transoms over each, and over each recessed opening there was a heavy metal beam. From the first to the fourth floor there were brick pilasters with beautifully ornamental capitals of classic design with the head of a woman in the center of each, all of plastic material. At each end of the building—First Avenue and Morris Avenue—there were circular balconies which took in practically the entire width of the bays and extended out over the sidewalk area.

The fifth floor, setting back in effect over the heavy cornice, acted as a parapet. There were towers at both ends of the building, each with six windows. The towers had circular heads and above them was rich and decorative terra cotta ornamental plastic work extending up into the large overhanging cornice. In the center of each tower was a flagpole and around the edges were four large ornamental terra cotta urns with handles.

The building was constructed of smooth, hard red brick with joints cemented with mortar one-eighth of an inch thick. The front of the building on First Avenue was divided by a wide court providing an open vestibule entrance, with two bays toward Nineteenth Street and one bay on the east side. The main entrance doors were twenty feet back from the sidewalk and opened into a beautiful arcade. The arched skylight over the arcade contained over two thousand panes of Belgian glass, each twelve inches square, which diffused the light.

The floor of the arcade was of Belgian tile, splendid in design and color. The color was baked into the tile and though the color was as thin as tissue paper, it never showed signs of wear or fading.

In 1889 Mr. Morris was stricken by paralysis, and the almost completed building was acquired by F. M. Billing, the half-brother of Mrs. Josiah Morris, and H. M. Baldwin. Mr. Morris died two years later.

Soon after the completion of the building in 1890, the Birmingham Trust & Savings Company (now Birmingham Trust National Bank) moved from its original quarters in the Elyton Land Company's building to the Morris Building. The bank remained in this location until 1901, when it moved to its present site on Twentieth Street.

When the Caldwell Hotel, then located on First Avenue and Twenty-second Street, North, was destroyed by fire in the summer of 1894, Birmingham suffered the loss of its finest hotel. By September 30, 1894, the upper floors of the Morris Building had been converted into hotel rooms, the choicest in the city. Prior to this time only part of the upper floors had been used for rooming purposes. C. H. Nabb, former manager of the dining room in the Union Depot (now L & N station) and later manager of the dining room in the Morris Building, leased the building and converted it wholly into a hotel.

Under Mr. Nabb's management, the Morris dining room was described as "A Scene from Fairyland; a vision of loveliness, a palace of enchantment; superlatives barely describing the new Eldorado, the Morris dining room, busy Birmingham's bright and beautiful buffet. The Eldorado is the finest arranged and equipped dining room in the South, unless one excepts the Plant and Rockefeller hotels in Florida."

The dining room is remembered for:

> Its beautiful lighting through the use of one hundred forty electric lights symetrically distributed. Chandeliers, arranged for lighting by gas or electricity, hung in profusion from the ceiling where the brass finished and highly polished fans made summer life worth the living while the woodwork, finished in mahogany and oak, added rest to the eye. Forty tables were arranged about the floor, each covered with the whitest of white linen, every piece being woven expressly for the house, each piece—having woven in the center a beautiful scroll bearing the words 'The Morris' in large Gothic letters and under the scroll the initials 'C. H. N.' Every dish served at the Morris is a gem, being the finest china, lightly flowered in pink and bearing the imprint 'The Morris.' The glassware is of cut crystal and hand-engraved, each piece having the Morris imprint. One of the

objects contemplated by Mr. Nabb—is the careful and especial attention which will be paid to meals a-la-carte for ladies who are out shopping and ladies without escort, will receive the best attention.

The Morris Hotel under the management of Mr. Nabb was Birmingham's leading hotel until the Hillman Hotel was opened in 1901. Mr. Nabb became the proprietor of the Hillman Hotel.

In the earlier days of Birmingham, the gay bachelors attended social events at the Morris. Among these were Erskine Ramsay, Culpepper Exum, R. A. Brown, Archie Carpenter, Chase Perkins, Ed Warren, and Paschal and Warner Shook. Social events at the Morris were "gay, glamorous and luxurious."

In 1890, Governor Thomas Seay was a guest at the Morris. John R. T. Rives, now editor emeritus of *The Railway Conductor,* was then the operator of the elevator at the Morris and had the honor of escorting Governor Seay to the roof of the hotel to view the city. It was at the Morris that Admiral Schley, who was in direct command of the American fleet that destroyed the Spanish ships at Santiago, had rooms for several days while a guest of the Alabama State Fair Association in 1899. In the early part of 1901, the present Southern Association of Baseball Clubs was organized at the hotel. It was here that campaigns for re-election of Senator John T. Morgan were directed. Oscar W. Underwood, in his early campaigns, had headquarters here. Joseph Jefferson, Robert Downing, Louis James, Maude Adams, Robert Edeson and scores of other stars of the stage stopped here while in Birmingham. Richard Pearson Hobson and William Jennings Bryan were also guests at the Morris.

Subsequent owners of the Morris Hotel have been F. M. Billing (1893), Birmingham Real Estate Association (1897), B. J. Baldwin (1906), M. L. Griel (1907), and J. E. Penny (1920). The property still remains in the Penny family. Prominent managers of the hotel were Michael Clifford, who succeeded Mr. Nabb, Levi Scoville, and George Scoville. Later the hotel was operated by the Howard Dayton Hotels Company. Before the hotel was closed it was being operated by the Milner Hotel Management Company as the Earle Hotel.

Though the Morris Building stood the years well, it became obsolete and was removed in 1958 to make way for a parking lot. The razing took from the city one of the remaining monuments to the memory of Josiah Morris, whose faith helped to establish Birmingham.

Nottingham Hotel

Nottingham, named for the English town, was a fanciful land development dream of the Nottingham Iron and Land Company. It was located in Talladega County, one mile northeast of Alpine and approximately five miles southwest of Talladega.

Perhaps no town in Alabama became a ghost town so quickly. It was a quick "boom and bust," although it was described as one of the most picturesque and beautifully located towns in Alabama, eight hundred feet above tidewater and entirely free from malaria and mosquitoes.

The Nottingham Iron and Land Company was organized in 1886 to promote the sale of lots. The first step in this promotional venture was the construction of the Nottingham Hotel in the spring of 1887, at a cost of about $15,000.

The hotel, consisting of sixty rooms, was of frame construction. It was a two-story building with a wide porch extending the length of the structure on the first floor. A conspicuous part of the building was the observation tower at one end, towering to fourth-floor level. This was intended for the prospective purchasers to view the lots and make selections. Living accommodations for the hotel employees were provided in attic rooms.

The hotel was situated one hundred feet from the newly constructed Nottingham station on the Selma, Rome & Dalton Railroad (now part of the Southern Railway System). The site of the hotel was five hundred feet from Talladega Creek; however, the land developers called the creek Nottingham River. It was advertised as a stream measuring about 150 to 200 feet wide when in reality the creek was only about fifteen feet wide. A large spring nearby supplied the hotel with pure water. Electric lights were advertised, but these were never realized. Each room was completely furnished, including a bowl and pitcher. The rooms were heated by fireplaces.

Extensive advertising by the Nottingham Iron and Land Company through its New York office at 47 Broadway told stories of the Pitman, Nix & Company Brick Works, forty thousand bricks per day capacity and to be increased to eighty thousand per day; Robinson Planing Mills Company, capacity of twenty thousand feet of planed boards per day; Blackman & Peacock Planing Mill, capacity of ten thousand feet per day; five saw mills; charcoal ovens; and a cotton gin.

It was further advertised that within sixty days after the completion of the hotel several new industries agreed to locate at Nottingham, including a one hundred-ton pig iron furnace, iron ore washing machinery, electric light and water company, machine shop and foundry, and nail and tack works.

According to announcements, several other enterprises contemplated locating at Nottingham, such as a dry goods store, grocery stores, boot and shoe shop, real estate exchange and a bank. The Lewis Block was advertised for the accommodation of stores, but the Lewis Block was never constructed.

On the day of the opening "big sale," in the spring of 1887, R. M. McClatchie, the railroad agent and Justice of the Peace, was employed by the land company to supervise the digging of a large hole in the ground near the railroad station, supposedly the foundation for the pig iron furnace. This made a good story for the prospects, and assisted in arousing interest in the lots. The hole remained there for several years as a reminder of the furnace, but no furnace was ever constructed.

The farmers in the vicinity furnished the hotel with fresh vegetables and supplies. Reports indicate that the hotel served delightful meals at a modest cost. The dining room accommodated at least one hundred guests for dinner and late evening dancing. A string band composed of Negro musicians was on hand during the day to entertain the guests and at night for the dancing.

The hotel was operated in grand style for perhaps six months after its opening. Many of the guests were purchasers of lots. Practically all who visited Nottingham were disappointed with the development. The comfortable rooms and good meals in the hotel, at a reasonable tariff, counteracted in some small measure the disappointment suffered by those who had purchased lots, as well as those who came to appraise the town of Nottingham. Nothing else was there except the hotel.

Many people came to see. The majority of would-be buyers of building sites were from New York. Groups also came from Chattanooga, where the company maintained offices. The main office was established at Nottingham, in a frame building located at Pennsylvania Avenue and Broadway. Though streets and avenues were never developed, the plan of the town called for streets with important names. The survey of Nottingham included approximately 540 acres divided into 1,830 lots.

After the first year the hotel depended upon patronage from nearby communities. This patronage was insufficient to support a hotel, and within a few years, because of the lack of repairs, the hotel was closed. In 1895 the sound timbers were removed to Talladega and used in the construction of the Talladega Chateau. Later the Chateau was torn down and the material used for a livery stable.

Older residents in the area have recollections of the cream colored hotel at Nottingham with its stained window glass, the fine meals, enjoyable dances, and especially the unhappy people who "bought and then came to see." The story is told that in some instances the people looked out the train window and then stayed on board after glancing at the "town."

Nottingham is probably the only town in Alabama that had a hotel as its only permanent building.

196

The Palings FORT DALE

It is quite evident that the Creek Indian Treaty stipulation that "stopping places for travelers through the Nation be provided" was generally carried out. The Federal Road, entering at Fort Mitchell and proceeding to St. Stephens, had many stopping places at an average of about fourteen miles apart.

The government regulated the charges for lodging and meals. Breakfast was fifty cents, dinner and supper seventy-five cents each. Stage horses were changed at each stopping place. The driver of the stage who drove for one relay would remain at the tavern until the arrival of the stage going in the opposite direction. This made one driver responsible for the travel in both directions over his regular route. A stage driver enjoyed an annual contract for his services at $400 and board.

The coaches were operated by corporations and individuals who obtained much of their income from the carrying of the mail. One traveler made this statement: "The drivers placed the mails in the stage, so as to very much annoy the passengers and give themselves no trouble about their baggage which must be constantly looked after from the interior of the stage. It would be far better for the passenger to give a regulated trifling fee, than to be subjected to this never failing sort of annoyance." Perhaps the traveler had in mind a "tip."

Fort Dale was erected in the spring of 1818 by order of Colonel Samuel Dale, who had charge of a garrison of soldiers at Fort Claiborne. The fort was named for this soldier who was instrumental in its erection for the protection of the whites against attacks by the Indians, who reluctantly saw their favorite hunting grounds turned into corn fields. All the people in this part of the county, now known as Butler County, sought refuge in this fort and remained there during most of 1818, although a red man was not to be seen.

After the excitement of 1818 was over, the settlers returned to their homes and resumed work. Colonel A. T. Perry entered the land on which the fort was built and lived there for several years, until he sold the property to Joseph Hartley of Putnam County, Georgia, in 1825. Mr. Hartley built "a good house of logs, which were sawed with a whipsaw, and cleared a large field around the fort." The house soon after became a stagecoach stop. It was quite adaptable as a tavern, since it was a two-story structure with the stairway on the front porch. The rooms were heated by fireplaces. The tavern was operated by "an intelligent man and in the tavern was a considerable library for that time. Travelers were accommodated tolerably."

Palings were at one time used to enclose the tavern yard, giving the appearance and service of a fence. Though the palings rotted away, the tavern became known as The Palings. It carried that name until it burned on Saturday morning, July 11, 1953.

The Palings, being the oldest building in Butler County, long reminded the people of the county of the Indian days when many of their ancestors were killed or frightened almost to death. Only two brick chimneys remain there now to tell the story of this "stopping place."

198

Phoenix Hotel CARROLLTON

Flourishing ante-bellum life is evident in the extent and beauty of the Phoenix Hotel in Carrollton, in historic Pickens County. The hotel was erected in 1841 by Benjamin F. Roper, sheriff of Pickens County, just seven years after Pickensville lost the county seat to Carrollton. The hotel was so named by Mr. Roper because it arose from the ashes of the Roper House, which had burned. Early financing of the Phoenix was done through "due bills" given by various planters who wished to "board out."

The two-story hotel, with twenty-seven rooms, is unchanged from the original except for the addition of a wing. It has always been immaculate in its coat of white paint. Also, like the Roper House, it has wide planking for flooring. Verandas skirt both floors, lending shade and shelter. Rows of comfortable rockers have been characteristic of the hotel throughout the years. The hotel has served as a companion to the courthouse, which is located across the street in the town square.

The Phoenix Hotel in its earliest years was not only popular among courthouse attendants; it was also well-located to serve the relay station for stagecoaches which took this route from Columbus, Mississippi, to points in central and southern Alabama. Its predecessor, the Roper House, served the post road, established in 1836, from Livingston, in Sumter County, via Horner's old store at Mount Sterling, McCarty's, and Carrollton, to Washington courthouse in Washington County. These points on the route had established post offices, with the mail carried principally by riders on horseback.

Mr. Roper operated the Phoenix Hotel and livery stable for twelve years and then conveyed his holdings to Mrs. F. W. Bostick, a widow, of Carrollton, who kept it for a few years. B. F. Wilson, a subsequent owner for a short time, deeded the property to W. G. Mustin in 1858.

During the War Between the States, the federals burned the courthouse at Carrollton, but the troops enjoyed lodging at the Phoenix.

The courthouse records today show the conveyance of the Phoenix Hotel and livery stable on October 22, 1866, from W. G. Mustin to his wife. The deed states that it was in settlement of dowry claims and interest through a court procedure. Mr. Mustin had entered into an agreement with his wife to repay her for money and slaves he used from the partial and final settlements from her mother's estate in the years 1856, 1857 and 1859. He had failed to comply with the terms of his agreement and when his wife threatened to enter suit, she was deeded the hotel and livery stable. As stated in the deed, the hotel had been her residence since 1858.

Following the war, with the carpetbag rule reaching unbearable heights, W. L. Duncan, Pleas Horton and Sam Nabers rode to Tennessee to familiarize themselves with the Ku Klux Klan. They returned with the information and established the charter of the first Klan in Alabama. The three men who made the trip to Tennessee, along with two additional members, T. J. Duncan and C. M. Lyles, whose sons were later connected with the Phoenix Hotel as proprietors, were the charter members.

Upon a visit to the hotel, one is apt to park his car beneath an ancient oak in front of the hotel building, a tree connected in legend with General Nathan

Bedford Forrest. In the early 'seventies, General Forrest visited Carrollton on his quest for votes for bonds to help finance his railroad from Selma to Columbus, Mississippi. Each county in Alabama and Mississippi through which the railroad was to extend was required to vote on the bond issue necessary to finance the project. Matt Thaxton of Carrollton had previously been engaged to plant young water oaks in the town. Arriving in Carrollton, General Forrest tied his horse to one of the young trees in front of the Phoenix Hotel. The horse gnawed the tree and almost ruined it, but the manager of the hotel would not have the tree replaced. The tree stands today and is luxuriant and beautiful.

Throughout the years the Phoenix Hotel has been admired for its fine features. The second floor stair newels are hand carved and well preserved. The rooms are large, well ventilated, and at one time were heated by big fireplaces. Tons of brick must have been used in the construction of the fireplaces, for each had a double chimney. All mantels and doors in the building are typical hand-carved colonial. Wide ceiling boards were used to finish the walls in many of the rooms.

On October 27, 1883, Mrs. Mary E. Mustin sold the hotel to Mrs. Henrietta R. Owings. During the time Mrs. Owings ran the hotel and the livery stable, she had a local carpenter build what was then called a "dumb waiter table" for the dining room, so called because the center section of the table is elevated approximately one foot above the outer section and revolves. Food is placed on the elevated section and is made available with a turn. Gardner Owings, a son of Mrs. Henrietta Owings, who helped with the livery stable operations when he was a small boy and who still lives in Carrollton, dates the construction of the table in 1895. This table is still in use at the hotel.

W. Pat Owings, the husband of the proprietor, was a most successful vegetable gardener. The hotel served vegetables from his garden when all other gardens for miles around were dead.

Other conveyances relate that on January 22, 1902, Mrs. Owings and her husband deeded the hotel to T. J. Duncan. During his ownership, Isaac Moss, a Negro, came to work for the hotel and remained through the years as a waiter and porter, highly regarded by the guests. On August 7, 1933, Mrs. Ann Eliza Duncan and Miss Ola Duncan, widow and daughter of T. J. Duncan, conveyed the hotel to another daughter, Mrs. Corrie Duncan Lyles. Mrs. Lyles and her husband, George Lyles, sold the hotel to Mrs. Olivia B. Sullivan on July 9, 1945.

Mrs. Sullivan is presently operating the hotel. Hunting horns bearing the Duncan family history for many years adorn the walls of the dining room.

The building which was used as the livery stable was torn down in 1953. The lumber of this building was found to be well preserved and was used by one of the workmen who assisted in the demolition work in the construction of a barn for himself.

The Phoenix Hotel for over one hundred years has been famous for its fine lodging and fine meals. It served the stagecoach days, the horse and buggy period, and now serves the automobile age. It is as beautiful now as it was when it was constructed in 1841. Each of the owners has taken personal pride in keeping the building modern. No hotel in Alabama has enjoyed a longer period of uninterrupted operation than the Phoenix in Carrollton.

202

Piedmont Springs

Ninety miles from Birmingham and an equal distance from Atlanta, on the Seaboard Air Line Railroad and the old Selma, Rome and Dalton Railroad (now part of the Southern Railway System) between Rome, Georgia, and Selma, was the Piedmont Springs resort in Calhoun County. Piedmont Springs is five miles west of Piedmont, 1,200 feet above sea level and halfway to the crest of Blue Ridge Mountain. The hotel building, which is still standing, is located there on an eighty-acre tract of land. The hotel was constructed in 1890 by the Piedmont Land and Improvement Company. This company made Piedmont a boom town in 1889 and 1890. In 1900 the company sold the property, including the hotel and a five-room cottage, to George D. Harris, who had served as president of the land company. Mr. Harris took over the management of the hotel.

The hotel building, with thirty-six bedrooms, is a three-story frame structure. The office, living room, linen room, laundry, kitchen and dining room which accommodated sixty persons were on the first floor. The entire lower floor, except for the kitchen and the laundry, is surrounded by a covered porch.

The guests were driven from the railroad station two miles up the mountain over a gravel road in a hack which met all trains.

There are three springs on the property, one producing freestone, one chalybeate, and the other a combination of sulphur, iron and magnesia water. The story is told that during the time this section was inhabited by Indians, they brought their sick to these springs to cure their maladies.

Recreational facilities at Piedmont Springs were meager, but enjoyable. They included a bowling alley and a dance pavilion, and mountain climbing was a favorite pastime. Guests always looked forward to clear days in order to view Lookout Mountain at Chattanooga in one direction and Sand Mountain beyond Gadsden in another. With the enjoyment of the mountain breezes and the mineral water, guests often commented on their wonderful appetites. Often this statement was heard, "Anything tastes good at Piedmont Springs." Perhaps the rest and quietude was the purpose for which many of the guests came.

Piedmont Springs was a popular place for picnics and week-end parties. Most of the guests came for a week, but many spent the entire summer there. Hugh M. Dorsey spent a full month there while writing the platform for his successful campaign for the governorship of Georgia.

George D. Harris personally operated the hotel for a few seasons until 1915, when he sold the property and hotel to a syndicate from Carrollton, Georgia. Under the new ownership, W. A. Jackson, formerly of Anniston, served as manager. Mrs. Butler Formby of Piedmont managed the hotel for a few months in the absence of Mr. Jackson after the death of his wife.

In 1920 the property was sold to Mr. and Mrs. Ed Alfriend of Alexandria, Virginia. Under their ownership, the hotel was never opened to guests. They had plans to recondition the hotel and improve the grounds, but their plans were never carried out. In 1945 Mr. and Mrs. Butler Formby, who for many years had owned and operated the Dixie Hotel in Piedmont, sold their hotel and moved to the Piedmont Springs Hotel. For the first time in many years, the doors of the resort hotel were opened to the public, although only for meals. Over a good road that has been constructed to the hotel, traveling men and special parties came to enjoy the fine meals. The Formbys operated the dining room for four years.

The property is now owned by the Alfriend estate. The hotel, closed and somewhat isolated, can easily be seen from Highway 11 between Anniston and Piedmont. The building is in a dilapidated condition and would be costly to repair.

During the prosperous days of the Piedmont Springs Hotel, two other nearby resorts, Borden-Wheeler to the east and Ingram Wells to the west, offered keen competition. These were also on the line of the Seaboard Air Line Railroad. Throughout its existence, the Piedmont Springs Hotel was dependent upon a regular clientele. It was largely supported by local groups, but some guests came from all parts of the South.

The Relay House BIRMINGHAM

There being a pressing necessity for hotel accommodations in the new town of Birmingham, Colonel James R. Powell, president of the Elyton Land Company, determined to build a hotel. Since the treasury of the company was empty, he decided to appeal to the stockholders to furnish the money, so he issued a circular describing the urgent needs of the town and asking them to pay into the treasury of the company an assessment of five per cent upon their stock. The amount asked for was $10,000, but the building cost $13,974.08.

At this time the stockholders, having high hopes of the future prosperity of the town, responded quickly and the thirty-seven-room L-shaped hotel, of frame construction, was built on the railroad reservation on Nineteenth Street near Morris Avenue. The hotel had modern improvements such as gas fixtures, earth closets, a cistern, an annunciator system connecting each room with the office, a brick baking oven in the kitchen, and four hose and a force pump for extinguishing fires.

The hotel, named the Relay House, was destined to become the main headquarters for coal and iron men of Alabama. It was opened in December, 1871, by William Ketchum, who came to Birmingham from Rome, Georgia, at the request of Colonel Powell to manage it.

Mrs. J. B. Francis, a pioneer resident, recalled: "The Relay House was opened with a grand ball, and no girl there could possibly have been a wall flower for there were five or ten beaux for every girl. The memories of that night are as sweet to me as the breath of roses, for it was my first ball. It was there I met Mrs. Ketchum and Mrs. William Berney. Mrs. Ketchum was like one of the colonial dames of the olden times that night, in the stateliness of her bearing as she graciously greeted one and all. . . . Mr. and Mrs. Berney, residents of the Relay House, led in the opening dance." This opening party was perhaps the birth of social life in the young city, and the gala entertainments that followed indicated that the town was booming socially.

Extraordinary furnishings in the Relay House included two high gilt-framed mirrors that people, especially the ladies, came to see. The mirrors were the property of Colonel Powell, and had formerly been used by Jefferson Davis, president of the Confederacy, in his residence in Montgomery The mirrors remained in Montgomery until the Relay House was built, at which time Colonel Powell moved them to Birmingham and placed them in the parlors of the new hotel.

Less than two years after Birmingham's incorporation in December, 1871, the Elyton Land Company's directors authorized the president of the company to build a water works. The first reservoir was located at Thirteenth Avenue and Tweny-second Street, North, and the pipeline was extended into town. Water was first turned on in May, 1873, and the Relay House was the first to use it.

Upon the invitation of Colonel Powell, the Alabama Press Association held its meeting in Birmingham in 1873. The visiting delegates were entertained at the Relay House. The following year, the bold Colonel Powell invited the New York Press Association to hold its meeting in the three-year-old city that boasted a population of approximately four thousand. What nerve Colonel Powell had! The New York visitors were astonished at the absence of anything that looked like a city, but were profoundly impressed by the show of coal and iron, and they sent back enthusiastic stories of Birmingham's natural resources. These visitors were entertained at the Relay House and at Blount Springs.

Close on the heels of three initial iron-making enterprises, the Birmingham Rolling Mills, the Alice Furnace, and the Sloss city furnaces, there came an incident of considerable interest—the first million dollar deal of the Alabama coal and iron trade. It happened when there came to Birmingham, to the Relay House, and to the welcoming arms of Major Tom Peters, an expert in ore lands, a Tennessee gentleman named Colonel Enoch Ensley. Colonel Ensley was looking for an investment in a coal mine. Through Major Peters, Colonel Ensley purchased the Pratt mines for $1,000,000. The first payment on the million dollar deal, a check for $600,000, was brought to the Berney National Bank. The check was exactly six times the capital stock of the bank. This was Birmingham's first sensational deal, and it originated in the Relay House.

Birmingham's first post office was located in the hotel, with Mr. Ketchum as postmaster.

Among those citizens who maintained residence at the Relay House at various times were Colonel James R. Powell, J. F. B. Jackson, D. M. Drennen, W. M. Malone, J. F. McCary, J. W. Brown, Miss Sallie Harrison (who later became Mrs. R. H. Pearson), Mr. and Mrs. William Berney, Mr. and Mrs. George R. Ward, and George B. Ward, who later became the mayor of Birmingham.

Mr. Ketchum continued as manager of the hotel until his death in 1877. Mrs. Ketchum then took over the management, with the assistance of her son-in-law, George R. Ward. The building was torn down and removed in the spring of 1886 to make room for the Union Depot.

Several years later, Mrs. R. H. Pearson, a member of Birmingham's Pioneer Club, had this to say:

> The Relay House served the purpose of the aristocracy and tourists. Its appearance was noble, indeed, it was the talk of the State. Throughout the state this house by reason of its superior cuisine and accommodations was commended by one and all. Both Mr. and Mrs. Ketchum were whole-souled, generous entertainers, always remembering their own youth and willing to go to any amount of trouble for the young people, for you must bear in mind that there were no 'old' people in those days. Among a large congregation there would scarcely be one gray head. The Relay was so popular that as I look back on it now, I am sure no invitation there was ever declined. The refreshments at the end of the evening were always delicious and in abundance.

THE RELAY HOUSE

On October 17, 1949, at a joint meeting of the Birmingham Historical Society and the Birmingham Rotary Club, a play was presented to revive memories of the famed old Relay House. The play was a re-enactment of the ceremonies and a reproduction of the speeches made at a dinner preliminary to the opening ball, in 1871, at Birmingham's first hotel. The descendants of those who took part in that memorable occasion were featured in the drama production. Mrs. Frank C. (Margaret Cameron) Spain, a great-granddaughter of William Ketchum, unveiled a historic marker, which is now located at Morris Avenue and Nineteenth Street, the site of the old hotel. The marker reads as follows:

THE RELAY HOUSE

Birmingham's first hotel was opened here between the Louisville & Nashville R. R.'s first train, Nov. 11, 1871, and the chartering of the city on Dec. 19th. Built by the Elyton Land Co., founder of the city, at a cost of $10,000. It was the home of Jas. R. Powell, its president, J. F. B. Jackson, one of the railroad builders, and other pioneers. Its proprietors were William Ketchum and George R. Ward. Ketchum was Birmingham's first postmaster, with post office in the lobby. The hotel was razed in 1886.

Birmingham Historical Society, 1949

Shelby Springs

The most notable resort in central Alabama was Shelby Springs, located in Shelby County between Calera and Columbiana. The history of this resort reaches back to the times the Indians enjoyed the healing qualities of the mineral waters.

John S. Washington advertised in the *Alabama Journal* of Montgomery on April 24, 1839, that:

> The subscriber has rented these well known springs, and fitting them up [with cabins] in a style not to be surpassed by any watering place in the Southern country. No expense or attention will be wanting to render those patronizing him comfortable. The medicinal qualities, together with the locality of these Springs are too well known to need comment. Having had

> long experience in the business, the subscriber flatters himself that he shall be able to please the most fastidious, and pledges himself to use every exertion in his power to add to the amusement and health of his guests. A line of stages will run direct from Montgomery and Selma to the Springs from the commencement to the close of the season. The Springs will be open for the reception of visitors the 1st of May.

Also in 1839, Mr. Washington, in addition to his duties as proprietor of the springs, was made postmaster of Shelby Springs post office.

When the Tennessee and Alabama Rivers Railroad was completed to Shelby Springs in 1855, Wimberly and Sparks & Company, a partnership, leased the springs and built a two-story frame hotel and a few cabins. The hotel building was "L"-shaped and contained approximately thirty rooms. A large porch encircled both floors, serving as a meeting place for the prominent families of the Black Belt of Alabama who enjoyed visiting there. The hotel was but a few yards from the railroad station, connected with it by a wooden floor.

A Ben Lane from Virginia Sulphur Springs wrote a letter in 1872 in which he described the resort as follows:

> One o'clock—Shelby Springs! Twenty minutes for dinner. A leather colored orator gives us a gushing description of the charms of the place, and the niceness of the dinner. A band of Ethiops, with wind instruments, give us a blast of salutory music—Most of us walk to the springs, and survey the premises. They look clean and cool, and there are worse places in the world than Shelby Springs, etc. Ah me! What memories do Shelby Springs recall! This day sixteen years ago [1856], I was here, with every so many beautiful girls, and how we danced, and carried on, and loved a little, and parted and forgot! And in a year or two they all went—Some to the bridal, some to the tomb—1:30 P.M.—Farewell, Shelby Springs! etc.

In 1856 J. I. Norris of Selma leased the property, which then consisted of 2,700 acres of wooded land, including the springs, hotel and cottages. He operated the hotel until the War Between the States, when the facilities were taken over by the Confederacy as a recruiting center and embarkation point for soldiers.

In 1862 Shelby Springs was known as Camp Winn. Several students in the University of Alabama Cadet Corps were sent there to drill troops for the Army. One of the students, Harden Perkins Cochrane of Tuscaloosa, wrote to his mother as follows:

Camp Winn, Shelby Springs, (Ala.)
March 28, 1862.

Dear Ma:

We arrived at this place yesterday at 2 o'clock after a very tiresome journey as we had to travel all that evening and that night and had a very poor supper and no breakfast, but we are getting on pretty well. There are 9 companies here but they are not full as a good many of the men have furloughs to go home. We were received politely by the Colonel whose name is Fraysier and we eat at the same table with him but we have two tents which we brought along and are staying in them just outside the lines of the regiment. Shelby Springs is a very pleasant place and seems to be very healthy. . . .

Your affectionate son,
H. P. Cochrane

To Mrs. S. S. L. Cochrane,
Tuscaloosa, Alabama.

During the latter part of the war, the Confederate government took over the hotel and cottages for hospital quarters. Peter A. Brannon, director of the Department of Archives and History, Montgomery, wrote the following statement after an interview with a Confederate officer several years ago:

> Captain Hubbell Pierce, who lived at Coosada, Alabama, was for a short time in a Confederate hospital at Shelby Springs. The hospital occupied the old hotel building and cabins. The chief surgeon was Dr. D. Warren Brickell. His assistants were a Dr. Bradbury, who later located in New Orleans; Dr. John P. Furness, who died long after the war in Selma, Alabama, and Dr. Jones, who lived in Meridian, Mississippi, after the war. Captain Pierce thinks the hospital was under the management of the Catholic Sisters. He recalls Father LeRay as a priest stationed there. Father LeRay was later made General Chaplain of the Confederate Armies, and after the war became Archbishop of New Orleans.

On March 16,1864, Lieutenant General Leonidas Polk ordered Surgeon Benjamin H. Thomas to proceed to Shelby Springs and take charge of the hospital. He was to take with him all hospital property in his possession, extend the capacity of the Shelby Springs Hospital to 350 beds, and make it a complete Soldiers' Home. It was known as a Soldiers' Home until March 31, 1864, when

Preston B. Scott, medical director of Alabama, ordered that it should be designated as General Hospital, Shelby Springs. This latter designation, which meant a home for invalid and disabled soldiers, was continued until the close of the war. Unfortunately many of the soldiers found a permanent resting place in the cemetery, located on a ridge overlooking the springs.

Surgeon Thomas continued in charge of the hospital until November 22, 1864, when he was succeeded by Surgeon D. Warren Brickell, who remained in charge until the end of the war.

Immediately following the war Mr. Norris again took over the proprietorship of the hotel. A letter to the Montgomery *Advertiser*, dated June 13, 1869, said:

> Here [Shelby Springs] is the breakfast and dinner house for the Selma, Rome and Dalton Railroad — The visitor is at once favorably impressed with the appearance of things here — The table is filled with such meats as these mountains can afford — venison, turkey, kid, mutton and beef are served in such a way as to meet the taste of the most fastidious. — The grounds are beautiful, the accommodations ample for five hundred people. In short, this is a delightful summer resort. . . .

Another visitor wrote of the springs to the Shelby *Guide* on July 8, 1869, and is quoted in part:

> Your correspondent took passage on the cars on the 1st inst., for Montevallo. Stopping twenty minutes at Shelby Springs for the hungry to breakfast, I strolled down among the tall oaks, where the gurgling waters mingle their music, with the singing of the birds. Truly this is one of the loveliest spots of the South. Nature has fashioned it for health and comfort. Sulphur and chalybeate springs of cold water slake the thirst, and give strength and vigor to the enfeebled frame, while the cool, refreshing breezes sport amid the branches of the old oak trees. The goodness of God is manifest in the rich provision he has made for the health and happiness of his creatures. . . .

In March, 1871, the Montgomery *Advertiser* contained the following article:

> SHELBY SPRINGS — This famous Summer resort, distinguished not only in Alabama, but all over the South, will be opened for the reception of guests on the 1st day of June. It will be under the personal supervision of Mr. Wimberly, of Wimberly and Sparks & Co., who is known far and wide as a successful caterer and manager. No watering place in the South is more beautiful or attractive than Shelby Springs. All kinds of mineral water, the

shadiest groves, and the healthiest climate in all the land. — Only three hours travel from Montgomery to Shelby Springs. Think of it. It is the very place for our people to visit this Summer.

The 10th Alabama Regiment, a part of the Army of Northern Virginia, held its first reunion here on July 27, 1871. The Selma, Rome and Dalton Railroad ran excursion trains. This was the first reunion of the soldiers since the surrender at Appomattox.

On July 4, 1876, the Democratic and Conservative Party celebrated the one hundredth anniversary of American independence with a grand rally. It was estimated that over five thousand people were present at the springs that day. Among the speakers were General John T. Morgan, who later became a United States senator, Governor Houston and Senator James L. Pugh. Other prominent persons present were Rufus W. Cobb, who later became governor of Alabama, and B. B. Lewis, who later was elected to Congress from Tuscaloosa.

Another Democratic rally, at which over three thousand were present, was held at Shelby Springs on July 30, 1880. General Morgan, "in his usual eloquent and forceful style," spoke for more than three hours.

It was quite evident that the buildings, equipment and furnishings were in need of repairs or replacement, for there were occasional suggestions in the newspapers that the springs properties should be improved. An interesting letter appeared in the Shelby *Sentinel* on July 21, 1881, part of which is quoted: "As has been previously published, the party of Selma gentlemen failed to come to an agreement with Mr. Norris in regard to the purchase and improvement of the Springs property. This is to be much regretted, as the place would soon become famous as a health resort should it be given all the improvements which its advantageous location, and surrounds, cause it so well to merit. . . ." Later in the year Mr. Norris sold his holdings to Hope Baker and wife, Mary M. Baker. The following year the hotel burned. It was not until November 17, 1885, that the Bakers took title to the property.

Soon after acquiring the property, Hope Baker leased it to Colonel J. M. Dedman of Selma, operator of the St. James Hotel there. In 1887 Colonel Dedman built another hotel on the same site as the former one, using the remains of the old foundation for the new building. In addition, he built bath houses for sulphur baths, which made the health resort more complete.

By an act approved by the legislature on February 16, 1891, the proprietor of

Shelby Springs was permitted to sell spirituous vinous or malt liquors to his guests or boarders from June 1 until the first of November each year.

Beginning with the 1892 season, Hope Baker again took over the management of the hotel. He advertised that his culinary department would be unexcelled and that the services of experienced physicians had been secured for the sick. The rates were $2.00 per day, $10.00 per week, $20.00 to $35.00 per month.

The Alabama Chautauqua Association, organized in 1893 by the Reverend Sam P. West, for two seasons held the sessions of the assembly at Shelby Springs, but it was found to be inadequate for the crowds. A movement was inaugurated to build a tabernacle or auditorium in Talladega, and the assembly was moved to that point.

The reputation of Shelby Springs as a resort gained prominence again to such an extent that additional sleeping apartments in the hotel were provided. An elegant dining room which measured sixty-seven by thirty feet was provided for dining and dancing. A billiard room, bowling alley, lawn tennis and game room were added, and several new cottages were constructed. A full-time string band was engaged to entertain the guests. The buildings were lighted with gas manufactured locally, and the grounds were lighted with lamps placed at intervals. These were but a few of the services and conveniences provided at the resort.

During the latter part of 1896 the hotel burned. Mr. Baker, following the destruction of the second hotel, leased the property to Ed Booker of Uniontown. Mr. Booker constructed another dining room and dance hall to accommodate the guests who lived in the cottages. For the next few years guests at the springs were dependent upon cottages for sleeping accommodations.

After the death of Hope Baker, Mrs. Baker married M. M. McMahon. Mrs. McMahon, in 1905, built another hotel on the same foundation that had served the two former buildings. J. A. MacKnight was manager of the resort for the 1905 season.

Members of the Birmingham Auto Club (there being approximately fifteen automobiles in the city at the time) assembled one fine Saturday morning in August, 1905, in front of the Athletic Club and, promptly at eleven o'clock, off they chugged to Shelby Springs. They took the Green Springs route out of Birmingham to Calera. All drivers of the cars wore goggles and dusters because of the terrific dust. By the time they reached Calera, Richard Massey, founder of the Massey Business College in Birmingham, became disenchanted with the idea and put his car on the train for the trip back to Birmingham. The line of cars moved on to Shelby Springs, arriving there at 8:30 P. M. Here the group spent a pleasant evening. On Sunday morning someone discovered there wasn't sufficient gasoline on hand for the trip back to Birmingham. One of the party returned to the city by train to obtain fuel. He returned on the afternoon train with several ten-gallon milk cans filled with gasoline. C. B. Ratliff, one of the members of the club who drove his new 1905 model Packard on the trip, recalls that no license plates were sold then, gasoline brought nine cents a gallon, and tires carried one hundred pounds of air pressure.

Beginning with the 1906 season, Mrs. McMahon took over the management of the resort. She advertised in a brochure as follows:

> Twelve acres of campus—the most beautiful in the State, shaded by hundreds of mammoth oak and spreading beech trees—just the place for the children to romp and play. Large crowds of pleasure and health-seekers attend this delightful watering place; belles and beaux here meet

for lovemaking, and many a duo of hearts have become one in this sylvan glade. . . .

These wonderful Springs have been celebrated for generations for their curative and cleansing properties, and are known to have cured innumerable cases of chronic stomach and bowel troubles, and diseases of the kidneys, bladder and digestive organs. They are also most salutary in all female complaints. It is not a punishment to drink them, as they are all mild and pleasant, cool and palatable, almost as sparkling as champagne.

In an enclosed park of ten acres are located a comfortable hotel and a large number of cottages, with a capacity for 300 guests. . . . That tired feeling cannot exist at Shelby. No insomnia there, nature's sweet restorative, balmy sleep, an all devouring appetite, rest and healthful recreation and the healing waters of Shelby will make you weigh more, feel better and will be far less expensive than a course of medicine.

Mrs. McMahon also advertised a list of patrons of Shelby Springs, to whom she referred with pride and pleasure. These were:

Hon. R. R. Pcole, Montgomery, Hon. W. W. Screws, Montgomery, Hon. E. W. Booker, Montgomery, A. H. Wilson, Montgomery, Col. J. M. Dimmick, Montgomery, Dr. Lamar Law, Montgomery, Dr. W. C. Hill, Montgomery, Dr. B. B. Simms, Talladega, Hon Cecil Browne, Talladega, Hon. Borden Burr, Talladega, Judge Camp, Talladega, Hon. Wellington Vandiver, Talldega, Dr. W. C. Hearn, Talladega, H. E. Hubbard, Talladega, Mrs. Rice Brown, Talladega, Hon. Morgan Smith, Autaugaville, James Nunn, Autaugaville, G. N. Hodge, Opelika, Mr. and Mrs. W. T. Wear, Opelika, R. H. Groswell, Deatsville, Mrs. Albert Elmore, Elmore, Judge Dan Greene, Birmingham, Hon. Sam Will John, Birmingham, Hon. W. H. Worthington, Birmingham, John Abbott, Birmingham, Dr. James E. Dedman, Birmingham, Hon. Jos. F. Johnson, Birmingham, Senator E. W. Pettus, Selma, Edmund H. Lacy, Selma, Hon. Minthrowne Woolsey, Selma, Dr. Clement C. Pitter, Selma, Hon. J. L. Clay, Selma, Mrs. W. R. Nelson, Selma, Mrs. P. I. Vaughn, Selma, Mrs. Wm. Wilby, Selma, Mrs. J. A. Mauldin, Selma, E. R. Kinsey, Selma, R. E. L. Neil, Selma, James Nunnalee, Selma, Hon. E. C. Meloin, Selma, Hugh Mallory, Selma, Hugh Hudson, Selma, Hon. W. B. Vaughn, Selma, W. M. Johnson, Selma, Miss Florence Guttman, Pensacola, Mrs. Hal Forbes, Pensacola, Mrs. J. W. Stewart, New Orleans, Mrs. F. M. Hendon, Meridian, Mrs. Willie Ogletree, Uniontown, Mrs. N. S. Knight, Uniontown, Mrs. J. D. Coleman, Uniontown, Mrs. Henry Robertson, Uniontown, Mrs. Frank Gist, Washington, D. C., J. R. Hill, Gulfport, Dr. E. C. Parker, Gulfport, Mrs. Hugh Cowling, Gulfport, Mrs. E. Stein, Demopolis, Mrs. H. Parker, Jr., Nadawah, Mrs. A. Farish, Nadawah, Misses Fuller, Nadawah, and Hon. H. S. Doster, Prattville.

The Reverend George B. Eager, a Baptist minister, in a letter to the Montgomery *Advertiser* said, "The present proprietor has left nothing undone to add to the natural attractions, such advantages as may be suggested by the mention of a herd of Jerseys, five hundred chickens, a new kitchen, a new dining room and a new pavilion, good servants galore, post and telegraph offices, etc., etc."

The first Baptist encampment in Alabama was held during the week of August 22, 1910, at Shelby Springs. Three hundred delegates from all parts of the state attended sessions in a large tent. Each day was devoted to different phases of denominational work, with such success that the delegates voted to repeat the procedure the following summer.

The hotel was destroyed by fire in 1910, after six successful seasons under the management of Mrs. McMahon. The resort, following the fire, was leased to W. J. Lloyd of Washington, D. C. Cottages were again used by guests at $2.00 per day or $10.50 per week. The dining room and kitchen, which were undamaged by the fire, were modernized. The management emphasized in a brochure, "The resort is drained perfectly, in itself alone a guarantee against malaria, typhoid and other fevers. The waters of these springs are so accurately compounded with medicinal properties they have become famous for their curative powers. They have cured thousands of cases of kidney diseases, stomach troubles of all sorts, intestinal and nervous disorders." Though Mr. Lloyd leased the resort for a period of twenty years, he lasted but two.

In 1912 the property was purchased by J. Ray McMillan. He rented cottages to guests and operated the dining room. In 1915 Shelby Springs was closed permanently as a summer resort. The McMillan family occupied the property as their home until 1926, when it was sold to Clyde H. Nelson of Birmingham and associates for the proposed site of the Yamakita Club.

Mr. Nelson laid out a superb eighteen-hole golf course, built a magnificent concrete swimming pool, and landscaped the grounds. A foundation was laid for a brick hotel and clubhouse to contain three hundred rooms, but the work on these buildings was never completed.

In 1938 Captain John Reid Irby, a prominent retired businessman, took title to the property and built a large colonial home near the springs. He enclosed the spring property but piped the mineral waters to the fence line so that the people in the vicinity could use the water. The original deed stipulated that the water could never be removed from public use.

Following the death of Captain Irby, the property was purchased in 1944 by Howard Hall of Birmingham for use as a summer home and cattle farm. It is a showplace of interest. On the grounds there is one remaining cabin, the only reminder of living accommodations at this famous central Alabama resort, now but a memory.

218

St. Clair Springs

As early as 1832 Marion Thomason owned vast tracts of land between Ashville and Sulphur Springs (now St. Clair Springs) in St. Clair County. During this same year, by an Act of Congress, a post road was established from Ashville, by Allen's Mills, Thomason's (Sulphur Springs) and Big Spring (Springville), to Elyton. By 1845, post roads connected Ashville with Huntsville, Jacksonville, Talladega, Blountsville, and Rome, Georgia. Ashville was the neighboring town to Sulphur Springs, thirteen miles to the northeast. In these early days, families came to Sulphur Springs during the summer months and lived in tents.

Prior to the War Between the States, Mr. Thomason built a four-room tavern on the small ridge overlooking the springs for the accommodation of guests at the Sulphur Springs. Following the war his brother, John I., a mineralogist, took over the springs and the acreage surrounding them.

About 1875 a small hotel and seven cottages were constructed near the springs by Ryland Randolph, a former resident of Tuscaloosa and a newcomer to the Sulphur Springs community. The buildings were constructed on property then owned by John I. Thomason. The one-story frame hotel building had seven rooms and each cottage had four rooms, two on each side of a central hallway. The hotel was called the St. Clair Springs Hotel. For several years Mr. Thomason managed the hotel, cottages and dining room.

Guests were beginning to come to the springs in large numbers for rest and for water treatment, though principally to avoid the malaria and the yellow fever epidemics. While there they enjoyed dancing at the pavilion in the spring lot a short distance from the hotel. A railing around the pavilion provided a place for the onlookers to lean or sit. A bowling alley was provided for those who were interested in that pastime.

Soon after the hotel was established, groups from Ashville and Springville began meeting at St. Clair Springs on the first Saturday in May each year for a day's outing. All business establishments in the two towns closed on that day and practically their entire population attended. At first the occasion was a picnic but later carnival rides and entertainment of every description were brought there for the amusement of the people. It was generally thought that if the Ashville-Springville picnic could survive for twenty years, this eventful occasion would become an everlasting tradition. On the nineteenth year, however, an unfortunate killing occurred and this bloodshed brought to an end these annual outings. Picnics on the grand scale lost their appeal. Often there had been several thousand in attendance on these occasions and the oldtimers look back upon them with joy and satisfaction, but also with regret that they did not survive.

In the early 'eighties, after the resort became well established, with guests arriving by train, J. E. Rogers drove a two-seated surrey which transported the St. Clair guests the 1.9 miles to and from St. Clair Switch, the nearest connection on the Alabama Great Southern Railroad (now Southern Railway System) where all slow trains stopped. Later Mr. Rogers drove a three-seated hack which carried twelve passengers. During the resort's busiest season, Mr. Rogers engaged his son, Raymond, to drive a second hack which carried twenty passengers. Often it was necessary for the hacks to make several trips back and forth to accommodate the crowds, especially for the week ends. The fast trains stopped only at Springville, therefore it was necessary to meet some trains there. Springville had a depot, but the St. Clair Switch was, as the name implies, only a stopping place. Raymond Rogers operated the hack service until 1917. Depot Street, which led from the resort to the switch, was the busiest street at the resort during the summer months.

In 1888, St. Clair Springs was listed on state maps as Cornelia, named for Francis M. Goodwin's daughter. Francis Goodwin was the son-in-law of John I. Thomason. Mail sent to residents of the community and guests was addressed to Cornelia, Alabama. At this time Mr. Goodwin took over the operation of the hotel.

The mineral waters at the springs were perhaps the principal attraction. Within the spring yard there are five springs along a brook. These are black sulphur, sulphur, freestone, white sulphur and red sulphur. A short distance away is the lithia spring. Across the road is the Big Spring. The waters come from the limestones overlying thin-bedded calcareous shales of the Flatwoods. They are pleasant to the taste, not too strongly sulphur. All of the sulphur waters contain lithium and traces of barium and strontium. The temperature of the waters is usually from 63.5 to 66.5 degrees.

During the 'eighties many private homes were built at St. Clair Springs. Many of the owners rented rooms and took in boarders during the summer months. Each of the houses had "water rights" for a certain number of guests. A large majority of the patrons of the resort chose to take accommodations in private homes, which assured them quiet and a home-like atmosphere. One of the most popular homes which accommodated guests was owned and operated by Mr. and Mrs. W. M. Fort. Mr. Fort was a retired railroad engineer. The Fort house is now located on Main Street and is owned by F. M. Jackson of Birmingham.

The St. Clair Springs Hotel became less popular following the bloodshed incident at the Ashville-Springville picnic. Towards the hotel's latter days, it was leased to Mrs. James T. Greene. Mrs. Georgia Breechin operated it during the summer of 1902, the last season it was opened. Three years later the dining room was temporarily used as a school room. The building finally became too dilapidated for use, was abandoned completely, and at length wasted away.

In 1902 Emanuel Lesser, proprietor of the Metropolitan Hotel in Birmingham, built the St. Clair Inn. This was a two-story frame building of twenty rooms with modern conveniences. The large white structure with colonial columns was located on the east side of Depot Street near Main Street. To the rear of the inn were a bowling alley, swings, a merry-go-round, and Mrs. Lovett's Dining Room, famous for fried chicken three times a day. A large underground area nearby was used for the storage of foods. On the premises Mr. Lesser built a bath house with showers for the convenience of his guests. No sulphur baths were available for the invalids.

Mr. Lesser, an experienced hotel man, was able to provide entertainment which would attract guests. Dances each Saturday evening were given in the dining room, with the best orchestras from Birmingham furnishing the music. Mr. Lesser improved the springs by installing a cement curb around each. He used hollow tree sections in each spring to beautify it and to make the water more accessible to the users. Though he did not own the springs, he provided these improvements at his own expense.

According to Mrs. Hal Copeland of Birmingham, the springs at St. Clair were "covered with cupolas and surrounded by comfortable benches. A description of the medicinal qualities of each spring was posted beside it. Each was prescribed for specific complaints, so visitors would know exactly which water to drink." Dr. B. F. Riley, noted Baptist author, reported that "the springs at St. Clair are worthy of special notice because of their well-earned popularity."

General procedure at the springs was for the family servant to go to the spring of the family's choice and bring back a jug of water to be drunk before breakfast. Around ten o'clock in the morning the ladies would gather at their favorite springs, sit on the shady benches, and alternately drink water, do fancy work and chat. After luncheon they would rest, then late in the afternoon gather at the springs again. Acetylene lights were added to make the paths safe for evening strolls to the springs.

One attempt was made to bottle the waters, and a bottling plant was set up, but the project was never a success. Proof of the water's purity was offered by the sediments left in the spring bowls . . . black as tar from the black sulphur, red as autumn leaves from the red sulphur, and "clear as the underside of wood on a frost morning" from the white sulphur.

Often there were three hundred to five hundred guests at St. Clair Springs for a week end. The guests who registered at the St. Clair Inn thought perhaps the name of the inn should be The Metropolitan, for Mr. Lesser moved much of his equipment, linens, dishes, silverware, and other objects from the Birmingham hotel, with its name still inscribed on them. Mr. Lesser personally managed the inn for three years and then leased it to several managers thereafter.

A cottage adjacent to the inn on Main Street was used for overflow crowds. Many guests came from Pensacola, Mobile, Gadsden, Selma, and nearby towns, but with the springs only thirty-five miles from Birmingham the largest patronage came from that city. Many house parties were given there by Birmingham groups.

The St. Clair Inn burned in 1925. A few years later another attempt was made to establish a hotel there, but the ten-room frame building was so small that it could hardly be considered a hotel. For several years, until the building burned, the rooms were rented to permanent residents for light housekeeping. It was never used in connection with the resort.

Various families have been identified with the social life of St. Clair Springs through the years. Some of the people were Hampton S. Smith, Ross Jones, William Fort, Dr. W. W. Perkins, A. R. McClendon, Frank Woodall, Edward Wilkinson, G. R. Harsh, Sr., Dupont Thompson, D. R. Talley, William H. Kettig, Raymond Rogers, Miss Ozella Rogers, Mrs. Charles McCormick, Mrs. Ruth Rankin, Carl Anderson, Ernest Simmons, Mrs. Annie Phillips, E. W. Riley, George Morris, J. R. Philips, John M. Woodall, Mrs. Charles Wolford, Mrs. Hal Copeland, C. H. Hilton, F. M. Jackson, Sr., and Mrs. James N. Merrell.

Several Birmingham families continue to maintain cottages at St. Clair Springs. The James N. Merrell cottage is perhaps the oldest in the vicinity. Originally it was located on the springs property but was later moved to Main Street. The framework of the cottage is held together with wooden pegs and the twelve-inch boards used as flooring are as good as the day they were installed. Many of the old homes which remain there are quaint in their design, rambling in appearance and structurally sound.

St. Clair Springs is located on the old Gadsden Highway and can be reached by a good paved road. The hotel and inn sites are easily detected; the spring yard is enclosed but the springs are easily reached. Depot Street is closed but Main Street gives evidence, as in the days of the resort, that "the place has ample provision for the accommodation of visitors."

224

St. James Hotel SELMA

On the northeast corner of Water Avenue and Washington Street in Selma, crowning a lofty bluff overlooking the Alabama River, is the old St. James Hotel building. Now dilapidated, it was once the pride of Selma. The hotel came into being in 1837, through the efforts of a group of men who were also interested in establishing the Selma and Tennessee Railroad Company. Though the railroad efforts failed at first, Selma did gain a hotel which became almost as well known as the city itself.

The stock company which sponsored the hotel was headed by Brigadier General John Brantley, and it was first named for him. The lower floor of the

Brantley Hotel housed the offices, bar, billiard room, and several stores. The spacious parlor was on the second floor and the ballroom was on the top floor overlooking the river. Twenty-five guest rooms were on the second and third floors.

After its opening, the hotel became a public meeting place for groups in Selma. It was here in 1838 that the Real Estate Banking Company of South Alabama, Selma's first bank, was organized; and here the plans for the first academy for the education of females in Selma were formulated. Many important social affairs were held. The Brantley shared social events with its competitor, the Railroad Hotel, formerly known as the Bell Tavern, which was erected in 1833.

In 1848 Major John Mitchell, a man with faith in Selma's future, took over the Brantley, making extensive improvements to the building and changing its name to the Planters Hotel. Major Mitchell also erected a three-story building, known as the Mobile House, across the street from his hotel.

The boat landing on the Alabama River was down the bluff to the rear of the hotel. Steamboat passengers disembarked from the boats and made the long climb up the hill to this popular hostelry, which was conveniently located for the river traffic.

In the courtyard of the hotel was one of the largest mineral wells in the city. The bold stream from this artesian well, rising to a height of thirty-five feet above the surface of the ground, supplied water to each floor of the hotel and to the fountain in the courtyard. Its depth was seven hundred feet and it discharged one hundred gallons a minute. The analysis of the water indicated that it contained iron, magnesia, sulphur, carbonic gas, and lime. The water was reputed to have had a fine effect upon the stomach and blood, increasing the appetite and facilitating digestion, and cases of dyspepsia are said to have been cured or greatly alleviated by it.

The hotel was extensively remodeled again in 1860 and taken over by Troupe Sturdivant, who operated it as the Troupe House. Under Mr. Sturdivant's proprietorship the hotel was especially the stopping place for planters awaiting the arrival and departure of Mobile boats.

Perhaps no hotel in the South saw more activity in the preparation of the War Between the States than the Troupe House. Two blocks south of the hotel was the Arsenal, where the Confederate munitions works were located; and two blocks north was the Confederate Naval Foundry, where many of the South's finest cannons and heavy ordnances were built. In the foundry the *Tennessee* and other ships which took part in the Battle of Mobile Bay were constructed.

In the spring of 1865, after a defense by General Nathan B. Forrest and his cavalrymen, Selma was finally captured by a federal army under General James H. Wilson. The city was plundered, buildings burned and the Confederate Arsenal and Naval Foundry were destroyed. The Troupe House was spared. Immediately following the War Between the States, Selma enjoyed perhaps its greatest period of prosperity.

In 1871, Captain Tom Smith bought the hotel and changed its name to the St. James. During Reconstruction days, competition among the hotels in Selma was very keen, and as a result the city council passed an ordinance "fining anybody $20.00 that did harass any person arriving on railroads or steamboats for patronage or handling baggage."

Through the efforts of Colonel James M. Dedman, mayor of Selma, the city council in 1871 constructed a cistern of thirty-thousand-gallon capacity at the center of the intersection of Water Avenue and Washington Street, in front of the St. James Hotel, and filled it with water from the river for fire protection. The following year the mayor was authorized by popular ballot to execute bridge bonds to finance the construction of a wagon bridge across the Alabama River. Completed in 1885, the bridge was located one block south of the St. James.

Early in the year 1873, John M. Keith took over the management of the St. James, and listed himself as superintendent. He advertised, "This 1st class hotel has been entirely refitted, renovated from top to bottom, rearranged and generally improved in all its departments and now presents greater attraction to the public."

In 1879, Colonel James M. Dedman became the proprietor of the St. James Hotel. It was the Colonel's desire to change the name of the hotel to the Dedman House, but the name St. James was now too deeply embedded as an institution of Selma, and it prevailed. Under Colonel Dedman's management the St. James became distinguished for its fine meals. An article appeared in the Selma *Times* in the issue of January 2, 1886, written by the editor, stating: "If there is any one thing that a hungry editor enjoys more than another, it is a good dinner at least once a year. And to Col. James M. Dedman, the popular proprietor of the Hotel St. James, are we indebted for a treat of this kind. Many of our citizens, as well as commercial tourists, ate their New Year's dinner at the St. James yesterday, and when you read the bill of fare you will be sorry you were not there as well as all the hungry newspaper men in the city." The meat, fowl and fish were always the favorite part of each meal served at the St. James and the one served the editor on New Year's day, 1886, was no exception. Colonel Dedman offered: "Roasts—Loin of Alabama beef, Southdown mutton, barbecued pig, brisket of veal with fine herbs, turkey with oyster dressing and quince jelly, and roast leg o' bear. Game—Oppossum with sweet potatoes, saddle of venison, prairie chicken, braised rabbit with mushrooms." The printed menu for this festive occasion covered two full pages.

It has been related that "a very interesting experience came to Colonel Dedman one afternoon about dark, when he was in the billiard room of the hotel knocking the balls around. A dapper and pleasant appearing stranger came in and asked the Colonel if he cared to play a game with him The next day, John Norris told Colonel Dedman he had been playing with the noted outlaw, Jesse James."

In 1887, Colonel Dedman sold the St. James because of ill health. He moved to Shelby Springs, in Shelby County, and leased the famous resort property. Here he constructed a hotel with modernized facilities which attracted guests from all over the South. In 1888, Colonel W. H. Tisdale became the owner of the St. James. The bar continued to be Selma's most famous meeting place. The hotel was always a rendezvous for farmers, politicians and sportsmen.

Often the courtyard was used for cock fighting, not game cocks but the ordinary barnyard variety. The story is told by C. C. Grayson, one of Selma's early citizens, that, "I used to creep through the fence to watch them fight. They gave me all the defeated roosters. Often they would not fight at all, and if he turned tail and ran, he was mine all the same. My first ownership of a business started right there. I sold those roosters for fifty cents apiece. Using the money to buy apples, oranges and peanuts, I peddled them on the streets of the city."

Late in December, 1890, the mayor tried F. P. Glass before a jury whose verdict was, "We the jury in the case of City of Selma vs. F. P. Glass declare the sewerage of the St. James Hotel a nuisance and recommend the same to be abated and that the said F. P. Glass be allowed till March 1, 1891, to abate same nuisance."

The St. James was operated until 1893, when the newly completed Hotel

Albert, on Broad Street, was opened. This new hotel, which covered almost a city block, became Selma's most up-to-date hostelry and attracted the patronage which had long been divided among the smaller hotels.

For many years the ground floor of the St. James Hotel building had been used for stores. The second and third floors were closed and the windows and doors boarded. This old hotel building continues to be of historical interest to residents of Selma and visitors alike, and is included on all historical pilgrimages sponsored in Selma. The iron grill-work around the floor balcony is of particular interest, and has been called the finest in Selma.

Talladega Springs

Near the southeastern border of Talladega County, below the Kahatchee hills, the beautiful Talladega Valley extends to the southern limits of the county. In this valley are some well-known sulphur springs, around which many Indian traditions still linger. Deer and other animals once gathered at the spot to lie for hours in the mud and drink the water, the sulphur content of which later caused the place to be called Sulphur Springs. It was then known as Talladega White Sulphur Springs, later as Franklin, and finally as Talladega Springs.

Fate seems to have played a part in the discovery by a white man of Talladega County's most famous springs. A soldier of Andrew Jackson's Tennessee troops, while tramping around, came across the springs, where he saw deer in large numbers. The springs were located within a few miles of Fort Williams, erected in 1813 by General Jackson with U. S. regulars, Tennessee volunteers, and friendly Cherokees and Creeks as an advance base for final operations in the defeat of the Creeks at the Battle of Horseshoe Bend on March 27, 1814.

Following the deportation of the Indians, a settlement was established at these springs and called Sulphur Springs, on a section of land numbered sixteen. Under the laws of Alabama, every section of land numbered sixteen was set aside for school purposes. In 1834, when the land in this section was sold, the money received was used for the schools. John M. McClanahan was the surveyor, Williams Watters, Henry G. Woodward and James Calvert were the commissioners, and Solomon W. Dunn and J. K. Steel were the chairmen of the board. The sulphur springs, according to McClanahan's map, were situated exactly in the middle of Broad Street in the town of Franklin. Though the town in 1834 was listed as Franklin, the name by which it had originally been known, Sulphur Springs, remained as a tradition.

From 1833 to 1835, the population of Talladega County steadily increased. With a sufficient number of "hands" to maintain the roads in the county, fifteen roads were established, one of which extended from Sulphur Springs to Mardisville, the location of the government land office. This road from Sulphur Springs to Mardisville was one of the four first-grade roads in the county, with a width of thirty feet.

The three-mile stretch of road from Fayetteville to Sulphur Springs was inspected August 19, 1838, by E. B. Stedman, Ephraim Pharr, William A. Reavis, J. W. Hazlett, Robert McGrady, W. Watkins and Milton Wood. On March 4, 1839, this road was established "by law," with William Watters as overseer. On the road from Averiett's to Sulphur Springs, Allen Jones was appointed overseer in 1840.

In the early days of Talladega County, the larger portion of the population settled in the southwestern section, mainly because of the nearness to the Coosa River ferries. The bulk of the travel and immigration into the county was from the north and west, largely because of the hostility of the Indians to the Georgians and the fact that Shelby and St. Clair counties, on the west and north respectively, were populated by the whites many years before a foothold was secured in the Indian settlements of Talladega County. With the attention Sulphur

Springs (Franklin) received with regards to roads, it is evident that this community enjoyed as much prestige as the town of Talladega, which was established about the same time.

In the *Alabama Journal* of Montgomery on April 24, 1839, B. W. Bell advertised:

> Talladega White Sulphur Springs—this celebrated watering place will open early the ensuing season for the accommodation of visitors. Ample arrangements have been made to render those who resort to it, either for health or pleasure, comfortable. The quality of the waters, the scenery which surrounds the place, and the opportunities for amusement and exercise, give to these Springs great advantages over most watering places, and enables the proprietor with much confidence to call public attention to them. They do not only afford an agreeable retreat for the general visitors, but they offer great inducement to the afflicted. Persons suffering under obstinate diseases which have resisted the influence of medicine have found relief here.

During the 1842 season, Mr. Bell reduced the price of board at the resort to $30.00 per month, and $15.00 for a horse. He pledged himself "to use every exertion to add to the health and amusement of his guests." He also announced a "line of hacks" which would run regularly to the Talladega White Sulphur Springs from Stewart's, fifteen miles above Rockford, connecting with the mail line from Montgomery to Talladega.

Beginning with the 1843 season, the proprietor announced extensive improvements for the springs, including a number of double cabins, adding "much to the beauty and comfort of the establishment." He also pledged himself "not to demand the payment of bills from any, on whose part dissatisfaction may arise." During the season the proprietor operated his own hack, which ran twice a week from Montgomery to the springs via House's. For those who brought their horses, board for the animals was reduced from $15.00 to $13.00 during this season.

The names Sulphur Springs, Talladega White Sulphur Springs, and Franklin had somewhat given over to the name Talladega Springs by 1845, for by an Act of Congress during that year a post road was officially established from Wetumpka, then in Coosa Couny, to Talladega Springs in Talladega County, by the old Jackson Trace.

From the minutes of a business meeting of the Fort Williams Baptist Church, held on Saturday before the Third Lord's Day in December, 1848, this information is obtained: "Inquired for miscellaneous business: Brother Ray laid in a complaint against Brother Averett [Averiett] for attending a party at Sulphur Springs. Brother Averett plead guilty and stated his reason for attending the party, when the Church decided she does not approve of her members attending balls or dancing parties. After hearing all the circumstances under which Brother Averett attended the Ball, it was moved and seconded the Church release Brother Averett of the charge, which was adopted." Mrs. John Oden Luttrell of Sylacauga has a sneaking feeling that Brother Averiett escaped the wrath of these good people because he was one of the most prominent and wealthy members of the church.

In the early 'fifties a "row," called the Talladega Springs Hotel, was constructed, consisting of approximately thirty rooms, each opening onto a narrow porch which extended the length of the building. It was a single-story structure about three hundred feet long. The proprietor used one room for himself, and the others were for the accommodation of guests.

Albert J. Pickett, the historian who published his *History of Alabama* in 1851, visited Talladega Springs for his health in 1857. He wrote home that the hotel was well kept, but on account of the absence of company, the place was extremely dull.

The post-war years brought an era of prosperity to the resort. By 1872, Talladega Springs became noted as a resort for invalids because of the sulphur and chalybeate waters. John B. Bachelder, in *Popular Resorts and How to Reach Them,* states in 1875: "Talladega Springs, the best sulphur springs in the State, are located on the line of the Selma, Rome and Dalton road, eight miles from Wilsonville. . . . Accommodations for visitors are fair and will doubtless improve in the future."

A letter published in the Talladega *Watchtower* on July 23, 1873, throws light on Talladega Springs:

> The trip can be made from Talladega to the Springs in about six hours, at a cost of $3.90. Leave Talladega with the freight train at 7 o'clock in the morning and you can reach the Springs in time for a good dinner. A ride of fourteen miles on a hack will put your appetite on edge (From Coosa station on Southern Railroad). The Springs are kept by Mr. J. B. Oden. Of those who have cottages here we can name Judge Leeper, and Rev. Bruce Harris

of Shelby; Col. F. A. Butt, of Kiymulgee, Mrs. Lessor and Mr. Cliett, of Childersburg; Dr. Fitzpatrick's family is here. Dr. Bethea's family, of Bullock, Dr. Bethea, of Marengo, and Mr. Bethea of Montgomery, Mr. Ben Averitt and family of this county and Mr. Ware of Shelby, Capt. Becker and Maj. Watson, of Selma, A. W. Plowman, Mr. and Mrs. Charley Jones, of Talladega, Major Lanier, of Montgomery, Miss Stafford, of Tuscaloosa, is the reigning belle. Major Pace has a beautiful residence near the Springs. Mr. Hamilton, who lives near here has a fine orchard. Mr. Blewster [Brewster] also has fine fruits.

By an act of the legislature in 1873, it became unlawful to sell intoxicating liquors within five miles of the Sulphur Springs Church, one of the churches in the vicinity of Talladega Springs.

Perhaps the most important event for Talladega Springs was the opening of the Louisville & Nashville Railroad's Alabama Mineral Line in 1891, which connected the resort with Calera, Columbiana, Sylacauga, Talladega, Anniston, Gadsden and Birmingham. The hotel was enlarged to fifty-two rooms, a large lobby was constructed, and a spacious front porch was added. The dining room, which accommodated 150 guests, and the kitchen were established across the road from the hotel. T. J. Law, a hotelkeeper in the nearby town of Fayetteville, was made manager of the enlarged Talladega Springs Hotel, and he operated the resort for the next three summer seasons.

Excursion trips, especially from Birmingham and Anniston, brought large crowds to the resort, often for all-day outings. The trains remained at the resort during the day and in the evening would make the return trip. Often there were five hundred men, women and children at the resort on a single day. Occasionally crowds went from Calera to Talladega Springs for the dances. When rules of the railroads were not quite so rigid, often a railroad crew at Calera would ask permission to take an engine and a car over to the springs for an evening. News "got around" in Calera that a special train would be leaving for Talladega Springs and anyone wishing to make the trip could "pile on" at no expense. This they did frequently, dancing away the evening and returning to Calera late in the night. For several years this was quite a favorite stunt.

Various recreational facilities were available at Talladega Springs. The male guests enjoyed skeet shooting on the hill to the rear of the hotel. Hunting in the nearby woods provided other recreation for sportsmen. A swimming pool across the road from the springs provided good entertainment for the children, as did dancing and bowling for the young people.

An often-spoken-of "haunted house" in the vicinity of the hotel aroused much interest, for it was here that a gambler was mysteriously killed. Near the house was a store, known as a "coffin house," operated by Misses Willie and Laura Boaz. Among the items offered for sale at the store were coffins. Though hotel guests visited the coffin house infrequently, it did provide a topic for front porch conversation.

For the 1898 season, George W. Holcomb of Calera and G. P. Beanland, a Louisville and Nashville Railroad conductor, became joint proprietors of the resort. Mr. Beanland resigned his railroad position to join with Mr. Holcomb in the management of the resort. These two were very social-minded and every means was used to attract large groups to Talladega Springs. The resort was well advertised and the crowds came, but because of the elaborate and costly operation and the low rates charged the patrons to entice them to visit there, the managers lost heavily. This unsatisfactory summer season brought to a close the proprietorship of Holcomb and Beanland.

At the turn of the century, William Yancey and Samuel Noble, both of Anniston, acquired the Talladega Springs Hotel and the acreage surrounding it. These joint owners both had cottages at the resort. Mathew Hendricks became proprietor of the hotel and managed it until Dr. A. A. Green of Anniston purchased the holdings of Yancey and Noble in 1905. Dr. Green moved into the hotel, but W. H. Jackson, a local resident, became manager and Gene Cooper, also a local resident, was made clerk. Rates for hotel accommodations were advertised by Manager Jackson at $7.00 to $10.00 per week.

Signor G. Moretti, the Italian sculptor who had designed the cast iron statue of Vulcan in Birmingham and who had moved to Talladega in 1906 to organize the Talladega Marble Company, for several years spent the summer months at Talladega Springs and was quite a favorite character among the visitors there.

In 1909 Mrs. A. A. Green, Dr. Green's widow, sold the hotel and the surrounding acreage to C. B. and A. L. Porter. The new owners improved, redecorated and modernized the hotel. The spacious grounds were improved with flowers, shrubbery and walkways. On leaving the hotel, you found a plank walk which dipped steadily down towards the white sulphur springs, the most popular springs on the grounds.

Perhaps the season of 1909 may be described as the most brilliant season Talladega Springs experienced in its history. An opening ball was given by the Talladega Springs Hotel Company on Friday evening, May 28, under the new management of the Porter brothers. It was a gala event with decorations, souvenirs and refreshments. Razzy Jones' Negro Band of Montgomery furnished the music for dancing. After the formal opening of the hotel under the new management, guests filled the hotel to capacity. People registered from New York City, California, and Connecticut. The elite of Alabama gathered at the hotel and cottages to enjoy the waters, the famous cuisine and fine entertainment. An orchestra played during meals. Often guests brought their riding horses and carriages. Talladega Springs became known as the "Queen of Alabama Watering Places."

Gaiety was not altogether the dominating attraction at Talladega Springs. People who were sick found the waters helpful in the treatment of diarrhea and rheumatism and diseases of the liver, kidneys, digestive organs, and stomach. The water was shipped all over Alabama and to many other parts of the South. The shipping of the sulphur water was an important part of the operation of the resort by the Porter brothers.

In 1912 the hotel and property were sold to a syndicate known as Hudson, Thompson and Durr, of Montgomery. The syndicate employed Tom Mabson of Montgomery to manage the hotel. He was there for two seasons. In 1914 the hotel was closed, and the glamor of Talladega Springs faded. The hotel could not compete with the more modern resorts outside the state, nor was it able to compete with modern transportation. Too, the backwater from Lay Dam on the Coosa River was within a mile of the resort, although the dam was fifteen miles down the river, and some feared that the water would eventually cover the site.

Following the official closing of the hotel, Powell Looney, Mrs. Kate Hall and Ernest O. Johnson, at different times, leased the hotel and operated it on a limited basis with little or no success. The hotel building finally wasted away. The hotel site and eighty-five acres of land surrounding the sulphur springs on the east side of the highway are now owned by D. B. Gooch, son of P. W. Gooch, a former owner. Charles Neal Porter, the son of Mrs. Bama Porter and the late Mr. A. L. Porter, owns the property on the west side of the highway on which the old dining room, kitchen and swimming pool were once located.

The community of Talladega Springs has several ante-bellum homes, a post office, churches and several stores. There are families presently living in the community who were identified with the ownership or proprietorship of the resort when it was a popular watering place. Abandoned walkways which were once used by the hotel guests and a covered springs are the remains and reminders of Talladega County's hospitable resort that was once almost as celebrated as French Lick.

The Tavern EUFAULA

Long before Alabama became a state, Eufollahs, a Lower Creek town, was on the east bank of the Chattahoochee River in what later became Quitman County, Georgia. In 1796 the town branched out and several settlements were established. Two of these were located on the west bank of the river. One was at the high bluff, at the present town of Eufaula, in Barbour County, and the other was lower, in Houston County. Carson Winslett, sometimes referred to as

"John," is said to have been the first white settler at the Chattahoochee site on the west bank.

When the legislature established Barbour County in 1833, the "bluff town" was known as Irwinton, named for William Irwin, a state senator representing Henry and Pike counties, who had used his influence in the legislature to make the place a landing for steamboats for the benefit of the people of the section.

The outstanding link of Eufaula with Irwinton is the sturdily balustraded dwelling known for generations as "the old house on the bluff," built in 1835. It was built by Mark Williams and James Edward Williams, early settlers who came from the vicinity of Cuthbert, Georgia. The land on which the house stands was deeded to James Edward Williams from Seth Lore and Company, composed of William Welborn, Alfred Iverson, Benjamin Iverson and John Forsyth, "by their attorney in fact, Seth Lore, on the 26th day of December, 1836, and of American Independence the sixty-first year."

The Williams house, a two-story English-type structure, was called The Tavern, and it was the first house to be built in Irwinton. One interesting feature of the house is the stairway, which has all the appearances of secrecy, shut off by a door and extending up between sturdy walls. The carved banisters of the stairway leading to the second floor show the splendid workmanship of pioneer days. Large porches extend across the front of the house on the first and second floors. From the porch there is a view up the river as far as historic St. Francis Bend.

The house was originally occupied by its owners, who also operated it as a tavern. According to Mrs. Caroline Copeland Clayton, her great-great-grandfather, Simeon R. Cannon, an émigré from South Carolina, later kept it open as a tavern. Mrs. William Clinton Russell remembers that one of the old innkeepers, known to the villagers as "old man Pease," operated the place under the name of Pease's Tavern.

During 1841 a bridge was built over the Chattahoochee River at Irwinton by John Godwin, formerly of Cheraw, South Carolina. Mr. Godwin, after building the first bridge at Columbus, Georgia, in 1832, had moved to Girard, in Russell County, Alabama. The Columbus and Irwinton bridges were identical. A toll was charged at Irwinton for the use of the bridge. After the river landing was established at Irwinton, the Georgia planters crossed the bridge to bring their cotton there to be shipped, and as a result the taverns and inns at Irwinton enjoyed good business.

In 1842 the name of the town was changed from Irwinton to Eufaula. During this same year, on October 15, James Edward Williams deeded The Tavern to his daughter, Cynthia. She later married Webster M. Rains, and they used The Tavern as their home.

The years have added to the history of the Williams place. In the 'sixties it became a Confederate hospital, and later, when the house was ransacked by Union forces, they left axe clefts in the wide flooring.

The main road leading into Eufaula curved narrowly by the north window of The Tavern, thus making it impossible to enter or leave the town without passing it. The planters stopped at The Tavern while waiting for their cotton to be loaded on the tiers, giving the guests sufficient time to hear the old tales of the river. Travelers through the wilderness also had time to swap stories while their horses were being shod at the nearby smithy. It was the principal meeting place in Eufaula.

Until the 'seventies the house remained unchanged. Older residents remember the outside stairs which led to the second floor. It was one of the few local houses of the pioneer period in that area which was constructed without a central hall. The three large rooms on the first floor ran across the entire width of the structure. The cooking was done in the outside kitchen. The roller towels, the gourd dippers, and the cedar buckets were familiar objects about the place.

The Webster M. Rains deeded the property to Ferdinand J. Hartung on February 22, 1871. Soon Mr. Hartung was married to Miss Josephine Hueur of Charleston. They occupied the property as their home. After the death of Mr. Hartung in 1891, Mrs. Hartung was advised by members of her family to move to a smaller house owned by her husband. She decided against this upon the advice of her niece, Mrs. Lizzie Hartung Ferrell, and her niece's husband, Captain George Archer Ferrell. Captain and Mrs. Ferrell lent money to Mrs. Hartung to purchase at public auction all of the property left by her husband "without issue" (no will). Mrs. Hartung remained in her home and rented rooms to transients until she married Thomas A. Mashburn. The Tavern again became a private home and was often called the Mashburn House.

Mr. Mashburn died in 1930 and Mrs. Mashburn in 1940. Much to the surprise of George Archer Ferrell, Jr., son of the Captain and Mrs. Ferrell who had befriended Mrs. Hartung (later Mrs. Mashburn) more than sixty years earlier, The

Tavern property was willed to him by his great-aunt upon her death. He presently occupies the house and has a nursery on the grounds.

Perhaps no property in Eufaula has been known by more names than the subject of this chapter. Besides The Tavern, it has been called the Williams House, Pease's Tavern, Irwinton Inn, "the old house on the bluff," Confederate Hospital, the Mashburn House and Ferrell's Gardens. Originally the address of the property was "where Broad Street turns to the bluff," but the present address is 105 Riverside Drive.

The Tavern enjoys the distinction of never having been mortgaged. The present owner is making improvements to the property to assure its preservation.

The Tavern MOORESVILLE

Mooresville, in Limestone County, dates back as early as March, 1816, when Llewelyn Jones, a Revolutionary soldier, was granted the sections of land now included in the town. Mooresville was chartered November 16, 1818.

On March 3, 1819, by an Act of Congress, Mooresville was linked to Huntsville by a post road, which authorized a post office for Mooresville and the delivery of mail to and from Huntsville. Mail was carried by a rider on horseback. On May 13, 1820, another post road was established, originating at Mooresville and extending to Russellville, in Franklin County, via Milton's Bluff, Courtland, Bainbridge and Big Springs (Tuscumbia).

THE TAVERN, MOORESVILLE

On May 8, 1822, still another post road was established from Huntsville by Triana, Mooresville, Athens, Eastport, and Bainbridge to Big Springs. This was an important and well-connected route of travel, for one ferry crossed at Triana and another crossed at Bainbridge, and since Big Springs was south of the Tennessee River, this gave an opportunity to serve a large patronage. A stage operated by James Eddington traveled this route in 1825, the fare being $6.00 from Huntsville to South Port, near Florence.

As early as 1822, Mooresville was served by stagecoaches from Huntsville to Triana, Mooresville, Cottonport, Milton's Bluff, or Marethon and Courtland to Russellville, three times a week, a trip of seventy-seven miles. A stage left Huntsville every Monday, Wednesday and Friday, at 1 P. M., and arrived at Russellville on Tuesday, Thursday and Saturday, at 11 A. M.; and vice versa from Russellville to Huntsville.

The outstanding landmark at Mooresville today is the old stage tavern, erected as the settlement's first post office. In the original map of the town, the site of this building was divided off into lots numbers 1 and 2. This tavern, an early weatherboarded "L"-shaped house, boasted the luxury of a second floor to assure guests the privacy not afforded on the first floor.

A visitor arriving on the coach or on horseback during the winter was ushered into the main room of the tavern, where a cheerful log fire burned in a huge fireplace beneath a hand-carved mantlepiece. A clock, its dial set with pictures of stately mansions surrounded by cotton, ticked rythmically near the traveler's head as he leaned over to warm his hands. A newspaper, often several weeks old, was usually found nearby.

During the summer months, the visitor's arrival was somewhat different. Even before he had time to shake the dust from his clothes, he was ushered to the well on the back porch for a drink of cool water or into the dining room where he might quaff his thirst with wine or liquor. Ice for his drinks was obtained from an icehouse a few feet away.

When the visitor had rested sufficiently, he was shown through a wide, low door to the outside of the building in order to reach a narrow stairway leading to the second floor. There he found two rooms, each opening into a small hallway. One of these chambers was smaller than the other and had no fireplace. The second, which was for guests who were willing to pay more, had a fireplace as well as a commanding view of the road entering Mooresville from the north.

Set off from the main room downstairs, a space which measured four by six feet was reserved for the post office. Mail was delivered inside through a latticed opening in the partition. To the residents of the community, who would congregate on the porch, mail was delivered through an opening fifteen by twenty inches at an average man's head height. Upon the arrival of mail, the people of the community were notified by the ringing of a bell which could be heard two or three miles away.

Records indicate that Griffin Lampkin was the builder of the tavern. He acquired the lot on which the tavern stands from James Clemens, who previously had purchased it from Green Roper. Lampkin paid $186 for the site in 1825. Three years later, when he sold it to David E. Putney, he was paid $1,500, covering "the houses and improvements thereon standing." Later owners included William and Patrick Sandifer, Thomas Thach, Amos Vincent, Fleming Douglass, Samuel DeWoody, Sarah A. Skinner and Mary E. Hayes.

The tavern was primitive in appearance, and accommodations were simple, but Mooresville was a popular stop, listed on *Tanner's Post Map* of 1825. Travelers on the established routes were charged reasonable amounts for their accommodations. Supper was "two bits" (twenty-five cents), that being the common price charged by the innkeepers. Corn sold at fifty cents a bushel for feed and $2.00 for eating. Fodder was three bundles for 6¼ cents.

The construction of the tavern was unlike many of the other buildings in the community. The majority of the plantation homes nearby were built of brick. The Methodist church, built prior to 1820, in which there was originally a balcony for slaves of the planters who attended it, was also constructed of brick. A mile away, at Belle Mina, is the beautiful home of Thomas Bibb, Alabama's second governor, with the year 1826 on the door knob. This home, like others nearby, is suggestive of the architecture of West Virginia and Maryland, from whence many of the early settlers of Mooresville came.

The tavern at Mooresville still stands. It is owned by Mrs. Henry W. Hill (formerly Mrs. Henry B. Zeitler) of Mooresville. The building is presently a Negro tenant house. The space used by the former post office, now a pantry and storeroom, has remained unchanged for over a hundred years, except for boards that have been nailed over the latticed partition. Moss covers the shingle roof and an outdoor stairway still leads to the second floor, but the part of the building which extended backward on the right side has disappeared.

The bell which called the people to the post office is a relic of the community.

244

The Tavern DECATUR

Decatur, in Morgan County, lies at the very apex of the watershed between the Gulf of Mexico and the Ohio River. From this point the Tennessee River flows towards the north and empties into the Ohio River. Some twelve miles south of Decatur, below the basin of the Tennessee River, all streams flow to the south and empty into the Gulf of Mexico.

Because of Decatur's geographical position in the Tennessee Valley and its railroad connections, it was considered the natural gateway of Alabama. It lies almost midway between Nashville on the north, Birmingham on the south, Memphis on the west and Chattanooga on the east. Decatur is connected directly to each of these cities by rail.

The town had its conception in 1820, when President Monroe directed the surveyor-general "to reserve the site for a town to be called Decatur." The project was turned over to the Decatur Land Company in 1820, but the land was still a part of the Cherokee Reservation until 1826. Though Decatur was the geographical center of one of the finest agricultural regions of Alabama, with almost unrivaled lands, the population grew only to 671 by 1870.

Decatur gained prominence with the establishment of the Decatur Land, Improvement and Furnace Company, chartered on January 4, 1887, for the purposes of promoting a city adjacent to Decatur, subdividing lands into blocks, lots or parcels, and promoting industry and transportation of every description. The capital stock of the company was fixed at $7,500,000. The company acquired nearly six thousand acres of land in and around Decatur, as well as fifty thousand acres of coal and iron lands in Tennessee and north Alabama.

The promoters of the new land company, headed by Major Eugene C. Gordon, the well-known railroad builder from Athens, Georgia, were determined to make Decatur a fine place in which to live, a manufacturing center, and a place for northern capitalists to invest their money. Building lots for residences were offered at $200 to $500, on most reasonable terms. To those who erected buildings on their lots within one year from the time of their purchase, a twenty per cent rebate was given by the company. The company donated building sites to manufacturers who wished to locate there.

In the promotion of the new city, one of the first buildings to be erected was a magnificent hotel, The Tavern, built at a cost of $140,000. The hotel was located on Grant Street and Sixth Avenue, East. It was constructed with day-labor, without a contract. The work was begun in 1887 and finished in 1888. Since the town of New Decatur was not incorporated until February 13, 1889, the hotel when constructed was on a site described as an Addition to Decatur, on the highest point in the area.

The Tavern, consisting of 125 rooms and built in the picturesque Queen Anne style, was constructed, owned and managed by the Decatur Land, Improvement and Furnace Company. Few hotels in Alabama have had such an elaborately designed interior or more handsome furniture. The wainscoting and furniture throughout the first floor were of polished oak, and the frescoing, done by Tiffany of New York, was in perfect harmony with the surroundings. The whole house was a marvel of artistic taste, cozy comfort and exquisite cleanliness. It was lighted by electricity, cooled in the summer by mechanical fans and heated in the winter by steam heat.

Externally the spacious verandas and porches would remind the traveler of the hotels at the best summer resorts. Massive arches of stone at the entrance porches added an element of solidity to the general appearance. The building was three stories plus the attics and a central cupola. The cupola was a favorite place from which to view the town. The building was constructed of stone, brick, wood and stucco, and the roof consisted of wooden shingles. It was advertised as fireproof.

The first or ground floor of The Tavern consisted of a parlor, dining room, ballroom, bar, bakery, steam laundry, and quarters for the management. Leading from the first floor was a broad and impressive stairway lined with expensive French plate mirrors.

The second and third floors were bedrooms which had wall-to-wall Brussels carpeting. The bedrooms were furnished with magnificent walnut and cherry wood furniture. The ceilings were high and the rooms large. Each bedroom had a bed, dresser, and a wash stand. On each wash stand was an elegant bowl, pitcher and soap dish, and a toothbrush holder. In the cupboard part of each stand was the necessary accessory, the chamber. On each floor there were two or three baths and toilets. Expensive cabinet mantels and open fireplaces were in all bedrooms.

The Tavern's opening ball was held in the fall of 1887, the grand march being led by H. B. Scott and Miss Cora Murry, who later became Mrs. Scott. Celebrities from many states attended this opening ball.

From the time The Tavern was opened under the management of John S. Reed, formerly of Huntsville, it became famous for its bill of fare, the cookery and the service. The dining room would accommodate 225 guests. Trains passing through Decatur at suitable hours stopped there long enough to permit passengers to take their meals at The Tavern. The old canopied surrey, with Tobe Stout as driver, met the trains at the depot, carried the passengers to the hotel for meals and returned them to the station.

By 1891 practically all civic groups in Decatur were using the facilities of The Tavern for meetings and dinners. At the meeting of the Decatur Commercial Club there on February 16, 1891, among those present were Major T. P. Branch, Major A. H. Howland, Major J. R. Stevens, W. A. Bibb, H. B. Scott, C. C. Harris, B. Crawford, A. F. Murray, W. W. Littlejohn, C. E. Hoy, W. W. Hedges, L. B. Wyatt, W. G. Skillman, J. F. Rodgers, L. W. Borton, G. A. Hoff, W. D. Clark, J. C. Eyster, J. D. Jervis, S. H. Gruber, D. T. Harris, G. O. Tenney, A. C. Nixon, Charles Bassett, G. A. Nelson, M. Marcus, A. C. Guth, M. C. Burch, Thomas Turner, J. C. F. Nelson and C. J. Hildreth. A resolution was passed by the club asking Major T. P. Branch of Augusta, Georgia, who was vice president of the land company, to solicit the aid of the New York Board of Trade to favor Decatur in any trade transactions, whenever possible. Messrs. P. Fitzgerald and Alexander Reed, New York and Philadelphia capitalists who were making a tour of the South, were at The Tavern during that week.

After the adjournment of Congress in 1891, President Benjamin Harrison, Postmaster General Wanamaker, and other Republican officials, while visiting the South, stopped in Decatur and took lodging at The Tavern.

With all the splendor of The Tavern, it proved to be an unprofitable operation, for it lost money for the company from the very beginning. As the Decatur Land, Improvement and Furnace Company experienced boom and bust, so did this fine hotel. During the Panic of 1893-94, The Tavern was closed to the public. The company rented the building for $1.00 per year to an occupant who lived there to take care of the property.

After the hotel was closed, it was not kept in good repair. On February 26, 1913, The Tavern was sold to C. E. Malone for $9,000. Mr. Malone converted the building into apartments.

On June 22, 1923, a most spectacular fire occurred and The Tavern went up in flames. The fire of unknown origin began licking at the big timbers of the roof at approximately ten o'clock in the morning and within thirty minutes the structure was doomed. This fire was one of the largest in Decatur's history.

At the time of the fire, the dining room was leased. The manager had scheduled the Brandon-Patterson political banquet for June 28, but Alabama's future Governor "Plain Bill" Brandon had to find another place for his banquet.

Decatur's earliest showplace, The Tavern, opened in a blaze of glory and closed in a blaze.

248

The Tavern TUSCALOOSA

According to William R. Smith, Sr., in his *Reminiscences of a Long Life,*

> The reign of Boniface was an era in Tuskaloosa. There was a time when our hotel-keepers held the keys of the money chests of the State. The fact is worth commemorating, as a part of the history of Alabama banking; it affords a signal illustration of the science of legislative log-rolling, and shows the potency of a well-flavored saucepan.
>
> In the number of the Chronicle before me (1827) I find the following curious and significant card:

"It is no less a pleasure, than we feel it a duty we owe to our friend Col. Chas. Lewin, to return him our most sincere thanks for his kindness and attention in giving a most sumptuous dinner on Sunday last (25th ult.), to which he invited many of our colleagues and friends in the participation. It was an entirely gratuitous act in Major Lewin, done only to afford satisfaction and pleasure to those whom he can acknowledge as friends—and we hope, sincerely, that all the success desirable may attend him, which his unremitted endeavors to please so fully entitle him.

Several Members."

I have a particular use for this card just now, as it opens a subject peculiarly in the line of my reflections, while it recalls the name of one of the earlier and most industrious of our pioneer citizens.

Major Lewin came to Tuskaloosa about 1818, perhaps earlier. He lived a while in Old Town, but cast his fortunes finally in New Town, where he built a fine brick hotel, and was smart enough to run it successfully for many years, long after the village had gone into general dilapidation.

He was industrious and active himself, and had a family equally so. His wife was skillful in the culinary department. Relying often on herself alone, she could prepare a breakfast quicker and better than any woman of her day. She was not above her calling, and was proud of the fame she had acquired as a queen of the kitchen.

It will be seen by the card above, taken from the Chronicle, that Major Lewin had the good fortune to please his patrons. Large numbers of the members of the legislature found accommodations at his house, attracted by the reputation for good cooking and attentive service.

The Bank of the State of Alabama, originally established in 1824, located at Cahawba, then the seat of government, was removed to Tuskaloosa, following hither the State Capital. According to the provisions of its charter, the directors of the bank were annually elected by the joint vote of the senate and house of representatives; and great was the struggle every winter amongst the numerous aspirants for those places.

Major Charles Lewin, in casting about for additional attractions whereby to induce wayfarers to seek entertainment at his hotel, became a candidate for bank director.

Now, with the hints in this little card, the reader will have but little difficulty in discovering that Major Lewin was actually engaged in electioneering and that the success he had already achieved was by no means contemptible. Who the several members were, it would be fruitless to inquire. This card is a very artful and delicate feeler. Major Lewin had secured the favor of his own boarders, and thus armed, he was ready for the conflict.

There were 133 members of the legislature; these were scattered among five hotels; it is fair to suppose that Major Lewin had about one-fourth, suppose we say thirty. Now, without any regular caucus to ascertain the inclination of his own force, Major Lewin could readily count his men; but without being tedious, it is only necessary to say that he fed high and was, of course, elected.

The Major had not overestimated the importance of this promotion. The news went abroad through the adjacent counties that Lewin was a bank director. Be it known that, at the time of which I now speak, there were vast numbers of people arriving at Tuskaloosa, seeking loans at the State Bank. These, of course, crowded toward Lewin's hotel! and for awhile the rival establishments were completely overshadowed by this more lucky and tricky old Boniface.

Lewin had his day of triumph and profit. But this monopoly was not to last. The Major's rivals comprehended the situation and were thoroughly aroused to the necessity of averting the calamity; so that at the next session of the legislature, or at least within a very few years, every hotel-keeper in Tuskaloosa got to be a bank director, and controlled with absolute and imperious sway the actions of the board, and the destinies of the Bank of the State of Alabama.

Let us look at these personages, and cast about for the results. Charles Lewin was a short, bulky man, hardly of the medium height—but fat, jolly and ponderous, weighing, perhaps, 200 pounds. He was genial and clever, how else could he have been elected a bank director? And how could he refuse to discount in bank the note of one of his guests, and then have the hardihood to charge him five dollars for a night's entertainment? *[Lewin's hotel was located near the southeastern corner of Eighth Street and Thirty-sixth Street.]*

Matthew Duffee, in figure, was the exact opposite of Lewin, but made up in height (six feet and some inches) what he lacked in bulk. He, too, was genial, clever, and Irish; how could he refuse to aid his guests in securing the favorable action of the board on a short accommodation for two or three thousand dollars? [Duffee operated the Washington Hall, located at the present site of the First National Bank building.]

Charles S. Patterson, in shape and figure, was a perfect specimen of his craft; something over the medium height, and considerably elongated crossways; really one of the best of men, how could he refuse? [Patterson operated the Lagrange Hotel, located on the northwest corner of Broad Street and Twenty-third Avenue.]

And William Clare, never to be forgotten for the generosity of his disposition, and the genial overflow of his native good-fellowship, how could he refuse? [Clare operated the Mansion House, located on Sixth Street where the Church of Christ is presently located.]

Then there was Thomas R. Bolling, a fine young Virginia gentleman, shouldering, with alacrity, the hospitalities and pride of the Old Dominion; how could he fail in his duty to take care of the aristocracy? [Bolling operated the Indian Queen, located on the southeast corner of Broad Street and Twenty-fifth Avenue.]

And last, but not least, there was Col. Peter Donaldson; he brought three hundred pounds of solid flesh and blood to swell this vast culinary sanhedrim, elected and impaneled to scatter to the winds of heaven the money of the people. [Donaldson operated the Bell Tavern, located at the site of the present post office. It was at this hotel the first session of the legislature in Tuscaloosa convened in November, 1826.]

At the time of which I now speak John L. Tindall was president of the State Bank, and in the management of that institution exhibited the finest traits of an accomplished financier. He was a man of quiet humor and prolific wit; a word from him would sometimes convulse a crowd. The following is one of his many hits:

"The money seekers who came to Tuskaloosa to borrow from the bank were in the habit of making fair weather with their hosts, and on discount days each hotel-keeper would earnestly press the claims of his particular guests for favors. It happened, on one occasion, that toward the close of the meeting of the board, when a large number of notes had been discounted (every one having had the earnest support of some of the hotel-keepers), that a note turned up for a moderate accommodation asked by some person who had no friend to advocate the loan. Not a Boniface raised his voice in favor of the disconsolate stranger. The suspicious waif passed around the board, from hand to hand, and was about to be marked rejected, when Tindall, looking quizzically upon the sentinels of the treasury, from the president's chair, quietly remarked: 'This man must have camped out last night.' "

This was a heavy thrust at Boniface, and had its effect in bringing into universal ridicule that pestiferous system of money-lending by which a log-rolling legislature had placed the people's money under the control of a particular class of men, who (with perhaps little reflection) used their positions to advance the popularity of their establishments.

The historian who searches for the secret causes of the utter annihilation of the banks, and the failure of the banking system of the State of Alabama, need hardly inquire outside of this simple but truthful chapter.

One of the remaining buildings in Tuscaloosa which was identified with the political life of the town, when the capital was located there, is the old tavern located at 2512 Fifth (Broad) Street. It is a two-story structure coated with gray stucco, and the original wide-planked pine floors are still in good condition. It was built about 1826, and was used originally as a tavern where only meals were served. A kitchen and dining area, both upstairs and downstairs, served many of the legislators. The structure has been known by various names during the last century, including Spanish House, Wilson House, Old French Tavern, French House, and Ewing's Tavern. It has erroneously been called Duffie's Tavern.

Many interesting, but somewhat doubtful, stories have been identified with this unusual building. In design the structure suggests the architecture of French houses in Mobile and New Orleans. In 1941 the building, although listed as Duffie's Tavern, was included in the *Historic American Buildings Survey* of the National Park Service, Department of the Interior. Presently it is a private dwelling.

United States Hotel DADEVILLE

Dadeville, in Tallapoosa County, was settled even before the lands had been acquired by the United States government through the Creek treaty of 1832. It was located on the road from Guntersville to Fort Mitchell, the road used by Jackson's army in reaching Horseshoe Bend where the Creeks were defeated in 1814. Dadeville, though not incorporated until 1858, was named for Major Francis Langhorne Dade, who was killed in the Seminole War in Florida in December, 1835. The town was laid out and the courthouse located by John Broadnax.

One of the notable landmarks in the town was the old Dennis Hotel, originally known as the United States Hotel, which was built in 1836. After the War of 1812, Sumeral Dennis came from York District, South Carolina, making his way first to Montgomery, then to Tallassee, and finally to the Dadeville vicinity with the opening of the Indian lands. Here he settled as a planter, and later established the United States Hotel. Prior to the construction of the hotel, he operated a log tavern as a stopping place for the stagecoaches. It is not known whether or not the tavern was located on the same site as the later hotel.

The property on which the hotel was built was deeded by the government to the Tallapoosa County Court House Commission in 1840. On February 23, 1842, the Court House Commission deeded the property to Sumeral Dennis, with "appurtenances thereon."

The United States Hotel, a spreading frame building two stories in height, extended out over the sloping rear lot. It had a decided "inn" aspect, resembling architecturally the old river inn in Eufaula. The sills and joists were hand-hacked. For years its dark brown paint with cream trim distinguished the hotel building. There were triple entrances, with windows at intervals across the front. An upper balcony which extended across the front served as shelter for the first floor porch. One wonders how the building managed to survive the jig saw era without gingerbread work.

The hotel contained sixteen rooms, which were heated by log fires. Meals were served in a large dining room. Steps connected the lobby with the corridors on the second floor.

It was in one of the rooms in the hotel that the establishment was made famous by the literary achievements of Johnson Jones Hooper. Mr. Hooper, while traveling around as solicitor, made Dadeville his headquarters for the Tallapoosa district. In the early 'forties he wrote here many of the notes and memoranda for *The Adventures of Simon Suggs,* a portrayal of a character which mirrors much of life in an ante-bellum atmosphere.

Although the Dennis family owned the hotel for many years, it was not until the 1890's that its name was changed to the Dennis Hotel, by Major Jere C. Dennis, the grandson of Sumeral Dennis. This hotel was the town's popular stopping place for nearly a century.

In 1900 the hotel was converted into a rooming house, occupied by several families. The interior stairway was closed, and steps to the second floor were constructed at one end of the front porch. Until 1956 the Dennis Hotel building was the oldest structure in Dadeville. The Dennis family finally removed the building to make way for a modern filling station.

Vanderbilt Hotel CALERA

Calera (Spanish for "lime-kiln") was known as Lime Station until 1855, when the Alabama and Tennessee Rivers Railroad brought in lime workers and the settlement took the name Calera. In the southern part of Shelby County, Calera is located on a plateau which stretches across the state dividing the mineral belt of north Alabama from the cotton belt of south Alabama. Its early settlers were attracted by the climate, virgin forests, an inexhaustible supply of lime, and fertile farm lands.

Calera is located at the intersection of the Louisville and Nashville Railroad and the Southern Railway (originally the South and North Alabama Railroad and the East Tennessee, Virginia & Georgia Railroad). A depot located near the tracks, just northeast of the crossing, served both lines. Adjacent to the depot and connected to it by a wooden walkway, the Vanderbilt Hotel was conveniently located.

The hotel site, 2.74 acres of land, was acquired from the South and North Alabama Railroad by Isaac N. Breazeale on August 8, 1881, for $274. The hotel site was developed by the railroad, and was recorded on September 20, 1878, as "Subdivision of lands between South and North Ala. RR & Jessie Kelley and others." In the Shelby *Sentinel* of September 22, 1881, in the "Calera Gossip" column, a report stated, "There are rumors afloat that Mr. Breazeale is to build a new hotel."

By March 9, 1882, the Breazeale House was under construction. In the Shelby *Sentinel* on May 4, 1882, in the "State Index" column, the following reference to the hotel was made: "The grandest thing not only in Calera but also in the State of Alabama is being put up by I. N. Breazeale who has been so many years in the hotel business at Calera."

Mr. Breazeale's hotel was completed in the latter part of 1882. It became known as the Vanderbilt Hotel, named for Commodore Cornelius Vanderbilt, who was a signer of the $100,000 bond for the release of ex-President Jefferson Davis. The hotel was a two-story frame building which contained twenty sleeping rooms and a large dining room. A porch on the first floor extended the length of the building on the two sides which faced the railroad tracks. The topography of the hotel site made it necessary for the building to be constructed on piers which measured from six to seven feet, so that it would be on a level with the tracks. The area between the hotel and the depot was improved with terraces and walkways, and beautified with planted flowers.

The Vanderbilt Hotel, managed by its owner, Mr. Breazeale, was the center of social activities for the people of Calera and the surrounding territory. The reputation of the hotel as a place where fine food was served regularly, where congenial company was always to be found, and as a quiet and restful place to spend the night, was well known among traveling men. The meals attracted guests who were willing to pay a higher price than was ordinarily charged by country hotels. Meals were priced at fifty cents each, but the extraordinary style in which they were served made the guests forget the price. Vegetables were always served in small individual dishes.

Water for the hotel was supplied by the South and North Alabama Railroad water tank, near the crossing, pumped from nearby New Town Springs. A deep well supplied drinking water.

On June 23, 1887, Mr. Breazeale sold the Vanderbilt Hotel to A. C. Wade and R. P. Thomason for $10,000. Mr. Wade became manager of the hotel, and Len G. Privett was employed as clerk. In 1890 J. S. Bridges was made the manager, but he had no ownership in the property.

After the Alabama Mineral Railroad (now a division of the Louisville and Nashville) was extended to Calera and began operations in 1891, the Vanderbilt served as a convenient overnight stop for the employees of that line. Many of the hotel guests were passengers who changed trains at Calera. Because Calera was located nearly in the cener of the state, railroad accommodations were available in all directions.

In 1893 Isaac Breazeale returned to Calera and for a short time managed the Commercial Hotel. He then again took over the management of the Vanderbilt and operated it for over twenty years. On April 3, 1899, his wife, Emma, purchased the property.

Many entertainments, such as church parties and oyster suppers, were given at the Vanderbilt by the local people. The hotel was the scene of elaborate dances which attracted people from Columbiana, Sylacauga, Clanton, Verbena, and Montevallo. There was never a bar in the Vanderbilt, but its nearby competitor, the Commercial Hotel, had a bar and it was not an uncommon sight to see guests from the Vanderbilt paying a visit to the Commercial.

The Vanderbilt was a haven for drummers. Many a drummer spent an evening on the front porch of the Vanderbilt, his tan shoes hoisted on the porch rail, a cigar in his mouth, his derby or straw hat pushed back on his head, swapping yarns with the other guests. He brought the romance of far-off places and the glamor of an exciting life to Calera. He saw and was seen. He was as romantic as one of King Arthur's knights because he came from out-of-town and was a man of the road. He looked over what the town had to offer, was a free spender, and was the chief character in popular stories that never reached the printed page. The Vanderbilt, the front porch railroad hotel of Calera, largely depended upon these men of the road for its regular livelihood. The town was in a prosperous agricultural section of the state, and prospects for good merchandising assured good business for the drummers as they made their trips into the rural sections of the county, using rented horses and buggies.

One outstanding feature of the Vanderbilt Hotel, as remembered by the older residents of Calera, was the spirit of friendliness which prevailed there. The managers were always congenial, and the hotel was of such a size that special attention could be given to the desires of the guests. Few hotels in Alabama were better located to serve the traveling public than the Vanderbilt, until it burned in 1905.

Presently at the railroad crossing in Calera there is nothing to mark the sites of the Vanderbilt Hotel and the old depot located northeast of the crossing. The present station is southwest of the crossing and is used only by the Louisville and Nashville Railroad. Passenger service into Calera by the Southern Railway and the Alabama Mineral division of the Louisville and Nashville has been discontinued. Only a few Louisville and Nashville trains carry passengers.

The Vanderbilt Hotel is but a memory in the minds of a few older Calera residents. Were it possible for Senator John B. Morgan, Senator Edmund W. Pettus, Hugh Mallory, General Joe Wheeler, or William Jennings Bryan to speak, the Vanderbilt Hotel's reputation could be verified, for these distinguished men were guests there on occasions.

Wilcox Mineral Springs

Majestic in their loneliness but standing on a favorite spot for picnickers, crumbled foundations are all that remain of the once famous Wilcox Mineral Springs resort in east Wilcox County.

In March, 1902, the Selma-to-Flomaton branch of the Louisville and Nashville Railroad was completed and opened for public service. Mushroom towns sprang up all along the line, each with its dream of being a city. One of these towns was Schuster, halfway between the stations of Pine Apple and McWilliams. This little village was one mile south of the once popular lumber center, Ruthven. Schuster was the railroad stop for the Wilcox Mineral Springs resort, approximately a mile away down a winding country road.

WILCOX MINERAL SPRINGS

The two Wilcox Mineral Springs hotel buildings were constructed in 1903 by George W. Stuart, owner of the property. He dreamed of a resort which would eclipse the then-famous Butler Springs in glory, and rival Hot Springs, Arkansas, as a health and pleasure resort. Four springs, clear as crystal, bubbled up in a space about fifty yards square.

The discovery of the springs was accidental. Mr. Stuart found them on a hot, sultry day when thirsty and tired. After drinking a quantity of the water he found it beneficial to his health and persuaded others to test it. They noted the curative effects. One spring tested to be lithia, one iron, one sulphur and the other freestone. Mr. Stuart advertised, "a man might blow his own horn for 100 years and avail himself nothing, but when the people are blowing it for him instead, there is merit in that man—so it is with Wilcox Mineral Waters."

In 1904, the resort with two hotels was opened for business and dedicated at a Fourth of July picnic to which the Louisville and Nashville Railroad ran a special train from Mobile, granting reduced rates. At this time Wilcox Springs was as nice a resort as could be found in a day's journey from Mobile and Montgomery. The hotels, called "The Upper" and "The Lower," according to their location on the hill, overlooked the springs. The springs were tiled and surrounded by a cement platform and balustrade, and were covered by a pavilion.

An amphitheater with a seating capacity of 1,500, built into the semicircular side of the hill near the hotels, was used for religious services, oratory, and moving pictures. Between the two hotel buildings stood a bandstand and a dance pavilion. A short distance away, to the rear of the hotels, was a municipal ball park with a grandstand. Among the tall trees of the five-acre pine grove in which the hotels were located, long tables were built for the convenience of picnickers.

Mr. Stuart also advertised his resort as "a scene of restfulness and peace where one can forget the clamor and noise of the great outside world with its bitterness and strife and fill the sick and feeble lungs with pure revivifying air under the shadowy arches of nature's faultless temple."

The waters at Wilcox Mineral Springs were advertised to be "most beneficial in Diabetes, Bright's Disease, Gastritis, Acute Chronic or Subacute Catarrh of the Stomach, many varieties of Dyspepsia, Chronic Cystitis, Irritable bladder, Subacute and Muscular Rheumatism, Gout and 'nervous wrecks'." People went there to be cured.

Here are two testimonials:

Camden, Ala., July 1, 1908.

Mr. George W. Stuart,

Dear Sir: Having been greatly benefitted by the use of the water of your Springs and also known many others who have by its use been cured of serious Bladder, Kidney and Stomach troubles, I most heartily recommend the water within my knowledge. The Wilcox Mineral Springs are held in highest repute by leading members of the Medical profession of this section who by their proximity to the Springs have the better opportunities of seeing the marvelous cures effected by the waters on their patients sent there and who in almost every case have returned entirely cured or greatly benefitted.

The situation of the Springs, in the piney woods, is all that could be asked by those who appreciate the beauty of hill and dale and the wonders of nature. The ceaseless attention of the management to the wants and comforts of the guests, and the untiring hospitality of the manager and his wife, makes a few weeks profitably as well as pleasantly spent.

Abner J. Smith, Editor,
"The Wilcox Progressive Era."

Camden, Ala., July 20, 1908.

Mr. George W. Stuart,

Dear Sir: I have recommended the use of the water of your Springs to a number of patients who were suffering from Bladder, Kidney and Bowel trouble and several with chronic indigestion with marked benefit in every case from the use of the waters and take great pleasure in recommending your Springs to all who are in search of water with medical properties that cannot be excelled for the complaints for which you recommend it. Very truly yours.

D. Bonner, M.D.

Mr Stuart boasted of the refined and cultured people who frequented his resort. He recommended Wilcox Mineral Springs

> to the business man in the city whose life was a humdrum drudgery, for the rest of mind, rest to the bloodshot eye that gazes upon field and tree, rest to the wearied frame that stoops from morning till night over the ledger, rest to the great organs of the body that have long ago rebelled against such treatment and are now ready to yield to that pitiless king under whose dominion we must all pass at last. But to him who will there is hope. Ponce de Leon in his wild search for the fountain of youth amid the orange groves of the Land of Flower, was ignorant of the fact that the prolongation of a life is not alone in the miraculous waters of a gurgling fountain but in the selection of one that experience has taught us is best suited for the eradication of our particular disease.

Wilcox Mineral Springs was sometimes known as Schuster Springs. The water was shipped throughout Alabama and adjoining states. The owner emphasized, "the waters of Wilcox Mineral Springs retains its virtues for an indefinite length of time, but naturally it will not do as much good as a visit to the springs."

In 1908, the Lower Hotel burned. It was never rebuilt. Within a few years the bandstand and dance pavilion burned. The resort was situated in the extreme southern portion of the state and resorts located in this section failed to attract a large number of guests, especially those who were seeking amusement. Because of the availability of the water by express, the sick found it easy to remain at home and still have the benefits of the water.

By 1930, time, wind, and rain had left only the decayed, ramshackled two-story hotel building to tell the story of the once-proud resort. Today no traces of any buildings can be found. During the life of the Wilcox resort, Mr. and Mrs. Stuart were its only managers.

Three springs have ceased to flow, and today only the lithia spring still bubbles. The property is now owned by Joe H. Bonner of Oak Hill, Alabama.

264
Windham Springs

Windham Springs, called the "Fountain of Youth" while the resort was in full operation, was visited by hundreds who came primarily to be cured of their ailments and hundreds more who came simply to pass the time away. The resort was located on the Crabbe Road, twenty-five miles north of Tuscaloosa, in the extreme uppermost part of Tuscaloosa County. Levi Windham, formerly of Pickens County, established this watering place which bore his name.

Hamlett Doss of Mobile entered government land in the northern part of Tuscaloosa County and was so impressed that he invited his brother-in-law, Levi Windham, to accompany him on an inspection trip of his new tract. After looking at the Doss land, the two visited the adjacent territory. Near the Doss property they found a beautiful site where several springs were flowing freely. Mr. Windham decided to enter 140 acres of government land on which these springs were located.

After obtaining title to the land, Mr. Windham returned to settle there. He brought along fifty slaves to clear the land, and upon completion of that work he possessed a beautiful farm. The immediate area surrounding the springs was left in its natural state because of its picturesque beauty, and became known as Windham Springs.

In 1850, Mr. Windham built a hotel and several cabins. The hotel building, a two-story structure which contained sixteen rooms, was built of poplar logs eighteen inches wide and five inches thick, and resembled a plantation house. A porch extended across the entire front, both downstairs and upstairs, with steps on the west end to connect the two floors. The eight guest rooms in the building measured twenty feet square. A large hall extended through the center of the downstairs area. A wing attached to the rear of the building provided dining room and kitchen facilities, as well as living accommodations for the owner.

After Mr. Windham discovered the curative qualities of the mineral waters on his place, the news spread throughout Tuscaloosa and the adjacent counties like news of a new patent medicine. Known as the "Fountain of Youth," it was regarded as a place where the ailing could be helped, especially by the use of the sulphur spring water which had a "pleasant taste and reputed medicinal quality." The water was "reputed to cure rheumatism, toe itch, colic, stomach acidity and most any other sort of ailments." For one example, George Christian, father of Northport businessman T. W. Christian, had a severe case of eczema on his legs which the doctors were unable to cure, so he visited Windham Springs. Inasmuch as there were no baths available there, he chipped the rock to make a bowl sufficient in size to soak his legs in the sulphur water, and after several days of this treatment the eczema was cured. People with body sores often had the water poured on them. Other waters at the resort included freestone, copperas, and another which had the appearance of Epsom salt water and produced the same effects.

The only recreational facilities provided by the hotel management were dancing and bowling. A separate building on the grounds was built for dancing.

Bowling was provided at ten cents per game. A saloon in the vicinity enjoyed good business until the church people objected. One of the nearby church groups was instrumental in persuading the legislature to pass a bill prohibiting a saloon within five miles of the church, and this took in the Windham Springs resort. Because of Mr. Windham's personal habits, he had no part in this prohibition measure.

The War Between the States had its unfavorable effects on Windham Springs. On April 4, 1865, Mayor Berry surrendered the town of Tuscaloosa to General John T. Croxton and his detachment of 1,500 troops. Factories and mills were looted and destroyed, and the University of Alabama was burned. On April 6, Croxton and his forces moved from Tuscaloosa to Northport, burning the bridge over the Warrior River behind them, and then moved towards Pickens County. The Union troops ran into General Wirt Adams, who was hastily moving to the relief of General Nathan Bedford Forrest at Selma, and General Adams' men gave Croxton's forces a severe tussle. Following the skirmish, in which the Union men came out second best, Croxton moved to Carrollton, where he burned the courthouse. He wandered almost to Eutaw, seemingly looking for "a way out," then retraced his steps to Northport, and from there moved to Windham Springs.

While the Union forces were at Windham Springs, they looted the hotel and used their rifle barrels to ram holes into the solid walnut furniture throughout the building.

Following the war, Mr. Windham lost his slaves and was unable to operate either his farm or the hotel. On one occasion he offered to give the hotel to S. C. Christian, the father of Professor T. E. Christian, who is presently a resident of Windham Springs, in exchange for five years of work on his farm. Later the acreage and the resort were sold to Sam Friedman and Company of Tuscaloosa.

Mr. Friedman built several new cabins, which brought the total to twenty, and leased the hotel and cabins to various operators. John M. Lawler was for many years the proprietor of the resort and, in words of Professor Christian, "Lawler kept things straight." The curative effects of sulphur water continued to attract people to the resort and often there were three to four hundred people there at one time. Traveling drummers who made trips "out" from Tuscaloosa, Jasper, Fayette and Carrollton stopped at Windham Springs regularly because of the good hospitality, cool nights and good meals. The hotel was used principally in the serving of meals, while the cabins were used for lodging.

In 1905, lots were laid out and streets and avenues were surveyed and named at Windham Springs. Eighty large lots were plotted but only a few were sold. The population of the community at that time was about one hundred persons.

Tragedy struck Windham Springs on the fourth Sunday in May, 1917, when a storm blew practically everything away. The cabins, stores, the Baptist church and all houses in the vicinity were leveled. Houston Clements, who had been the proprietor of the hotel for two years, and his family were in the hotel at the time and their lives were miraculously saved by their being in one of the two rooms which withstood the pressure of the wind. The remainder of the hotel building was demolished, and neither it nor the cabins were ever rebuilt.

In 1933, Joe Christian of Northport, a veteran Tuscaloosa County rural mail carrier, purchased the Windham Springs property from Friedman and Company, through Bernard Friedman of Tuscaloosa. In 1945, Mr. Christian offered his holdings for sale, advertising in the Tuscaloosa *News* that "Windham Springs [is] for sale, including a store, 140 acres of land where the springs are located, a dwelling and four rental houses." It was later said that "the police and fire departments" were also included in the sale, but Mr. Christian denied having any part in this frivolity. The property was sold to Franklin Fields for $6,500.

Family names closely identified with Windham Springs in its earlier days included Clements, Christian, Fields, Dunn, Bolton, Lollar, Doss and Collins. Presently, one of the most prominent men living there is Professor T. E. Christian, who taught school in various parts of Tuscaloosa County and at Windham Springs for eighteen years.

Many important people, especially from Tuscaloosa, drank from the waters at the springs during their heyday. Among these were William (Plain Bill) Brandon, once Alabama's governor; George Johnson, Tuscaloosa County tax assessor who lived there as a boy; Dr. William A. Leland; Dr. Reuben Searcy; and Henry A. Snow.

Mrs. P. A. Doss, widow of the Reverend P. A. Doss of Tuscaloosa, says about the sulphur water at Windham Springs, "I still drink it any time I can get any." Professor Christian relates what he heard a doctor at the springs say on one occasion: "They drank themselves healthy. Apt as not they could have done the same thing at home. Lots of water is good for most anything."

Today, the only reminder of the resort is a shelter over the bubbling sulphur spring. An old roadside store and several homes are also located there, and the Baptist church and a modern school building are the latest additions. The people of the community still boast of the fine water, and there are some who still make trips there to taste of the "Fountain of Youth."

Bibliography

In writing this book I have used many sources, some obvious, some obscure, and some which, unfortunately, are impossible of positive identification. The following have been most helpful:

Acts of the General Assembly of the State of Alabama, 1818, 1854, 1855, 1860, 1866-1867, 1873, 1888-1889, 1890-1891, 1894-1895, 1896-1897, 1898-1899.

Alabama, A Guide to the Deep South, American Guide Series, by the Alabama State Planning Commission, New York, 1941.

[Alabama Historical Society] *Transactions of the Alabama Historical Society at the Annual Meeting in the City of Tuscaloosa, July 9 and 10, 1855,* Tuscaloosa, 1855.

Alabama State Gazetteer and Business Directory, 1887-88, Atlanta, 1888.

Alabama White Sulphur Springs, 1880, [Chattanooga, 1880].

Anderson, William H., *The City of Mobile and the Contiguous Country about the Gulf Coast as a Winter Resort for Health and Pleasure of Invalids and Others from the North and Northwest,* Mobile, 1882.

Annals of the Alabama Baptist State Convention, 1922-1932.

Anniston, The Model City of the South, Bureau of information, City of Anniston, 1887.

Anniston in North Alabama, The Model City of the South, Anniston Land and Improvement Co., Baltimore, 1885.

Armes, Ethel M., *The Story of Coal and Iron in Alabama,* Birmingham, 1910.

Avequin, J. B., *Analysis of the Mineral Springs of Charles Cullum, Choctaw County, Alabama,* New Orleans, 1854.

——, *Analyse de la Source de la Pointe et de la Source du Pont L'une et l'autre sulfureuses, de M. Chs. Cullum,* New Orleans, 1854.

Bachelder, John B., *Popular Resorts, and How to Reach Them,* Boston, 1875.

[Bailey Springs] *Conception and Proposed Plan of Creation of Bailey Springs, an All-Year Around Health and Recreation Resort,* Birmingham, n.d.

[————] *A History and Description of Bailey Springs, Lauder-*

dale County, Alabama, Memphis, 1860.

[————] *Proposed Natural Health and Recreation Development at Bailey Springs,* Birmingham, n.d.

Beers, Fannie A., *Memories,* Philadelphia, 1889.

Berney, Saffold, *Hand Book of Alabama: A Complete Index to the State; with a Geological Map, and an Appendix of Useful Tables,* Mobile, 1878.

Bessemer City, Alabama, South Publishing Co., New York, 1889.

Besson, J. A. B., *History of Eufaula, Alabama, the Bluff City of the Chattahoochee,* Atlanta, 1875.

Betts, Edward Chambers, *Early History of Huntsville, Alabama,* Montgomery, 1916.

[Birmingham] *City Directory of Birmingham and County Gazetteer* 1883-1890.

Bladon Springs, Choctaw County, Alabama, the First Watering Place in the South, B. Ward, Agent, Mobile, 1876.

Blue, M. P., *City Directory and History of Montgomery, Alabama,* Montgomery, 1878.

Boyd, Minnie Clare, *Alabama in the Fifties,* New York, 1931.

Brannon, Peter A., *By-Paths in Alabama and Some Houses by the Side of the Road,* Montgomery, 1929.

————, "The Confederacy at Montgomery," *The Pageant Book,* Montgomery, 1926.

————, *Historic Highways in Alabama,* Montgomery, 1929.

————, *Lilies, Lions and Bagpipes, Tales of Other Days in Alabama,* Montgomery, 1934.

————, *Little Journeys to Interesting Points in Alabama,* Montgomery, 1930.

————, "Little Journeys Through Alabama," *Alabama Highway Magazine,* May, 1930.

————, "The Roads to Huntsville," *Alabama Highway Magazine,* August, 1929.

————, *Turning the Pages,* Montgomery, 1932.

Brewer, W., *Alabama: Her History, Resources, War Record, and Public Men,* Montgomery, 1872.

Bridgeport, Alabama, 1890-1900, Bridgeport Board of Trade, Chattanooga, 1900.

Burroughs, P. E., *Fifty Fruitful Years, 1891-1941, the Story of the Sunday School Board of the Southern Baptist Convention,* Nashville, 1941.

Caldwell, H. M., *History of the Elyton Land Company and Birmingham, Ala.,* Birmingham, 1892.

Campbell, T. J., *The Upper Tennessee,* Chattanooga, 1932.

Carmer, Carl, *Stars Fell on Alabama,* New York, 1934.

Carney, Mary Owen, *Gateway to History,* Daphne, Ala., 1954.

——————, *The Yanks Take Over the Eastern Shore,* Daphne, Ala., 1949.

Clinton, Matthew William, "An Historical Sketch of Tuscaloosa," *Annual Labor Day Program,* Tuscaloosa, 1947.

——————, *Tuscaloosa, Alabama, Its Early Days, 1816-1865,* Tuscaloosa, 1958.

Coleman, John S., *Josiah Morris (1818-1891), Montgomery Banker Whose Faith Built Birmingham,* Birmingham, 1948.

Comings, L. J. Newcomb and Martha M. Albers, *A Brief History of Baldwin County,* Fairhope, Ala., 1928.

Cook's Springs, Alabama, Mountain View Hotel, Annex and Cottages, L. Cooke & Co., n.p., 1907.

Craighead, Erwin, *Mobile: Fact and Tradition, Noteworthy People and Events,* Mobile 1930.

——————, *Mobile, Ala., The Gulf Coast Winter Resort,* Mobile, 1889.

Crane, Mary Powell, *The Life of James R. Powell and Early History of Alabama and Birmingham,* Brooklyn, N. Y., 1930.

Crumpton, Washington Bryan, *A Book of Memories, 1842-1920,* Montgomery, 1921.

Culver, I. F., *Alabama's Resources and Future Prospects,* Birmingham, 1897.

Cumming, Kate, *Gleanings From Southland,* Birmingham, 1895.

——————, *A Journal of Hospital Life in the Confederate Army of Tennessee,* Louisville and New Orleans, 1866.

[Decatur] *Decatur, the Gateway of Alabama,* Decatur Land, Improvement and Furnace Co., Decatur, Ala., 1887.

Dowling, H. G., *Tuscaloosa, Alabama, the Druid City,* Tuscaloosa, 1939.

DuBose, Joel C., *Notable Men of Alabama,* Atlanta, 1904. 2 vols.

DuBose, John Witherspoon, *The Mineral Wealth of Alabama and Birmingham, Illustrated,* Birmingham, 1886.

——————, *The Life and Times of William Lowndes Yancey,* Birmingham, 1892.

Fattorusso, Joseph, *Wonders of Italy,* Florence, Italy, 1950.

Fitzgerald, W. Norman, Jr., *President Lincoln's Blockade and the Defense of Mobile,* Madison, Wis., 1954.

Fleming, Walter L., *Civil War and Reconstruction in Alabama,* New York, 1905.

Fort Payne, Alabama, Illustrated, Fort Payne Coal and Iron Co., Elizabeth, N. J., 1890.

Foster, Henry B., *History of the Tuscaloosa County Baptist Association,* Tuscaloosa, 1934.

Garrett, William, *Reminiscences of Public Men in Alabama for Thirty Years,* Atlanta, 1872.

Glennon, John F. and Rosemary Glennon, "Where Time Bears Witness to Sound Building," publication of reprints and advertisements appearing in the Mobile *Register* during 1934 and 1935 for the First National Bank of Mobile.

Goodrow, Sister Esther Marie, *Mobile During the Civil War,* Mobile, 1950.

Grayson, Claude C., *Yesterday and Today, Memories of Selma and Its People,* New Orleans, 1948.

Green, Fletcher M., ed., *The Lides Go South and West, the Record of a Planter Migration in 1835,* Columbia, S. C., 1952.

Hamilton, Peter J., *Colonial Mobile,* Boston and New York, 1897.

Hardy, John, *Selma: Her Institutions and her Men,* Selma, Ala., 1879.

Harrison, Karl C., *A Brief History of Shelby Springs,* Columbiana, Ala., 1941.

Historic American Buildings Survey, United States Department of the Interior, National Park Service, Washington, 1941.

Historic Homes of Alabama and Their Traditions, National League of American Pen Women, Alabama Members, Birmingham, 1935.

Hodgson, Joseph, *The Alabama Manual and Statistical Register for 1869,* Montgomery, 1869.

——————, *The Cradle of the Confederacy; or, the Times of Troup, Quitman and Yancey,* Mobile, 1876.

Holt, Thad, *Old Gainesville, 1832-1875,* Birmingham, 1955.

Hoole, W. Stanley, *Alias Simon Suggs, The Life and Times of Johnson Jones Hooper,* University, Ala., 1952.

——————, *The James Boys Rode South,* Tuscaloosa, Ala., 1955.

Jackson, Walter M., *The Story of Selma,* Birmingham, 1954.

Jones, Charles H., ed., *Appletons' Hand-Book of American Travel, Southern Tour,* New York, 1873.

Jones, J. B., *A Rebel War Clerk's Diary at the Confederate States Capital,* New York, 1935. 2 vols.

Jones, Walter B., *The Greene Springs School,* Hale County Historical Society Publication, Havana, Ala., 1947.

Jordan, M. H., "Cholera at Birmingham, Ala., in 1873," *U.S. Executive Documents,* House of Representatives, 2nd Sess., 43rd Congress, 1874-75, Washington, 1875.

Jordan, Thomas and J. P. Pryor, *The Campaigns of Lieut.-Gen. N. B. Forrest and of Forrest's Cavalry,* New Orleans, Memphis and New York, 1868.

Kennamer, John Robert, *History of Jackson County,* Winchester, Tenn., 1935.

Land and Rail, publication of Planters' Journal and Southern Iron Worker Co., Birmingham, January, 1887.

Lathrop, Sallie B. Comer, *The Comer Family Goes to Town,* Birmingham, 1942.

Lemly, James Hutton, *The Gulf, Mobile and Ohio,* Homewood, Ill., 1953.

Little, John Buckner, *The History of Butler County, Alabama, From 1815 to 1885,* Cincinnati, 1885.

Lorenz, Lincoln, *The Life of Sidney Lanier,* New York, 1935.

McClellan, Captain R. A., *Early History of Limestone County,* Athens, Ala., 1881.

McMahon, Mrs. M. M., *Health and Happiness at Shelby Springs,* n.p., 1906.

Martin, Thomas W., *French Military Adventurers in Alabama, 1818-1828,* Princeton, N. J., 1937.

Maury, General Dabney Herndon, *Recollections of a Virginian in the Mexican, Indian and Civil Wars,* New York, 1894.

Maxwell, James Robert, *Autobiography,* New York, 1926.

Memorial Record of Alabama, Brant and Fuller, Madison, Wis., 1893. 2 vols.

Miller, Francis Trevelyan, *Photographic History of the Civil War,* New York, 1912. 10 vols.

Miller, L. D., *History of Alabama,* Birmingham, 1901.

Mineral Springs Hotel, Mineral Springs Hotel Co., Gadsden, Ala., 1910.

Minutes of Annual Conference, North Alabama Conference of the Methodist Church, Birmingham, 1912.

[Mobile] *Highlights of 75 Years in Mobile,* First National Bank of Mobile, Mobile, 1940.

Montezuma University Medical College, Catalogue for Second Annual Session, 1897-1898, Bessemer, Ala., 1897.

[Montgomery] *Modern Montgomery, the Capital City of Alabama,* Montgomery, 1895.

[North Alabama] *Historical and Statistical Review and Mailing Guide of North Alabama, Illustrated,* New York and Birmingham, 1888.

Olmsted, Frederick Law, *The Cotton Kingdom,* New York, 1861. 2 vols.

Owen, Thomas McAdory, *History of Alabama and Dictionary of Alabama Biography,* Chicago, 1921.

Parker, Foxhall A., *The Battle of Mobile Bay,* Boston, 1878.

Pioneers Club, *Early Days in Birmingham,* Birmingham, 1937.

Powe, Esther M'Elrath, "Romance, Life and Tragedy of Bladon Springs Painted," undated clipping from Mobile *Press-Register.*

[Ravesies, Paul] Sub rosa, *Mobile Oyster and Its Destiny and Other Attractions,* Mobile, 1884.

[Red Mountain] *Advertisement of the Mineral Lands of the Red Mountain Iron and Coal Company of Alabama,* New York, 1868.

Riddell, J. L. and W. P., and R. T. Brumby, *Analyses of the Bladon Springs,* Mobile, 1870.

Riley, B. F., *Alabama As It Is; or, The Immigrant's and Capitalist's Guide Book to Alabama,* Atlanta, 1888.

Scruggs, J. H., Jr., *Alabama Postal History,* Birmingham, 1954.

Selma and Dallas County, Alabama, Chamber of Commerce, *Suggested Tour and Description of Historical and other Interesting Attractions,* Selma, n.d.

Shackelford, Edward M., *The First Fifty Years of the State Teachers College at Troy, Alabama,* Montgomery, 1937.

[Shelby Springs] *Getting Acquainted with Shelby County,* bulletin of Alabama College, Montevallo, 1945.

Sherman, Senator John, *Recollections of Forty Years in the House, Senate and Cabinet, An Autobiography,* Chicago, 1895.

Slocomb, Ala., *School Bulletin,* 1907-08.

Smith and De Land, *Northern Alabama, Historical and Biographical, Illustrated,* Birmingham, 1888.

Smith, Eugene Allen, *The Underground Water Resources of Alabama, Geological Survey of Alabama,* Montgomery, 1907.

Smith, Nelson F., *History of Pickens County, Alabama, from Its First Settlement,* Carrollton, Ala., 1856.

Smith, William R., Sr., *Reminiscences of a Long Life; Historical, Political, Personal and Literary,* Washington, 1889.

Spratt, R. D., *Brief History of Livingston,* Livingston, Ala., 1931.

Stuart, George W., *Wilcox Mineral Springs,* Schuster, Ala., 1908.

Sulzby, James F., Jr., *Annals of the Southside Baptist Church,* Birmingham, 1947.

————, *Birmingham Sketches,* Birmingham, 1945.

Taylor, Thomas J., *Early History of Madison County, and Incidentally, of North Alabama,* Huntsville, Ala., 1883-84.

Teeple and Smith, *Jefferson County and Birmingham, Alabama, Histori-*

cal and Biographical, 1887, Birmingham, n.d.

Thompson, Mattie Thomas, *History of Barbour County, Alabama,* Eufaula, Ala., 1939.

Tintagil Club, *Official Guide to the City of Montgomery, Alabama,* Montgomery, 1920 and 1948.

Towner, J. D., *Guide to the Great Southern Health and Pleasure Resort, Blount Springs, Alabama,* Nashville, n.d.

[Tuscaloosa] *The City of Tuskaloosa,* Tuskaloosa Coal, Iron and Land Co., Cincinnati, 1887.

Walker, Anne Kendrick, *Backtracking in Barbour County,* Richmond, 1941.

Walker, Robert Sparks, *Lookout: The Story of a Mountain,* Chattanooga, 1952.

West, Anson, *A History of Methodism in Alabama,* Nashville, 1893.

Woodward, Joseph H., II, *Alabama Blast Furnaces,* Woodward, 1940.

Other resourceful information was derived from the following manuscripts, magazines and printed articles: Anderson, James A., "The Federal Raid into Alabama, April 1865," address delivered before the Kiwanis Club, Tuscaloosa, 1935; Bailey Springs Hotel Register, 1858-1870; Brannon, Peter A., "A Story of a Road through the Pine Belt Country," *Alabama Highways,* Vol. VI, No. 7, 1932; Chapman, Elizabeth H., "Changing Huntsville, 1890-1899," Huntsville, 1932; Dillard, A. W. *History of Sumter County,* Livingston, 1859; "Historical Sites in Alabama," "Talladega County," by various historians, *Alabama Historical Quarterly,* Vol. 15, No. 2, 1953; Jones, Pat, "The Green Bottom Inn," *Alabama Highways,* Vol. VI, No. 7, 1932; "Madam Le Vert's Diary," *Alabama Historical Quarterly,* Vol. 3, No. 1, 1941; Parkes, Holcombe, *The Southern Railway System and Birmingham, Alabama,* Washington, n.d.; Pickett Papers in Alabama Department of Archives and History, Montgomery; Vandiver, Wellington, "Pioneer Talladega, Its Minutes and Memories," *Alabama Historical Quarterly,* Vol. 16, No. 2, 1954.

In addition to the printed sources, as suggested above, I have also received a great deal of help from individuals who have granted me the benefit of their personal time and information. Many of these individuals also have assisted me in securing numerous pictures and illustrations. For all information and the use of pictures, many of which have lain undiscovered for years and are here used for the first time, I am indebted to a host of friends throughout the state. They include:

Reese Adamson, Birmingham
Rucker Agee, Birmingham
Mrs. Mary Livingston Akin, Montgomery
Judge Henry L. Anderton, Birmingham
Jack T. Atchison, Columbiana
Colonel Harry M. Ayers, Anniston
Thomas Ballard, Birmingham
Bernard C. Bass, Memphis, Tenn.
Mrs. Elizabeth Parks Beamguard, Huntsville
W. B. Blevins, Calera
R. E. Bowden, Sr., Calera
Hon. Frank W. Boykin, Mobile
Peter A. Brannon, Montgomery
William H. Brantley, Jr., Birmingham
A. B. Bristow, Shelby
H. E. Brown, Millry
Judge Joel E. Brown, Montgomery
Mrs. R. C. Bruce, Birmingham
E. V. Caldwell, Huntsville
James A. Carney, Fairhope
F. W. Carr, Jr., Bridgeport
Elbert R. Chandler, Decatur
Luther C. Chandler, Chandler Springs
Mrs. M. F. Chandler, Chandler Springs
Dr. James H. Chapman, Birmingham
Dr. Frank L. Chenault, Decatur
Joe Christian, Northport
T. E. Christian, Windham Springs
Judge C. J. Coley, Alexander City
Mrs. Sebron Colson, Eutaw
Mrs. C. M. Cook, Birmingham
Gene Cooper, Talladega Springs
Mrs. Susie H. Copeland, Birmingham
Mrs. P. O. Davis, Auburn
Judge W. E. Dearman, Livingston
Caldwell Delaney, Mobile
Mrs. Corinne Demetropolis, Mobile
Brewer Dixon, Talladega
Miss Ella Dobbs, Birmingham
Mrs. Frances J. Doss, Tuscaloosa
Mrs. Richard V. Evans, Birmingham
Mrs. G. B. Fallow, Birmingham
Judge W. E. Farrar, Carrollton
Hill Ferguson, Birmingham
Mrs. Hill Ferguson, Birmingham
G. A. Ferrell, Eufaula
Mrs. T. M. Floyd, Birmingham
Butler Formby, Piedmont
Mrs. W. M. Fort, St. Clair Springs
Mrs. F. D. Gamble, Birmingham
Roy W. Gilbert, Birmingham
Mrs. Carolyn Ingram Gillespie, Birmingham
Miss Mildred Goodrich, Anniston
Neeham Graham, Jr., Birmingham
Sam Graham, Birmingham
Mrs. W. T. Graves, Birmingham
Oscar Green, Cloudland, Ga.
Miss Frances M. Hails, Montgomery
Mrs. Elizabeth Hanby, Birmingham
William E. Hargrove, Birmingham
H. P. Harris, Anniston
Karl C. Harrison, Columbiana
Mrs. W. W. Hazzard, Birmingham
Walter E. Henley, Birmingham
G. E. Hill, Fort Payne
Henry W. Hill, Mooresville
Mrs. Henry W. Hill, Mooresville
Casper P. Hilty, Birmingham
G. W. Hodges, Ashville
Mrs. G. W. Hodges, Ashville
Mrs. J. D. Hood, Ashville
Dr. W. Stanley Hoole, Tuscaloosa
John Horn, Brighton
Hal Howe, Mentone
L. H. Hughes, Sr., Bridgeport
Oscar V. Hunt, Birmingham
Mrs. Susie Nabb Illingworth, Birmingham
Francis H. Inge, Mobile
Miss Jessica Ingram, Birmingham
Richard M. Ingram, Jr., Birmingham
Dwight M. Jackson, Clairmont Springs
Jenkins Jackson, Livingston
W. V. Jacoway, Fort Payne
Joe B. Jeffers, Birmingham
Miss E. Grace Jemison, Talladega
William H. Jenkins, Decatur
Malcolm C. Jeter, Birmingham
Judge Jim A. Johnson, Fort Payne
Mrs. C. P. Johnston, Somerville
Judge Thomas W. Jones, Huntsville
Mrs. W. J. Jones, Oak Hill
Mrs. Ted Joy, Birmingham
Mrs. W. S. Knight, Healing Springs
Dr. George Lang, Tuscaloosa
Mrs. Scears Lee, Talladega
Mrs. Henry Lide, Sardis
Mrs. David D. Lindsey, Hartselle
Duke Logan, Anniston
Mrs. John Oden Luttrell, Sylacauga
Doy L. McCall, Monroeville
C. E. McCartney, Fort Payne
Carl F. McCool, Birmingham
Miss Bertha McElderry, Talladega
William H. McGowen, Birmingham
Julian F. McGowin, Chapman

Mrs. J. W. McKinnon, Talladega Springs
Mrs. J. D. McLaughlin, Blue Springs
R. E. McLean, Birmingham
Dr. James B. McMillan, Tuscaloosa
Miss Lena Martin, Gadsden
Thomas W. Martin, Birmingham
Hardeman S. Meade, Birmingham
Chapman Meadows, Selma
Mrs. James N. Merrell, Birmingham
Miss Minnie J. Michael, Mobile
Lee Moody, Bessemer
Ed H. Moore, Birmingham
Will W. Moore, Blount Springs
Hugh Morrow, Sr., Birmingham
G. H. Mosher, Selma
P. A. Nash, Oneonta
Jack Nelms, Selma
W. W. Newman, Huntsville
W. M. Parks, Fayetteville
Harry A. Peters, Jr., Point Clear
Cameron Plummer, Mobile
Mrs. Frank Polk, Cook's Springs
Edward Ponder, Chandler Springs
Mrs. Calvin Poole, Greenville
Mrs. Bama Porter, Talladega Springs
John B. Privett, Birmingham
Mrs. Frances Byars Quarles, Blount Springs
Mrs. Walter B. Raymond, Fort Payne
H. L. Reeder, Florence
Louie Reese, Jr., Birmingham
Ira Rhodes, Alpine
John R. T. Rives, Birmingham
David Roberts, Jr., Birmingham
Mrs. Mary W. Roberts, Gainesville
Barnes A. Rogers, Gainesville
Miss Ozella Rogers, St. Clair Springs
Raymond Rogers, St. Clair Springs
Miss Anna L. Russell, Nashville, Tenn.
George Rutledge, Bessemer
Mrs. Harriet Fitts Ryan, Tuscaloosa
Mrs. F. J. Sauer, Mobile
Mrs. Sarah P. Sawyer, Fort Payne
Mrs. Ruth T. Sessions, Bladon Springs
Mrs. J. Bolin Shirly, Birmingham
George P. Shurbet, Birmingham
Mrs. Cornelia M. Simpson, Florence
Judge Robert T. Simpson, Florence
Henry Upson Sims, Birmingham
Alvin H. Sinclair, Jr., Blount Springs
Marvin B. Small, Gadsden
Charles C. Smith, Chatom
James Arthur Smith, Birmingham
Richard Smith, Florence
Zac Smith, Birmingham
Alden H. Snow, Tuscaloosa
Mrs. Frank C. Spain, Birmingham
Senator John J. Sparkman, Huntsville
Murray Stevenson, Mobile
Mrs. Annie Lorrie Carroll Stutts, Slocomb
Mrs. Olivia B. Sullivan, Carrollton
Dr. Charles G. Summersell, Tuscaloosa
Mrs. J. D. Sutter, Birmingham
Willard F. Suydam, Birmingham
Pratt Tartt, Livingston
Mrs. Pratt Tartt, Livingston
Mrs. Sallie Lowry Thompson, Somerville
Mrs. William M. Thompson, Russellville
Fant H. Thornley, Birmingham
Morris Timbes, Mobile
Miss Pattie C. Turner, Bladon Springs
J. J. Tyson, Talladega Springs
Mrs. J. J. Tyson, Talladega Springs
Mrs. Sarah Hunt Vann, Birmingham
Leon Waite, Jr., Mobile
Mrs. Alyce Billings Walker, Birmingham
Mrs. Cullom Walker, Sr., Birmingham
Tobe Washam, Talladega
Mrs. H. H. Wefel, Mobile
Gordon Welch, Talladega
G. H. Welden, Rising Fawn, Ga.
Mrs. G. H. Welden, Rising Fawn, Ga.
Mrs. T. V. White, Livingston
Mrs. Temon Williams, Birmingham
H. G. Williamson, Earle, Ark.
Mrs. Virginia G. Wilson, Birmingham
C. A. Wolfes, Fort Payne
Mrs. Eliza Mae Woodall, Stevenson
Joseph H. Woodward, II, Birmingham

In addition to the books, personal interviews, magazines, pictures and other sources of information, I have also used many contemporary newspaper files. These papers contain not only information concerning the springs, hotels, etc., but also countless advertisements and social notes of the day. Without the use of these materials this book could not have been written. I am indebted to the publishers of the *Alabama Journal (Montgomery),* 1839, 1842, 1843; Albany-Decatur *Daily,* 1923; *Baldwin Times,* 1939; Birmingham *Age Herald,* 1892, 1894, 1899, 1903, 1905; Birmingham *News,* 1894, 1902, 1904, 1905, 1915, 1931, 1938, 1940, 1944, 1949-1954; Birmingham *News-Age Herald,* 1932, 1935-1937, 1943, 1944, 1949; Birmingham *Post,* 1939; Birmingham *Post-Herald,* 1954, 1955; Chattanooga *Times,* 1954; *Daily News* (Birmingham), 1891; Dothan *Eagle,* 1954; *Evening News* (Anniston), 1889, 1932; *Evening News* (Birmingham), 1889; Gadsden *Journal,* 1914, 1915; Gadsden *Times,* 1901, 1949, 1950, 1952; Gainesville *Dispatch,* 1875; Greenville *Advocate,* 1953; Huntsville *Advocate,* 1878, 1882; Huntsville *Democrat,* 1883; Huntsville *Southern Advocate,* 1825, 1828; Huntsville *Times,* 1935, 1940, 1955; Mobile *Daily Register,* 1869, 1871; Mobile *Press,* 1930; Mobile *Register,* 1851, 1863, 1935; Mobile *Weekly Register,* 1869, 1872; Montgomery *Advertiser,* 1855, 1905, 1922, 1930, 1937, 1941, 1946; Selma *Daily Messenger,* 1866; Selma *Times,* 1866; Selma *Times-Journal,* 1954; *Shelby Guide,* 1873; *Shelby Sentinel,* 1882; *Sumter County Journal,* 1956; *Sumter Democrat,* 1854; Talladega *Democratic Watchtower,* 1840; Talladega *News,* 1954, 1955; Tuscaloosa *News,* 1955; *Voice of Sumter,* 1836; and *Weekly Iron Age* (Birmingham), 1886, 1887.

I am particularly grateful to Mrs. Martha McDade (Mrs. A. C. McDade) of Livingston, who produced the sketch of the Choctaw Tavern which appears on the title page. This sketch was made from a faded newspaper picture not suitable for reproduction.

Index